Praise for *Why We Need to Be Wild*

"This book is in the tradition of the best immersive journalism, in which the author tries on a lifestyle that offers unforeseen benefits, amidst difficulty, and then discovers that she can't go back to the way she used to live. It will get many of us thinking about whether we also need to immerse ourselves in more Stone Age living to thrive in the coming era of massive change."

—A. J. Jacobs, author of *The Year of Living Biblically*

"An engrossing, illuminating, and personal journey into how humans have become so disconnected from nature, and how to rewild ourselves back to health."

—James Nestor, author of *Breath* and *Deep*

"This is the life-changing magic of going wild—Kraft shows us how we could all benefit from being a little less civilized."

—Tiffany Shlain, acclaimed filmmaker, Webby Awards founder and author of *24/6: The Power of Unplugging One Day A Week*

"A brave book by a courageous human. With intellectual and emotional honesty, Jessica Carew Kraft offers a first-hand account of the badass pioneers of personal rewilding. She reports their various visions of the future with a good journalist's skeptical eye and an idealist's imaginative hope. In the vernacular of her movement, Jessica is one happy hominid."

—Richard Louv, author of *Our Wild Calling* and *Last Child in the Woods*

"How should we live? Global change has transformed our existential angst into a matter of physical survival, a realm in which few of us feel competent or prepared. Luckily we have Jessica Carew Kraft ahead of us, questing to the heart of nature and bringing back practical information about how we might thrive in the Anthropocene. In a narrative full of joy and empowerment, she posits a plausible future for our children and ourselves."

—Mary Ellen Hannibal, author of *Citizen Scientist: Searching for Heroes and Hope in an Age of Extinction*

"*Why We Need to Be Wild* shares the author's journey of extracting herself from urban living to rewilding herself and her children. Her journey toward conviviality with the rest of the natural world, her stops and starts, courageous leaps, and relentless efforts inspire the reader to make their own forays out of the strictures of civilized society to reconnect with the rest of Nature and become a respectful, skillful community member again. Read and be inspired to rewild your life!"

—Darcia Narvaez, co-author of *The Evolved Nest: Nature's Way of Raising Children and Creating Connected Communities* and *Restoring the Kinship Worldview: Indigenous Voices Introduce 28 Precepts for Rebalancing Life on Planet Earth*

"In this book, Kraft not only engages with a range of bad-ass skills for living more wildly, but she shows us how learning and passing along these skills can be a path towards a thriving future. We could all be a little more wild, not just with long beards and the occasional campfire feast, but with a deeper engagement with nature and a better understanding of Stone Age life."

—Adam Conover, comedian and host of
TruTV's *Adam Ruins Everything*

"Sometimes, the best wisdom lies behind us, in our distant past. Jessica Carew Kraft has focused her quest in that direction, seeking to learn venerable, largely forgotten skills for simple living in sync with nature. In this time of increasing anxiety about the health of our only planet, it is both urgent and invigorating to read about her adventures on this path. That Jessica is a mother—in addition to being a very good writer—adds depth to this essential, resonant topic."

—Mollie Katzen, author of *The Moosewood Cookbook*

"We face enormous challenges and choices as civilization itself seems to be displaying the beginning of its end days. Jessica, an accomplished professional and mother of two, faced up to this reality and has given us a remarkable piece of writing about her odyssey, what she decided, and what she has learned. This is a gift for all of us to take to heart."

—John Zerzan, author of *A People's History
of Civilization* and *Future Primitive*

"Kraft's is a quest that's never been needed more in our age of overstimulation, this moment in time that leaves us feeling stressed out and empty. Modern hunting and gathering reminds us that the oldest tools, ideas, and indeed crafts are not only timeless but never more vital to fill the void of the digital age."

—Larry Smith, founding editor *SMITH Magazine* and originator of the Six-Word Memoir

"In the nick of time comes a manuscript that urges us to get off our computers and out of our houses and head into the backcountry. Like Kraft, I've ditched the magical thinking of tech and capitalism as solutions to our dwindling happiness and our looming climate catastrophe, and I love Kraft's concept that the best answers may lie in 'rewilding' and our more primitive selves. I would pick up this book in a heartbeat."

—Caroline Paul, author of *The Gutsy Girl* and *Fighting Fire*

"A compassionate, reasonable, curious, fascinating exploration of the concepts and practices of rediscovering our place in the natural world. Clear-eyed, honest, and with an open heart, Jessica Carew Kraft takes us on a journey filled with excitement, connection, contradiction, gore, and tenderness—and it's a wild ride!"

—Sy Montgomery, National Book Award finalist and *New York Times* bestselling author

"Jessica Carew Kraft has gone boldly down a difficult path that diverges from the frantic and often absurd mainstream life of this wobbling nation. Things are coming undone fast, and we'll have to figure out a lot of other ways of doing what needs to be done. Some of these are ancient ways imprinted in our *Homo sapiens* DNA. It's a helluva learning curve, and Jessica's journey on it is a great job of social map-making for the rest of us.

—James Howard Kunstler, author of the World Made by Hand novels and *The Long Emergency*

"Kraft has discovered through the stories of rewilders that love, strength, and happiness are the birthright given to each of us by Mother Nature; if we only get back to her, she will hold us, so we feel safe and capable. The skills she details in this book add to what millions are discovering about tapping into their innate physiology to live wild and free."

—Wim Hof, the Iceman

"*Why We Need to Be Wild* shows how connecting deeply to nature provides the inspiration to make major life changes and start correcting the damages we all suffer living in high-tech civilization. In the world of wilderness skills, historically dominated by men, Kraft also champions the important role of women and mothers."

—Doniga Markegard, author of *Dawn Again* and *Wolf Girl*

The ecosystem-devouring megamachine called technoindustrial civilization, with its economics of endless growth, is primed to implode in the not-too-distant future, likely in the lifetimes of our children. Jessica Kraft shows us the psychological, material, and logistical journeys needed to prepare for ushering in something totally different: a societal order based on abundance in simplicity, an economics of sufficiency, and the beginning of true sustainability.

—Christopher Ketcham, author of *This Land: How Cowboys, Capitalism, and Corruption Are Ruining the American West*

WHY WE NEED TO BE

Wild

WHY WE NEED TO BE

Wild

ONE WOMAN'S QUEST FOR ANCIENT HUMAN ANSWERS TO 21ST CENTURY PROBLEMS

JESSICA CAREW KRAFT

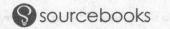

sourcebooks

Copyright © 2023 by Jessica Carew Kraft
Cover and internal design © 2023 by Sourcebooks
Cover design by Elizabeth Yaffe
Cover images © Chansom Pantip/Getty Images, ksushsh/Getty Images,
Sebastien Clark/500px/Getty Images, victor s. brigola/plainpicture
Internal design by Tara Jaggers/Sourcebooks

This publication is designed to provide accurate and authoritative information in regard to the
subject matter covered. It is sold with the understanding that the publisher is not engaged in
rendering legal, accounting, or other professional service. If legal advice or other expert assistance
is required, the services of a competent professional person should be sought. —*From a Declaration
of Principles Jointly Adopted by a Committee of the American Bar Association and a Committee of
Publishers and Associations*

Published by Sourcebooks
P.O. Box 4410, Naperville, Illinois 60567-4410
(630) 961-3900
sourcebooks.com

Cataloging-in-Publication Data is on file with the Library of Congress.

Printed and bound in the United States of America.
MA 10 9 8 7 6 5 4 3 2 1

To my mother's granddaughters

Table of Contents

A Note about Terms

In this book, I refer to the activities of our *Homo sapiens* species before the rise of agriculture and civilization as "Paleolithic." This term has historically been used by scientists to classify those *Homo* species that created tools made of stone, going back at least 2.5 million years (but perhaps as early as 3.3 million years ago), which invites questions about whether the earliest toolmakers were indeed part of the genus *Homo* or something else. The Paleolithic period is more specifically divided into Lower, Middle, and Upper periods and coincides almost exactly with the epoch of geologic time known as the "Pleistocene," which spanned from 2.6 million years ago to 12,000 years ago.

Because the focus of rewilders falls mostly on the habits, skills, and lifeways of our particular species, I delve into human technologies that can be dated from the Middle Paleolithic onward, starting about 250,000 to 300,000 years ago. It is cumbersome to specify Middle in each instance, so the terms Paleolithic and Pleistocene stand in for ways of life that span most of *Homo sapiens'* existence, but not early progenitors. The popular vernacular synonym for this historical period—"Stone Age"—has come under criticism because it can imply that the skills and tools stemming from this time are obsolete because it was human destiny to progress toward more and more complex technologies. This is not the case, as there are contemporary *Homo sapiens* cultures today, including many bands of existing hunter-gatherers, whose skills and tools have been in continuous use for hundreds of thousands of years. The development of civilization is not an inevitable end state for all human populations. Therefore, the imprecise term "Stone Age" is only used in this book when the sources have said it directly.

Introduction

Why would anyone want to learn the wild skills of our ancient ancestors today, when our lives are full of advanced technologies, quick conveniences, and the joys of instant communication? What could their Paleolithic wisdom have to offer us when a blockchain digital utopia is on our horizon?

It's hard to believe, but the world of our ancestors is never far from us, especially considering that our bodies and brains are essentially the same as those early humans who lived as hunter-gatherers for nearly three hundred millennia. These highly intelligent, spiritually attuned people roamed across wide territory in small, supportive groups searching for wild food. They didn't build permanent structures, they didn't plant seeds, and they didn't keep livestock. Contrary to popular ideas about "cavemen," these cultures, which never died out entirely, value women and live peacefully, in sync with nature's cycles. There are still numerous groups across the globe who never gave up this original human lifestyle and survive by hunting animals and gathering plants and fungi. They are nothing like the Flintstones.

Yet for most of us, the prospect of finding all our meals in nature and making our own stuff *is* cartoonish and completely out of the question. Just a few years ago, I would have found skills like foraging, hide tanning, and crafting stone tools totally irrelevant to my life as a working mother of two young girls. At the time, I was like any other resident of tech-boom San Francisco, ordering meals on apps and summoning GPS-coordinated rides around the city, constantly glued to my cell phone. I had a hectic life with constant stress, but I was also filled with the excitement about a future in which the repetitive, annoying tasks of nuclear family life might evaporate with the touch of a button. While I was frightened by the coming era of climate change and deeply objected to ongoing environmental destruction, I could still see myself years ahead, never lifting a spoon in the kitchen or pressing my foot to the pedal while my children and I indulged in all the possibilities of a healthy, digitized, clean-energy future. But I'm lucky that a few experiences steered me off that course and toward a more wild life.

One of the initial sparks was grief. Just after my first daughter was born, my mother died from complications of multiple sclerosis. MS is an autoimmune disease in which the body's defense system attacks not just foreign bodies, bacteria, and viruses but also its own nerve cells. Like mourning children do, I wondered why she had to be taken, right when I needed her the most? Who would be there to guide my new motherhood journey? Was there something my mother could have done to avoid this disease that she was diagnosed with right after I was born? I came across some alternative health practitioners who found success in treating their MS patients with diet, supplement, and lifestyle changes. While none of the science about these treatments is settled yet, it does seem that our Paleolithic ancestors and today's hunter-gatherer communities don't get MS or most of the degenerative, metabolic, and mental illnesses that we suffer from at increasing rates. I was starting to wonder about the differences between how hunter-gatherers and people in mainstream society live. Could some of those differences explain differing rates of disease and mental health issues?

When I went to graduate school for anthropology, I learned that researchers who spend time with hunter-gatherer societies agree that there are major benefits to living a nonindustrial and nonagricultural lifestyle. In addition to robust health, these groups enjoy a network of fulfilling relationships and thrive with plenty of leisure time. Their consumption of resources rarely exceeds what can be replaced through natural cycles. They live in the present moment, connect face-to-face, and don't endure emotional pain for long, perhaps due to the strong emotional support systems surrounding them. Women and men have equal control over their lives and the activities of the group. These cultures roughly represent how humans evolved to live for most of our history, proving that it is not our fundamental nature to destroy the environment and traumatize each other.

While some might regard a daily routine of securing food, caring for people, and staying alert to surroundings as possibly boring and repetitive—or even completely backward in the trajectory of human cultural development—the more I reflected on the difficulties of contemporary living and the damage we were doing to the environment and ourselves, the more I yearned for that life of basic pleasures. Was it completely out of reach? Or could I still pursue my wild birthright? What would that even mean in a world so completely dominated by human influence?

By spending time with anthropologists, I learned that there is a big difference between hunter-gatherers who share food equally among their group versus the more recent, "complex" hunter-gatherers who hoard food sources to accumulate power and prestige or who begin controlling the production of resources through planting crops. Remarkably, domination over food production caused the most profound change in the long history of *Homo sapiens*, setting off a cascade of negative social outcomes like slavery, warfare, oppression of women, and environmental destruction.

The groups that share equally were identified by the anthropologist James Woodburn in 1978 as "immediate return" societies. If their deer hunt is successful or if they harvest from a fig tree, the whole group will share the food right away. Sometimes they will store the leftovers for a few weeks, but they will continue to dole them out to whomever is hungry. As they move across the landscape in search of more food, they set up temporary camps where adults and kids are free to do what they want. They keep only a few personal possessions because they need to travel light, and they can usually find what they need along the way. The groups that live this way today—numbering roughly ten thousand people scattered across Africa, South America, and Asia—provide examples of how our human ancestors lived for the vast majority of our species' history.

Woodburn contrasted these groups with more recent societies in our evolutionary history, such as complex hunter-gatherers from around 30,000 years ago, farming societies from 10,000 years ago, and our own 250-year-old industrial civilization, calling these "delayed return." For people in these societies, it takes months, if not years, to harvest the crops they plant, raise livestock, or cash out on the Bitcoin they invest in. Individuals hoard the surpluses, using these to accumulate wealth, which creates classes of extreme haves and destitute have-nots as well as almost every negative social consequence you can think of. When we stopped getting our meals immediately from nature, the new mode of domination completely changed our way of relating to each other and the earth.

The more I looked into the differences between how I live now and how humans once lived, it seemed likely that our disturbing trends of poverty, chronic disease, violence, and environmental degradation are the price we moderns have to pay for our increasingly comfortable, high-tech, delayed-return lifestyle. This observation has been employed by advocates of the Paleo diet, who say that it's beneficial to eat the foods we evolved to eat in our hunter-gatherer past because refined, industrial food is making us sick. And indeed, there has been a surge of recent innovations incorporating our ancient hunter-gatherer blueprint. These include products and services like Paleo-diet-approved foods sold in big-box retail stores, barefoot running shoes, squatty potties (which help you eliminate in the more beneficial primal position), ancestral medicine, and athletic events like the Spartan Race, which encourages the running, climbing, carrying, and bending that used to be a regular part of our Paleolithic lifestyle. All these developments help us align with how our bodies evolved to thrive. But they are all focused only on the health of the individual and not on the health of communities or eco-systems. Any industrial product is still dependent on a system that will eventually run out of resources. We're not staving off extinctions and ecological collapse by drinking plastic bottles of collagen and green-tea extract shipped across the globe, even though our health might improve from consuming antioxidants and healthy fats. We're not improving environments by going camping with the latest high-tech gear from REI and hauling all our trash out of the woods with us. The truth is that all this producing, consuming, and throwing away—even if it's "green"—cannot reverse the damage that it causes. Our economic system further distances us from fostering commu-nity and planetary health; we are shackled to fast food, cheap oil, and chronic debt, while our social worlds have collapsed from the lively village commons to the tiniest handheld screen.

There is a way to live as lightly on the earth as a deer does, to feel whole, healthy, connected, and sustained by nature and sup-ported in raising a family. Indigenous cultures know how to live without massively disrupting ecosystems, as did every one of our ancestors before the dawn of civilization. (Note to the award com-mittee of the MacArthur Genius Grant: your winners have nothing on every single ancient culture ever.)

Folks who I encountered in my research told me that eating at the Paleo buffet is only the first step toward aligning with our evo-lutionary blueprint. We need to move, work, sleep, socialize, raise families, and produce goods the way early hunter-gatherers did, all from nature, if we are to survive on this teeming planet hurtling toward collapse and extinction.

The growing movement of human "rewilding" challenges us to readapt to our environment in just these ways and start going on one long minimalist camping trip. Any effort that keeps the industrial system intact, like electric cars, renewable energy, and reusable shopping bags, will only put off the collapse a few years, they say. The concept of human rewilding offers novel ideas about addressing the impending threat of global climate change and future pandemics, using evidence of how humans best lived and adapted through periods of climate instability, guided by perspectives from today's Native communities and the observations of anthropologists about how immediate-return groups subsist.

The concept of rewilding originated in conservation biology during the nineties and refers to the process of allowing natural areas to return to a state unaltered by humans in order to protect a wide variety of species. This is somewhat established as a conservation method, spearheaded by the late Earth First! founder Dave Foreman, who called for the creation of contiguous networks of wildlands instead of isolated protection areas to create a connected wildlife habitat and a larger rangeland for top predators. His organization, the Rewilding Institute, works to create this in North America. So far, the rewilding land movement is vastly more influential and well-known in Europe and Australia.

Searching Google for "rewilding" is thus going to uncover reams of conservation biology literature. Yet deeper into the digital hive mind, rewilding has been appropriated as a catch-all term for any kind of revival that involves nature. You can rewild your garden, your career, your sexuality, your consciousness. The term is picking up currency. In September 2018, *Outside* magazine's cover story, "Rewilding the American Child," proclaimed that modern childhood lacked any sense of adventure. Let kids roam free outside, the article preached...to the choir of outdoor folks. There are Christian rewilding groups that aim to show believers that the American consumer path is not Jesus's way; he was more like a hunter-gatherer. Likewise, rewilding as it is used in non-Western spiritual traditions now takes the form of meditation in the woods, shamanic power workshops, and radical self-care for women with all-natural materials.

Is rewilding, then, devolving into a New Age trend, or worse? These popular uses don't involve conservation and don't call on the wild origins of humans. Yet they speak to the fact that people are longing to recapture something of their wild nature, especially in this digitally saturated moment.

The extent to which a person feels this disconnect is an indicator of the amount of change they need to make to feel whole. Some people—most people—may never feel it, so they will never respond with an intense attraction to the nearest forest or wild space. But for many, the feeling that our way of life has gone very, very wrong will send us down some initial path in search of reconnection. We can sync our behavior with our environment of evolutionary adaptation through changing our diet, fitness, and sleep routines, gaining autonomy at work, spending weekends out in nature, or building a close-knit social support group.

If you follow it long enough, the path might eventually lead you to "rewild yourself," which is, incidentally, the name of fitness expert Daniel Vitalis's popular podcast that I listened to devotedly for several years and which provided a thorough curriculum for a newbie rewilder.

There is something else rewilding offers that might be more useful for those of us who live in industrial civilization and don't feel equipped to abandon it anytime soon. Becoming self-reliant for some of our basic needs instills confidence. Understanding how most humans lived up until the modern era points the way toward freedom from social structures and institutions that no longer serve us well. Knowing that our birthright is a fearless, happy, low-stress, and socially supported way of life provides a baseline to strive toward. The overall upshot of the COVID-19 virus was that the mainstream seemed more receptive to rewilding practices. Across the world, people experienced a partial collapse of global supply chains, economies, and social structures during an extended quarantine. As many people discussed online, it was like a dress rehearsal for the apocalypse. Those practicing rewilding proved to be their own "essential workers," and they didn't suffer as much as others from the interruption of goods and services. They reliably provided for their daily needs from what nature offered for free. Wild skills also afforded them the mental and physical challenges that build a type of resilience that is hard to come by in a sedentary, civilized life.

For several years, rewilding took over all my free time as I learned from experts, studied my local ecosystem, and acquired survival skills in nature. I harvested wild food with my kids and practiced weaving baskets, tanning hides, and making friction fires.

Wildlife trackers showed me how to read the land for animal signs, and hunters prepared me to skin, gut, and butcher game. I learned how Native groups lived before colonialism and studied what they are still doing to maintain their traditions. Yet after each foray into the wild, I couldn't shake a sense of loss and deep contradiction when I returned to consumer convenience after experiencing the thrilling joy of surviving in the forest with minimal gear.

For a while, I accepted that our current way of life was irreconcilable with the ways of the hunter-gatherers, and I took comfort in the fact that even the most passionate environmental thinkers felt the same. "We can't go back," they intoned, over and over again. Many of them said that abandoning our technological advances was too difficult to imagine. They said that we had to ask if life was really worth living without the pleasures of a bestselling novel, a long-awaited tropical vacation, or Beethoven's symphonies blasted on Bose speakers.

But then I looked deeper, and I met folks who had thrown out the Beethoven with the bathwater. These rewilders had grown up in mainstream consumer society, but now they live off the land with very few concessions to contemporary life. They weren't cobbling together various ancient human habits as many Paleo enthusiasts and Silicon Valley life hackers were doing. They were trying to live a fully integrated wild life. Some spent periods every year living in primitive shelters, sourcing their sustenance and materials from nature, and then returning to towns, jobs, cars, and coffee shops. Some kept a few durable industrial goods but carved out a feral life in the woods for most of their days. Others roamed the

West in bicycle and horseback caravans, harvesting and planting back wild species.

Despite my tame, urban upbringing and total lack of experience with nature, I was surprised by how deeply I connected with these rogue folks and their ideas. I felt comfortable on their remote lands, and joining them to forage, craft, make fires, build shelters, and navigate without devices made me feel more invigorated and purposeful than I ever had. I saw that even technologically advanced, educated folks could enjoy a simpler way of life and find unexpected fulfillment, and even love, in the process. Superficially, I was also attracted to the healthy, sexy lifestyle they lived close to the earth, free of the repression of polite society and the burdens of bureaucratic institutions maintained by the threat of force. I often found myself asking them, "Is that legal?" and hearing the retort, "I don't care!"

I was captivated by how rewilders deepened their knowledge and skills by following the long-overgrown ancient paths of Native people across the land, reintroducing similar planting traditions, shelters, stone toolmaking, and hunting techniques with a few modern innovations. I saw rewilders helping to revive traditions that had nearly been lost. While fearful of being accused of cultural appropriation or "going Native" (rightfully so, in many cases), these individuals carefully navigated issues of Indigenous rights, colonialism, and economic and racial privilege in the realm of rewilding. They were motivated by how human cultures had once been fiercely egalitarian, never subjugating anyone or exploiting resources to ruin. I had to acknowledge that only certain groups of people with access to nature, education, and some financial resources were the ones exploring rewilding today—these folks were predominantly white, heterosexual, nonurban, and mobile. They were able to sometimes leave their families and communities, and they felt comfortable being away from medical services, grocery stores, schools, and typical employment. Despite the fact that living wild was once the birthright of all humans, it is now a privileged endeavor that can often be exclusionary to minority groups, perhaps even completely anathema to folks who are struggling to get by.

I also became increasingly convinced by the scientific evidence rewilders presented to back up their practices. I cross-checked their experiments with Paleolithic skills against recent research in anthropology, archaeology, evolutionary psychology, ecology, and genetics. Beyond the brainy stuff, I also acquired some fierce skills that I never imagined I'd practice in midlife or teach my children. Through harvesting roadkill, collecting and spreading wild perennial seeds on public land, and tracking animals and ancient human artifacts across the West, I sought my original birthright as an intelligent, omnivorous, bipedal, female hominid. I found that I was like so many of the rewilders I encountered who were dissatisfied with modern life and looking for an alternative.

It became apparent that my perspective as a mother provided a valuable corrective for this emerging movement. From wilderness guides and survival experts to bushcraft teachers and participants on reality TV shows like *Alone*, the majority of folks actively rewilding are male. I learned to recognize that *solo* survival, in which nature is a brutal combatant that only the strongest individuals can contend with, was a myth that didn't reflect how humans actually live in the wild. Ethnographic studies overwhelmingly show that instances of solo survival are scarce in human history, because what truly allows humans to survive is caring and sharing in small communities. We require a multigenerational group to thrive; we are social primates who need each other. I feel strongly that the role of women—as gatherers, nurturers, and wild tenders—is far more crucial to the survival of the social group than the actions of a single heroic male, yet this is downplayed in rewilding circles.

Breaking the cultural barriers that keep women and children from leaping into the wild is very challenging, yet I persisted. Learning and strengthening my nature knowledge became the most direct and successful approach to finding my way in what is currently a male-dominated quest. Looking at how hunter-gatherer groups equally valued the roles of each sex also offered a way out of the gridlocked feminist culture wars that, for instance, pit working women against stay-at-home moms.

Acquiring the capabilities to thrive outdoors without modern technology soon opened the door to much more than self-sufficiency and physical hardiness. I discovered that rewilding at the extremes reaches beyond the rising popularity of alternative ways to live more sustainably, such as homesteading, permaculture, or wilderness camping. Spending time with more hard-core rewilders, I wondered if they might be the vanguard of a movement demonstrating the only proven way to survive the onslaught of climate change and diminishing resources. After all, humans had endured hundreds of thousands of years living only with Paleolithic skills and tools, while our current civilization is short-lived and clearly unsustainable by comparison. Could we learn from their experiments and start on our own paths to rewilding? After a few years, I was no longer an impartial journalist chronicling this movement. I was all in.

Falling for a romanticized back-to-nature fantasy was always a danger as I explored the possibilities of rewilding. There's a prominent criticism of rewilders and people who reject civilization that says that they are beholden to their own myths rooted in how they wish people could live. And many of my encounters forced me to look critically at the deprivation and depression that emerged for individuals when they abandoned the structure of institutional society and stopped relying on industrialized goods and the internet. Though I was trying to envision and build a more wild life, I didn't want to lose my social support or my sanity or create hardship for my family. As I returned home again and again after testing my emotional and physical limits, making radical changes in how I lived, I wondered if I could ever make the wild my home. And who would join me?

This is the story of my journey.

CHAPTER 1

Mismatch

"It's a fox!"

I gleefully screamed and pressed the brakes of my rented camper van as my two daughters scrambled to the window to glimpse what I'd seen. A furry orange lump rested on the shoulder of the freeway.

"We have to get it! This is our fox."

Adrenaline coursed through my body as I pulled over. It was just past 8:00 a.m., and we were making our way home from a primitive skills family camp near Santa Barbara. We had spent the evening before dancing to drums on the edge of a giant fire pit after telling ghost stories inside a tent used for herb storage. My hair still smelled of smoke, sweat, and sage beneath my brimmed hat.

I'd never grabbed roadkill before. "We can do this," I announced to the girls, pumping my fist victoriously. Then, bravado fading, I asked them, "Should we do this?"

My older daughter answered clearly, her green eyes wide and encouraging. "You have to, Mommy."

As I exited the van, I grabbed the latex gloves I'd used to serve bean soup to two hundred people at the previous night's dinner along with an empty canvas tote bag. Cars, trucks, vans, and SUVs scattered dust over me as they whizzed by at seventy-plus miles per hour. My girls, aged six and nine, were barefoot but still intent on jumping out of the van to accompany me on my quest.

"Mommy, don't get hit!" my oldest screamed.

I didn't want them walking down the narrow shoulder as semis careened by, so I left them standing under a road sign in thigh-high needle grass as I sprinted the last fifty meters to the fox. I waited for a break in traffic before darting onto the road to grab it by its stiff front and hind legs. I was moving rapidly, but I noticed how elegant and perfect this creature was: not a nick or a scratch on its russet fur. With its stiffened muscles, it looked suspended in motion, forever leaping across the lane into eternity. I took a deep breath and thrust it upside down into the bag. Hooking the handles onto my shoulder, I sprinted back to the girls, now fearing that someone would see what I'd done.

In the van, I deposited the fox in the footwell of the front passenger seat. The corpse smelled slightly skunky, but there were no flies, no blood, no mark or clue as to where it had been hit. We sped away, the fan on high, a bit stunned from picking up this unlikely hitchhiker. Later, I looked up how long rigor mortis lasts (up to eighty hours) and estimated that the fox had been lying on the shoulder for less than a day. Given the species' nocturnal habits, it had likely been hit the night before. I would also learn that processing an animal should be done before or while it is stiff to be sure decay has not begun.

One million vertebrate animals, mostly mammals, are killed each day on U.S. roads, according to an estimate by an independent wildlife biologist.[1] It is impossible to account for all the invertebrates that die in traffic, spattering our front grills with carapaces, antennae, and flattened wings. These dead creatures are collateral damage from the roads and highways that are designed without taking their needs into account. Because the animals don't belong to anyone— they are neither pets nor livestock—their lives have little value in the economic system. Birds, lizards, amphibians, and furry creatures are unwary trespassers on dangerous human territory. While they are not intentionally killed, they are blatantly ignored, and their widespread, isolated deaths are never tallied or identified by any agency.[2]

Until I had seen people processing these animals at gatherings for ancestral skills, I viewed roadkill as an eyesore, as most people do: it is something gross, just nature's trash. We actively turn away from these kill sites in learned obliviousness. Passing unsightly carcasses at highway speeds, I would think: *When will that disappear?*

Yet the status of road-killed animals is slowly changing. Instead of dismissing the mass death as a necessary consequence of accelerating transportation speeds and the increasing development of open land, some policy experts and planners are devising ways to mitigate wildlife casualties. One promising direction is the construction of ecopassages—tunnels and bridges that animals can traverse safely.

A more immediate response to roadkill, however, is to prepare the meat, if fresh, for consumption. People who consume roadkill place a high value on making use of the animal, and by doing so, they decrease their engagement with the industrial food system. Roadkill is organic, local food that carries the spiritual significance of redeeming lost life.

Despite my initial aversion, my kids had no trouble appreciating the practice of harvesting freshly dead animals. They had just seen many such unfortunate animals' skins turned into beautiful pelts at the skills gathering. Our friend Tom and his two daughters had spent a couple of afternoons assiduously scraping small pieces of flesh from the hide of a bobcat they had picked up on a Santa Barbara freeway. They told us another driver, with a Prius, had stopped for it first but was hesitating to take the animal. Tom said he swooped in and carried it away, judging that anyone with a Prius wouldn't know what to do with a bobcat. I had to admit that watching them work the flesh with a draw knife that spewed out pink shreds of slime made me queasy. The ease with which Tom and his kids handled the viscera, fascia, and fur had come from years of hunting and processing game. I was not accustomed to touching raw flesh—I bought precut meat at the store precisely because I didn't want to handle it. Yet Tom's finished product was quite appealing. My oldest begged me to buy a similar tanned fur on sale at a vendor's tent; she tried it on like a glamorous cape.

Technically, it is illegal to remove deceased wildlife from public land in California unless you are an agent from the Department of Fish and Wildlife. Stopping along a California freeway for anything but an emergency is also unlawful. Yet some states do allow drivers to pick up roadside animals, and California is beginning to explore this option. In Montana, a prominent nature skills program run by Tom Elpel depends on road-killed deer, elk, moose, and antelope to feed its participants. By regularly patrolling local highways, Elpel's students quickly become proficient in skinning, gutting, butchering, and preparing hides without needing to hunt.

My ambivalence about the process wasn't caused by the illegality, the moral issues, or even the animal's unsavory scent. What prompted me to instruct the girls to keep our fox completely secret was my avoidance of a cultural taboo. I didn't know how I would explain my newfound feral interest to our friends, or even to my husband, without alienating them. They all bought precut meat too.

Once back to Berkeley, I stashed the fox inside an empty garbage bin in our garage. The carcass was not quite a ticking time bomb, but it had to be dealt with quickly to avoid attracting decomposers and scavengers, or worse: suspicion. I had neither the courage nor the knowledge to skin it right away. When it materialized on the roadside, I had no plan. It was more like the fox grabbed me, offering the opportunity to transform myself, which I desperately wanted to do.

I sent urgent texts to a few contacts, including our new pal Tom, asking how I should skin it. (I knew that I wouldn't want to eat it, even if it could be done.) No one could come help me, but a couple offered advice.

Check out the tutorials on YouTube, they urged. *Do it quickly, before bacteria make the fur slough off. Get the guts out, and then you can store the body in your freezer.* (My freezer? Filled with edamame, mangos, pizzas, and Popsicles?) *And be sure to save the skull—it's useful for kids to learn from. Don't be too hard on yourself; we have lost these skills and there are no elders to teach us.*

I procrastinated. After a week away camping, there was so

much to catch up on, and I'd been a solo parent the whole time since my husband stayed home to work. For the rest of the day, I stayed busy with unpacking, showering, laundry, answering a week's worth of emails, and throwing mounds of unopened mail into the recycling bin.

Furthermore, I found it jarring to return to living in a clean house in a tidy neighborhood in the world's most politically correct city. We had just been sharing communal outdoor space, eating with our hands, squatting over holes to relieve ourselves, and ignoring the dust, grease, feathers, fish scales, burrs, and splinters of wood that clung to our hair and clothes. The endless housecleaning and yard maintenance that made up our daily routine in the city now seemed like so much pointless busywork. Was there a purpose to all of it besides keeping up appearances? I'd been cavorting with folks who have stripped away the conventions of modern life to bare essentials. The rules that held our makeshift clan together during the weeklong gathering were truly primitive: wash your hands before meals, monitor young kids with knives, and the last one to bed puts out the fire. I felt like I had been unconfined for a week, only to return to a cage.

This trade-off of individual freedom, wildness, and adventure for security and social conformity is what generations of European social theorists blamed for widespread urban discontent. Sigmund Freud argued in *Civilization and Its Discontents* (1930) that our highly regulated and structured lives in an urban, capitalist society defy our basic instincts for autonomy and equality. Marxist theorists from Émile Durkheim to Theodor Adorno proposed that the hierarchical

division of labor and social classes in society deprived individuals
of autonomy and alienated them from their fundamental human
nature. They were speculating about how individuals feel when
they've never had a chance to experience their primal instincts and
drives. City-dwelling Europeans were very far removed from any
kind of wild state, as they had experienced multiple generations of
alienation since the Industrial Revolution. Yet the American experience always offered an escapist path (and still does), initially because
of the proximity of European colonists to Native Americans.

In a letter Ben Franklin wrote in 1753 to his English patron,
Peter Collinson, a member of the British Royal Society, he described
what he found to be an alarming trend in colonial life:

> When white persons of either sex have been taken prisoners
> young by the Indians, and lived a while among them, tho'
> ransomed by their Friends, and treated with all imaginable
> tenderness to prevail with them to stay among the English, yet in
> a Short time they become disgusted with our manner of life, and
> the care and pains that are necessary to support it, and take the
> first good Opportunity of escaping again into the Woods, from
> whence there is no reclaiming them.[3]

Not all these colonists were initially captives, as Franklin
described. Hundreds, perhaps thousands of them deliberately
chose to become so-called "White Indians," attracted to the lifestyle of egalitarian social roles, mobility, adventure, and freedom
that prevailed in Native societies.

I understood the appeal. The lifestyle of freedom and discovery I had gotten a taste of at the gathering—while in no way a substitution for Native society—was a tantalizing contrast to the structured, regulated, and repetitive lifestyle I lived in the city. "Escaping again into the Woods" was on my mind.

The morning after we arrived home from that week in the woods, I woke up having dreamed of the dead fox and felt compelled to skin it. I couldn't bear the guilt of letting it rot in my garage after I had made such a huge effort to claim it. My husband, lying next to me, who tolerated and sometimes encouraged my wild adventuring, would not have been enthused about this project. He's a fantastically intelligent class-action attorney who spends his days in an urban office tower, plugging away on legal briefs. At night, he sometimes retreats to his study to read and write more. He loves order, cleanliness, and great jazz. He was admirably loyal to friends from his youth, many of whom we still hung out with regularly. But the dirty parts of life are like typos in a court docket to him—they must be eliminated immediately. Just dealing with the kitchen compost made him wince.

Making the excuse that I had to take the car to get gas, I entered the garage and gingerly strung the fox up from the rafters with kitchen twine and pushed the large municipal compost bin beneath it. Its muscles were beginning to loosen up, which was concerning. After donning rubber gloves, I tried out a couple of knives until one sliced cleanly through the fur and skin on the hind leg, mimicking a tutorial I had watched on the internet. Soon, that first clean cut devolved into a mess of pulling, scraping, cursing, and sweating. I was trying to load the DIY video on my phone in the concrete Wi-Fi-challenged garage. "Skinning is not easy!" I yelled to the competently macho hunters on YouTube. I struggled to release the bushy tail in one piece from its archipelago of meaty bones. It separated: a small victory. I packed the tail, still smelling of skunk, into a ziplock bag and rotated the animal toward myself to find four sets of small nipples. *Oh, God. It's female!*

Somehow, I had assumed that the animal was male. I gasped and stepped back upon seeing her abdomen—I had torn up the vixen. Was this a mother who still had hungry pups waiting for her back on the far side of the 101 freeway? People have long observed vixens going to great lengths to protect and dote on their offspring, who aren't able to hunt for themselves until they are five or six months old. When the pups are first born, the mother cares for them constantly for weeks, and she needs the father fox to hunt for her. If he disappears, she finds a way to feed and care for them on her own, even taking time to play with them to build their hunting skills. In England, a fox pup once got snared in a trap where it remained alive and healthy for two weeks until it was rescued. Experts on the scene said it was only possible because its mother brought it food every day. Reflecting on this, I felt my stomach turn over, even though *I* hadn't killed her or left her pups without sustenance. I dropped the knife.

Shocked back to my senses, I realized that on a lovely Sunday morning in the spring of 2018, I was perspiring over a carcass in the prosperous hills of Berkeley, lying about my whereabouts and trying to devise a good location to bury a stolen, dead animal so that I could later retrieve its skull for my children's education. Any other Sunday, I might have been at a child's birthday party or walking through a museum with my family. What had brought me to this wildly different moment?

———————

From the vantage point of my life three years earlier, my behavior with the fox would have seemed absurd. To all outward appearances, my consulting position for one of the world's top venture capitalists was a cushy gig with all the clichéd perks. The office had biometric security check-in, daily catered lunch, and private glass-walled cubicles in a sprawling, too-big office complex just off Sand Hill Road near Palo Alto. I had gained fluency in digital marketing language after a year of working in tech PR, and in my new job, I was charged with increasing the firm's output of quality content. I manufactured blog posts, LinkedIn updates, press guides, media trainings, and Q and As with startup founders. Yet I felt strangely mismatched there and had started wondering what I could do differently. Even though the office's indoor setup was casual and on-trend, I would grow irritable from the LED lights and recirculated air and took frequent breaks to try to restore myself. I'd wander outside in the landscaped office park, planted with hardy native species in undulating garden beds.

Wondering why the gardens weren't as exotic as the offices, I imagined that there must have been a series of meetings between the office managers of the various companies that shared the compound. These were likely followed by dozens of emails, Slack chats, and leafy emojis going back and forth over weeks, maybe months, until a committee was formed and the wider community was consulted. Perhaps due to the environmental concerns of nearby homeowners who objected to the use of pesticides and unsightly irrigation pipes, the managers eventually decided to install the same species that would have grown there naturally, just in a more orderly fashion.

Once, near the parking lot, I spied a thrumming hive of bees hanging low in a live oak tree. Could it be that I had never seen a wild hive before? I drew closer and watched the circles of frenzied flight around the hole in the tree. The hundreds of insects were so in sync—none of them collided. I could have stayed there watching for hours in rapture. The bees' activity seemed so much more purposeful and fulfilling than my own. They were making food and cooperating. I mused on this for several minutes until a grounds worker pulled up in his truck behind me, cueing me to head back to the office. The next chance I had, a week later, I tried to find the bees again, but they were gone. Were they removed because they posed a threat? Did they swarm elsewhere? I had no one to ask. I doubted anyone in my office had seen them. My coworkers often raised their eyebrows when I chose to work outside or take strolls on my breaks. Nature was only interesting to them if it could fuel a multimillion-dollar enterprise.

This firm funded one company that catalogued the human microbiome, another that was developing novel human genetic tests, and a third that was designing organisms for industrial applications. This last startup modeled new enzymes, engineered novel

strains of bacteria, and designed never-before-seen metabolic path-
ways. The company intended to ferment beer more efficiently, grow
more robust GMO grains, synthesize sleeker cannabinoids, and
increase human longevity.

Their website declared that the human body was no longer
constrained by mere biology. When we hack our DNA to reroute
our molecular functioning and insert new genetic algorithms, they
claimed, the aging process shuts off and cells replicate infinitely.
They implied that this radical development would enable humans
to focus more diligently on the bigger problems of the world. I heard
similar messages at conferences for digital health, at discussion
panels on neurotechnology, and in the laboratories of researchers
trying to treat mental health patients with FDA-approved video
games. Humanity would soon be able to transcend our messy biological reality and program a healthier, more prosperous future. It
was an enticing vision that was already playing out in the subculture
of biohackers who were mastering their biology, increasing their
"peak-performance" feats through sophisticated supplements, bio-
feedback devices, and AI-assisted workouts.

While writing the script for this epic change in human history,
I became fascinated by the prospect of continual human optimiza-
tion, trying out many of these tracking devices and potent herbal
formulas for leveling up my brain and body. Sometimes I did feel
that surge of amped-up energy that allowed me to write better,
faster, longer. I enacted the metaphor of my body becoming a pro-
grammed machine that could propel my success and, therefore, the
world's. But more often than not, I felt empty and confused. Was all

this technologically enhanced progress doing anything more than keeping me and everyone I knew tethered to apps on screens?

I saw that the quality time I could allot to my family and friends was shrinking as I dashed around dealing with strangers and other folks I didn't particularly like. I adhered to a fixed schedule in which I executed tasks that higher-ups had assigned me without any input into the rules I had to follow. I wore uncomfortable dry-cleaned tailored clothing and sat in a stiff chair eight hours a day, mindful of always appearing productive to my coworkers. When my lack of sleep would catch up with me, I'd down more coffee and supplements and even chew nicotine gum to boost my energy. My ninety-minute commute to and from our house became a circus of multitasking as I spun the plates of overflow work and balanced on the tightrope of the family calendar. If using tech, working in tech, and promoting tech just led to more time with tech, which equaled more stress, then what was the point?

But no one I worked with asked that question, even though they never stopped complaining of fatigue, busyness, pressure, and their lack of time. They believed in a future where everything would be digitally streamlined, asking only: What more could we do to further tech? Techno-optimism was the only lens with which to examine our lives and the issues of the wider world. *Alexa, what's the meaning of life?* I felt guilty that I was obsessing over ways to eject ourselves from the progress-driven rat race. Was that need to escape just a symptom of depression—one that I should consider getting treatment for? Yet sometimes, I didn't totally believe that thought. My studies in anthropology had taught me to be critical of my culture, and I knew that there were infinite ways to approach life, many of which might be more fulfilling than what I was living in twenty-first-century digital capitalism.

For instance, the types of stressors we experience from today's obligatory deskbound work are ones that our ancient ancestors never knew because, as evidence suggests, they didn't have to work so hard—no more than three or four hours a day. In fact, the concept of toil was not in their vocabulary because their productive activities were interspersed with hanging out, playing, and expressing themselves with song, dance, and ritual.[4] An entire band cooperated to find and prepare food. All other materials for daily life, including shelters, clothing, weapons, toys, and medicines, came free from the environment. They did not experience economic stress. Life was not rushed and hectic, as each day included plenty of movement and exertion as well as ample time to rest and recreate. These foraging bands also enjoyed the security and well-being that comes from living in a tight-knit social group. Today, many of us are further stressed out because we are isolated from supportive community and positive social contact.

In the late 1970s, anthropologist James Larrick studied the health of the Waorani, Native inhabitants of the upper Amazon jungle. He proclaimed them "among the world's healthiest people," with no discernible heart disease, cancer, stroke, or diabetes.[5] These hunter-gatherers didn't suffer from autoimmune or neurodegenerative diseases, and they weren't crippled by back pain, anxiety, or depression. Similar studies over past decades have confirmed Larrick's findings and have also shown that hunter-gatherers develop natural protection from Alzheimer's disease and allergies of all kinds through, oddly enough, exposure to various parasites.[6] They also do not habitually engage with supposedly stress-abating substances like tobacco and alcohol, and their use of psychoactive plants is limited to infrequent rituals. Their lack of addiction may be connected to the absence of alienation. In a small forager band, individuals have a strong, unwavering lifelong identity uncomplicated by existential questions that might plague many of us moderns. Anthropologist Colin Turnbull reported that the Mbuti, an immediate-return group in Africa, were a people "who had found in the forest something that made their life more than just worth living, something that made it, with all its hardships and problems and tragedies, a wonderful thing full of joy and happiness and free of care."[7]

For all these reasons, hunter-gatherer populations have a reputation as models of public health. But none of this is to say that they don't endure their own miseries or forms of social domination. Calories are harder to come by in the wild, and shortages of food sources do cause periods of hunger, although there is no evidence of long-term famine. Infections and parasitic diseases are common, and infant mortality rates are much higher than in modern societies. Much of their original land has been completely destroyed through human industry, leaving these communities on the least desirable spots for foraging. Enforced sharing of resources among the group and complex taboo structures about purity and sex can make daily life for individuals socially stressful on occasion. So, life in civilization obviously offers many undeniable benefits and improvements over the hunter-gatherer lifestyle. Today, we in the industrial world have relatively easy access to calories, clean water, climate-controlled shelter, health care, and entertainment (yet it's still a struggle to find something good on TV!). However, in contrast to hunter-gatherers, most of us don't have adequate leisure time, healthy social support, or a purposeful sense of belonging from birth to death.

Furthermore, humans gained survival advantages in their ecological niches through the hardships they endured, and also by hunting game, fishing, and foraging edible plants and fungi in small, nomadic bands and seasonal settlements. The environment that shaped our genes is no longer the environment we live in. We still have hunter-gatherer minds and bodies, but we don't live as they do. Biologists call this "evolutionary mismatch."[8]

Many of us intuit this deep disconnect, though we don't call it evolutionary mismatch. We just know that something's not right with how we live. We are overweight, sleep-deprived, stressed, lonely, depressed, anxious, diseased, addicted, unable to pay attention. We have an inkling that sitting all day, staring at screens, driving cars, and living alone or just with a few people may not be the best way to live. Yet we don't know any other way, and we don't comprehend just how many skills we have lost in the last couple hundred years. If we lose our way at sunset on a hiking trail without cell service, death is a very possible outcome. How is this possible, when this is the environment we evolved to survive in? It seems that we have traded away the social, psychological, and physical benefits of our ancestral lifestyle in favor of convenience, comfort, and technological progress without accounting for the massive toll of stress on every aspect of our lives.

As I continued to feel unhappy in my corporate job, I began to wonder if evolutionary mismatch was setting me up for health problems. I had seen how my mother's MS ripped her slowly away from every activity she loved to do, and it ultimately deprived me of a mother when I needed one most.

MS is an autoimmune disease in which the body's defense system attacks not just foreign bodies, bacteria, and viruses but also the body's nerve cells. Neurons are sheathed in a fatty casing called *myelin*, which protects nerves as they relay messages around the brain and body. The immune system's damage to the myelin—a process called *demyelination*—causes various symptoms that flare up, then recede but ultimately worsen over time until functions are completely lost.

As a toddler, I learned to walk by holding on to my mother's portable IV pole when she was hospitalized for an exacerbation of her symptoms. Her disease progressed gradually as I grew up. As I gained mastery of my body, she was slowly declining. She had been a quick runner and a graceful dancer, with the five-ten frame of a prima ballerina. When I was four, she taught me the rudiments of ballet. We cartwheeled across our yard together when I was six. We used to have family dance parties on Saturday nights where my father would deejay from his vast collection of seventies rock and jazz.

Her arms and legs would periodically go numb and then reached a state where they permanently tingled. When I was ten, she invented a game of winter tag played on a maze of snow trails. Four years later, her gait grew unsteady, and she quit running altogether, soon walking with a cane. As she lost control of her legs, bladder, and bowels, she sat in a wheelchair, like at my college graduation. In a rare moment, holding tightly to my brother's arm, she triumphantly shuffle-stepped down the aisle at my wedding.

In advanced MS, the brain becomes spotted with demyelinated zones of inflammation leading to memory impairment, depression, and inexplicable rage. In my twenties, my mother wanted me to accept that she was approaching death. We had long, teary talks while I sat at the foot of her bed that she only rose from a few times a week. But when she did get up and go out, she looked fabulous.

Her diagnosis did not bring her down until she was nearing the end. Throughout her thirty years of illness, the disease solidified her commitment to living a fun life and reinforced her stubborn streak. This was a woman who talked back to limits and pushed hard against cultural norms. As a young girl, she demanded that her mother let her play football with the neighborhood boys, even though she repeatedly broke her glasses. She defied company regulations when she worked for a Campbell's soup factory, reporting to work in the men's uniform instead of the flirty skirt they required women to wear while deboning chickens. One summer, she was the first woman to operate a truck weigh station for the Minnesota Department of Transportation. In the workaholic get-ahead eighties, she pushed in the other direction, becoming a leader of "New Games," which encouraged people to play in large groups in cooperative, not competitive, ways. If you've ever done a "group sit" and ended up tumbling to the ground in laughter with thirty of your closest friends, you know the spirit of New Games.

Meeting her grandchild was very important to my mother, and she was able to hold my first baby girl a few weeks after birth. I think this link to the future kept her going during the last year of her life. When she contracted pneumonia six months later, she was too weak to fight it. Her MS endured for one full generation, from the birth of her daughter to the birth of her granddaughter. If we judge a life based on biological reproductive success, my mom achieved it. Yet it saddens me every day that my kids don't know their beautiful, vivacious, fun-loving grandma.

As I sought bigger-picture reasons for my mom's decline and death, I fell away from the mainstream narrative about illness. People tried to comfort me by saying that she just had the bad luck to get sick, and I had to accept that degenerative disease is an unfortunate part of life. Yet the more I looked into it, the more I grew convinced that the lifestyle of Western civilization had done her in. She was, as I still am, enjoying the most comfortable and convenient living conditions humans have ever attained, and yet this environment seemed to have damaged her. Was it damaging me and my kids too? Determined to do everything I could to avoid her fate, I became obsessed with possible precursors for autoimmune disease.

The granddaughter of Danish and British immigrants, my mom was likely the first generation in her entire ancestry to be raised mostly indoors. And while she had what we now call an "active" lifestyle, as a college-educated professional, she had nowhere near the amount of movement in her day that her farming and factory-working relatives did. The majority of her waking hours since she hit puberty was likely spent sitting in chairs. She also ate a lot less animal protein and fat than her lineage was used to consuming because she became vegetarian in college. Even if she was predisposed to an autoimmune condition, her lifestyle probably helped it along. She wasn't getting the fat, protein, movement, sun exposure, and even the bacterial load that everyone she was descended from had received. And the absence of bacteria may be a very important factor for a whole host of ailments we suffer from; numerous studies have demonstrated that children who grow up on farms near animals and in wilderness settings have a reduced risk of developing autoimmune conditions.

As I waded through my grief, finding out that several health advocates claimed to have eradicated their MS symptoms with a full-on Paleo lifestyle caused me to turn alternative scenarios around in my head. *What if she had eaten more meat? What if she had spent more time in the sun as an adult? What if she had cut out the chocolate mints and other treats she loved to indulge in?* (At a lot of meals growing up, we not only had dessert...we had dessert dessert.) With the same genes and basic lifestyle as my mom, I wondered if I could avoid her fate. I decided to eat a gluten-free, anti-inflammatory diet made up primarily of veggies, meat, healthy fats, and chocolate chips—couldn't give those up.

While my vitamin D levels went up, my blood sugar was perfect, and I was in great shape, my stress levels were still increasing with every passing week. I was approaching burnout at work—particularly because of the obligations I was dealing with at home. During the years that I worked full-time in an office, my kids were very young. Half of our monthly income paid for child care. After my job, I served the proverbial "second shift" doing domestic tasks. Like most working mothers I knew, I made nearly all my kids' meals, spent most of my nonworking time with them, and was responsible for most of their activities and possessions, from playdates to pajamas. To keep it all going, I would often wake up around four in the morning, pack some carefully chopped food into the slow cooker, scour the internet for weekend activities, and then run and bike my kids to day care and preschool. Then I'd commute to my job, work there till five o'clock, pick up the kids, orchestrate dinner, and direct evening playtime until I collapsed with my daughters in their bed. I didn't even have the mental space to figure out how this arrangement could be less taxing. Meanwhile, my husband was putting in eleven hours a day at his law practice (including a two-hour commute downtown), and he'd do as much with us as he could. His love and devotion to our kids was obvious. No time together became the norm as we operated in our separate spheres, unless one of us decided to splurge on a babysitter.

I was like most of today's workers who simply accept the predicament they are in, even when their social or biological needs conflict with the imperative to be economically productive. I wasn't sure that I had ever actively chosen this life though; it was more like I was herded into a corral like a work horse who could still view, off in the distance, the free-flowing manes of galloping wild horses.

My "motherwhelmed" state started after the birth of my first child in 2009, when I stayed at home while my husband went to his office. I would fit my work in during evenings and baby nap times, trying to avoid paying for child care. Without any relatives or close friends nearby to help with the day-to-day tasks, living in a nuclear family arrangement seemed to exponentially multiply everything I had to do: care for an infant, work, maintain the house, make food, and try to return to my prebaby body. Like most new moms, I experienced my highest-ever levels of stress, anxiety, loneliness, and overwhelm in the first year of my daughter's life.

Throughout the ensuing years, it was difficult to get enough rest or time away from constant caregiving, and my situation was not exceptional. Mothers are accustomed to putting everyone else's needs first in order to measure up to an ideal of the good mother. The expectation is that moms are superhuman and inexhaustible and that we derive our self-worth from deprivation. In popular movies, TV, and social media, an idealized version of the fashionable, fun, well-organized, ready-to-serve mother is everywhere. Moms internalize these unrealistic expectations, earnestly blaming personal inadequacies for why we are so fatigued. I too believed that everything about my children was primarily my responsibility, and I had to attempt to be the perfect parent in order to have a happy child.

While we modern moms don't have to harvest and process food, make clothing, or build shelters for our families, we do have to work longer hours to have all this industrially produced for us than we would if we were living in a small foraging society. Ironically, we've made motherhood more labor-intensive than ever. Mothers not only carry the responsibility for their kids' basic needs, but we also serve as social coordinator, nurse, therapist, and chief procurer for all the goods that they require.

This is not what being a mother was about throughout most of human history. Ideally, and as we see in today's intact traditional communities, motherhood is a more supported period of time in which the tending and caring for children is parceled out to all sorts of helpers in the tribe: the father, grandparents, aunties, uncles, and older children nearby. When you can share food and child-rearing responsibilities while in the company of adults, being a mom can be fun—or at least not monumentally draining. Women maintain strong social bonds with each other as they collect food, prepare it, tend to their kids and hearths, and offer one another support and advice. The women are still primarily responsible for children in these settings and interact with them most frequently, but it's not an unrelenting context of isolation as it is for us now living in nuclear families. Furthermore, girls are immersed in caring for younger children and know what to expect when they have their own. By contrast, I had no idea what I was in for as a mother. I only hung out with people in my stage of life. Babies just looked cute. Who wouldn't want one?

Then, getting a full-time office job made everything worse, but I needed to do that to enter the Bay Area real-estate acquisition game. Rentals were dicey and overpriced, and my husband and I wanted a solid family home to grow into. But my time spent in the office left huge gaps at home that only I could fill.

When my older daughter, who was six at the time, was having intense anxiety about transitioning from school to summer camp, she really needed me around. Every morning, she begged me to stay home and help her get through the day. How do you turn away from those plaintive tears that only *you* can wipe away? But I wasn't allowed to work from home, and our babysitter wasn't skilled at deflecting her worries. My daughter got worse, losing sleep and not eating properly. When I approached my boss about letting me stay home with her, he told me no, because it was important to the people I managed to see me there working. "Think about the optics," he said. Instead, he suggested that I bring my daughter to the office. So I tried that out, and she was happier because she could be around me, but she started distracting my coworkers with her antics, dancing around in red cowgirl boots and raiding our snack cabinet. I was preoccupied with keeping her busy, so I fell behind.

Everyone (except the boss) could see how absurd the situation was. I was torn between two vital commitments, and the rigid workplace expectations (be visibly productive in the office, observe stated working hours) meant that I could not be the mother I needed to be. I knew that even amid this heart-twisting double bind, I was lucky. So many women have no choice but to leave their children in unsatisfactory care while they go to work (and many of them to care for other people's children!). My group of working mother friends sympathized with my dilemma, admitting that they had run into the same contradictions. A couple of them urged me to quit, telling me that nothing—especially a job that I wasn't fulfilled by—was worth sacrificing my child's mental health. But these were high-earning women with nannies and house cleaners, who had no trouble taking a mother away from her own children to serve their households.

In striking comparison, I heard a Native mother on the radio being interviewed about whether she found parenting "stressful." Mayan villager Maria de los Angeles Tun Burgos didn't even understand the concept. After hearing more explanation of the English term "stress," she admitted to once feeling "worried" about her son. But that feeling quickly passed, she said, and like most humans throughout time, her perspective on raising children and making a living was that these were enjoyable activities.[9] Yet these are the exact pursuits that make urban, professional people crack under pressure.

It's unreasonable that today, the concerns of parents at home are often seen as detracting from their commitment to their jobs. This is part of modern civilization's confining approach to an organic life, of which I was growing increasingly wary. Native plants grow in orderly garden beds, workers override their need for the outdoors hunched at computers all day consuming stimulants, and children are sequestered from their parents. Nature must be dominated and institutionalized within a rigid structure; errant growth must be weeded out. As I pieced this tragedy together, I felt my inner wild mother rear up, buck, and jump over the corral fence. My mom's stubborn will to push the limits was alive and well within me.

I wanted to live permanently outside, not just on office breaks. I also wanted to become deeply connected to what really matters. I wanted to write a script objecting to techno-utopia, a new story in which my life and everyone else's lives—CEOs, biohackers, and landscapers alike—were irrevocably tethered to that wild beehive in the live oak tree. This new story would demand that we stop making apps just to make money so we could go to the store and buy honey but instead learn to harvest the honey ourselves.

I feared that if I didn't do something drastic to alter their trajectory, my two grade-school-aged daughters would spend the bulk of their childhoods indoors. Their education would consist of preparing for an adulthood of screen-bound work that did not connect directly to nature or their own subsistence from it. I fantasized that nature immersion could show them a different way of life not reliant on technology, one that challenged their perceptual faculties and physical capabilities in ways their current lifestyle failed to do. I wanted my daughters to become fierce, independent, and physically strong while interacting with the environment they had evolved to live in, the world of their ancient ancestors. This kind of experience didn't fit neatly into time slots after school; it would require radically altering our family routines. I wanted to learn with them how to really *be* outside—to rewild.

My first liberating decision was to quit my office job in favor of freelance work. Getting back my daily autonomy brought some relief, and my kids benefited from more time with me. I also enrolled in a training course to become a naturalist, which required studying and spending lots of time in nature. I gained familiarity with the flora and fauna of my area, discovering a special passion for edible plants and fungi. I geeked out on taxonomy and how science has cataloged and named species according to physical and genetic similarities. While looking scrupulously under leaf debris for elusive fungi, observing the myriad ways chlorophyll manifests, and becoming emotionally invested in the welfare of coyote cubs in my local park, I started to feel like I had a stake in the more-than-human natural world. These pursuits also improved my outlook in general. In contrast to the previous clock-in, clock-out years of working in an office, I was able to spend half the day out in the sun, never glancing at my watch because I was focused and having fun.

But in my quest to rewild, the closest I ever came to experiencing something like a hunter-gatherer band was by attending week-long primitive skills events. These special times within a healthy rewilding community would become the most important punctuation marks in my year. They accelerated my acquisition of wild skills and integration with nature, perhaps when I wasn't even ready for it, like when I was returning from the gathering in Santa Barbara and picked up the roadkill fox—a moment that signaled to me that I had really started my rewilding journey. As I stood with her mangled body in my garage, that mama fox brought home everything I was beginning to reconsider. She symbolized the sacrifice of mothers and the deadly confines of civilization. She also became a memento mori of the mother I had lost.

Looking further into the origins of the red fox, *Vulpes vulpes*, I learned that these animals were imported from the Great Plains in the 1870s to provide for the booming fur trade. Red foxes are one of the most widespread and populous land mammals in the world now because of their adaptability to a variety of habitats, and they are sometimes considered invasive species. They can live in areas as diverse as tundra, salt marsh, and even in cities. Once released into the California landscape, red foxes occupied a different ecological niche than they had in their original habitat and quickly became fierce predators of ground-nesting birds. In recent decades, they have been blamed for the decline of several endangered avian species like clapper rails, least terns, and snowy plovers, none of which evolved defenses against predators like the fox. As a result, foxes have been targeted in extermination campaigns run by the state under the directives of the Endangered Species Act.[10] In light of this, my roadkill foray was not the straightforward act of reclamation that I imagined it to be.

My fox was ensnared in a web of dysfunctional relationships. First, she was living outside her evolutionary context. Second, the natural predators that might have prevented her from decimating various bird populations had been rooted out by people who wanted more control over the land for ranching, farming, and development. The wolves, bears, mountain lions, and eagles that may have kept her numbers in check are no longer a dominant part of California's Central Valley ecosystem. Coyotes do kill these foxes, but not enough to keep the web balanced, and they are widely exterminated as well. From an ecological perspective, the speeding vehicle that took the fox's life likely saved dozens of endangered birds that she and her kin would have eventually consumed.

Humans too function like an invasive species. Currently most of us live like the red fox: an exotic species out of our context, causing havoc in global ecosystems. Yet humans, like foxes, once had a beneficial impact on ecosystems, keeping populations in check. Ecologists have shown in several instances that foraging bands of humans, with their regime of controlled fire, migration, and seed transport, also function as a keystone species on the land. Keystone

species create an overwhelmingly positive impact for other creatures relative to a small amount of disturbance in the environment.
There is evidence that other species, like small seed grasses and
large wild fruits, evolved in relation to human influence and now
don't thrive without us creating areas of disturbance for seeds to
flourish or assisting with fire germination, for example.[11] Can we
imagine a future where our activities on the land are not to be feared
and proscribed with "stay on the trail" signs but are welcomed for
their regenerative qualities? Can we once again become reciprocal
partners with the nonhuman living world?

The observation that humanity has lost an essential link to
an original, natural state of being has a long history in Western
thought, from ancient Greece through the Enlightenment to the
transcendental era and the back-to-the-land hippies of the 1960s.
The experimenters from these eras sought to spend more time in
nature; they criticized increasing industrialization and rejected new
technology and consumerism. This urge to recapture the purity and
simplicity of a life governed by the body, the seasons, the earth, and
our ancestors has been a through line in history, a constant tension
pulling against the advancement of industrial civilization.

I identified with the sentiments of these predecessor movements
and had at various times in my life romanticized American pioneer
settlers, Thoreau and Emerson, the communal living gurus of the
Farm in Tennessee, and other hippie-era communes. Rewilding
builds on this succession of utopian movements, yet it is rooted in
a much longer timescale of tens of thousands, if not hundreds of
thousands, of years. It aims to reconnect us to our shared heritage

of hunting and gathering—one in which, I would learn, it was the women in the band who most often made animal skins into clothing, blankets, and adornment. I intuitively knew that I needed to participate in this work to feel fully human, but it would take many tries to get it right.

On that Sunday when I made my first attempt to skin the fox in my garage, I gave up. I dumped its mangled corpse into the compost bin that would be emptied the next morning. As I pressed the button to close the garage, my stomach tightened. I imagined where the mother fox was going—first to a vast warehouse to be combined with the rest of the city's food scraps and heated up to 180 degrees, and then, once alchemized back into soil, she'd be dumped on the fields of a Napa vineyard to enrich the grapevines. Perhaps her elements would make their way into a fine wine, one that would be drunk by someone who would drive the 101 late at night, never knowing what animals they might collide with. I shuddered at this thought because I wanted her encounter with humans to be done. I didn't want her looped back into the system that destroyed her. I wanted to immediately return her to nature. Somehow, I could make up for her untimely death on the freeway, and life could be regenerated. I also wanted to be able to watch the process, because I had never experienced what one of my favorite poets, Robinson Jeffers, had captured when he wrote, "I sadly smiling remember that the flower fades to make fruit / the fruit rots to make earth / Out of the mother; and through the spring exultances, ripeness and decadence; and home to the mother."[12]

Next to our house was a tract of wild sloping land that had never been developed. Grabbing the fox's legs once again—this time with my bare hands—I carried her to a bay laurel tree and placed her in a hollow on the hillside under the fragrant branches. I softly pressed violet vinca flowers on top of her dim eyes. For weeks afterward, my daughters and I visited her to see how her body was changing. We noticed that she was scavenged a bit, perhaps by a coyote or a turkey vulture, and after a few weeks, her skin turned black and leathery. When the rains came, mushrooms grew at the base of the tree. She helped us understand the natural life cycle of death and decay. It would be almost a year before I came back to find that all that was left of her was her skull. Her tiny sharp teeth were like ivory puzzle pieces lodged into the smooth curve of her jaws. Yet my failure to properly harvest this fox made it clear that I didn't have the skills to change my life yet. I needed to seek the wisdom of those who knew how to live wild.

CHAPTER 2

Weaving

Later that same year, on a sunny Saturday afternoon in fall of 2018, fifteen other women and I were gathered in a natural history museum in San Francisco, trying out an ancient art form perfected by women. As the wind riffled through the grassy hills of the surrounding landscape of Twin Peaks, my hands tightly gripped the reeds I had chosen from a bundle of dried tule, a giant bulrush plant that towers over inland waters in extensive patches across the country. Native Californians made huts, mats, canoes, hats, decoys, dolls, skirts, and baskets from its pliable stalks. Tule reed is identified by a golden toggle of flowers at the tip of its stalk and by its three-sided stem, which can reach ten feet tall. It often appears with cattails (the giant stalks that look like hot dogs on sticks) in dense clusters surrounding ponds, lakes, and estuaries.

I was twining the "earth end" of the reeds in circles around the bottom of what would become my first handmade basket, woven in the style of the Miwok Indians of Central California. When I had reached the "sky end" of the reed, I spliced in another stalk with a double twist and kept going. The reed is spongy in its interior, and as I wove the basket, it compressed into a tight pattern that would create a flexible, durable container for collecting and storing natural materials and food. Baskets can be woven from some grasses such that they become airtight, tolerate heat, and hold water. When hot stones are placed inside these sturdy baskets, they can be used for cooking.

Guiding my unschooled fingers were four generations of Native women, led by the matriarch and legendary Coast Miwok–Kashaya Pomo basket weaver of Yosemite Valley, Julia Parker. She was assisted by her daughter, granddaughter, and great-granddaughter. Witnessing this multigenerational family practicing their age-old tradition amplified my longing to be part of a woven net of relatives embedded in nature. The Parker family told us that Native women formed deep bonds while sitting and sharing the weaving techniques.

Julia had learned how to make baskets in a variety of Native California styles in her twenties from her husband's grandmother. She didn't just learn intricate technique, patience, and artistry; she also learned how to interact with the living beings and spirits that inhabited the tule marshes and willow stands. She had inherited the songs and prayers of gratitude for the plants and the power of creation. "We take from the earth and say please. We give back to the earth and say thank you," she told us. "Our baskets are living things. They start as tiny seeds and grow into something beautiful."

To someone unfamiliar with Native ways, this gesture might seem valuable only within the realm of ritual and religion. Yet it is accepted in Native communities that people who learn to respect the spirits of plants and exhibit gratitude to nature in general will both protect natural resources and respect their ancestors, elders, and other community members.[1] Acting within this integrated net-work of relations isn't just spiritual; it can transform how humans treat the physical world.

Julia and her daughter Lucy had collected these reeds, which they generously shared with the class, from their traditional lands where they have special rights to harvest. Before California was set-tled by Europeans, tule and other basket stock material grew all over, but by the early nineteenth century, European grasses and other invasive annuals brought to feed livestock had overtaken the landscape. Now, less than 1 percent of California grassland is made up of native grasses. The last two centuries of logging, mining, ranching, agriculture, and urban development damaged more hab-itat. So much land is now taken over by invasive Scotch broom and thistle that it is managed through aggressive pesticide spraying, making the environment more toxic. Yet in the 1980s and 1990s, government initiatives started allowing Native artisans to gather plant materials in areas that could be officially designated as their ancestral homelands.

Tule is less common now across the state because massive bodies of fresh water have been diverted for agriculture and city water projects. It would be hard to source enough of the plant from public land to build a shelter or a boat today without depleting the stock or depriving nesting ducks of their home. Given these factors, it would be easy to say that basket weaving is dying out here. In most Native Californian communities, people don't have the time to practice their traditions, occupied as they are by the demands of modern living. They also don't maintain the land as they once

did. Hundreds of years ago, Native communities would stimulate regrowth by digging in soil, pruning plants, spreading seeds,
and lighting controlled fires to remove dead leaves and debris that
would block sunlight for sprouting grasses.

Yet Julia has kept her tradition alive. Over the last sixty years, she
has become one of the most well-known Native American basket
makers in California. From 1960 to 2015, she worked as a cultural
specialist at the Yosemite Museum, sharing her techniques and
knowledge. Her work has been exhibited at the National Museum
of the American Indian, and she was tapped to make a gift basket
for Queen Elizabeth II when the British royals visited Yosemite in
previous decades. She also helped establish the California Indian
Basketweavers' Association, which has trained hundreds of people
in making baskets, which was necessary to keep the art alive. "This
is ancient Tupperware!" she quipped to our class with a grin, adding
levity to the fact that she was doing nothing short of resuscitating an
art almost lost under genocide.

Weaving is not easy to master, as I learned through messing up
repeatedly, pulling out lengths of reed from mistakenly twined rows,
and starting over and over. But as the basket took shape, I began to
feel a sense of satisfaction. My hands were learning the algorithm
as each twist took less effort than the last until I began sensing the
pattern of maneuvers without looking. Through the process, I was
learning a new way to observe so many objects I had never taken
a closer look at before. In the weeks after the workshop, baskets of
all kinds popped out at me in three dimensions, posing a challenge
to decode how they might have been made—*Which method of twist?*

What materials? How were the ends secured at the top of the vessel?
The basket on my bike, the straw hat my friend wore, the laundry
hamper—these were all handmade objects carefully constructed
with skill that became newly legible.

Baskets made from natural fibers are likely the oldest and most
diverse form of craft, though because they biodegrade quickly, it's
hard to know exactly when people started making them. To this
day, nearly every basket available in stores has been assembled by a
human, even ones you can buy at Target. Despite all the latest high-
tech advances in fabrication, they're still difficult to manufacture
with machines, making them some of the most human objects.

The tradition of weaving can also bind a society together. From
what is known about Julia's ancestors from four thousand years ago,
basketry would have been a central component of women's lives, and
baskets would be central to material culture for everyone from birth
to death. They were used for gathering, transporting, processing,
storing, and preparing plant materials and foods. Before the birth of a
child, mothers would weave infant carrier baskets so that they could
continue working while tending the baby. At the end of life, baskets
were sometimes woven as coffins for the dead or containers for the
bones of the deceased. Women maintained the knowledge about
useful plants and stewarded their growth, claiming certain patches
and territories for their families' use, year after year. Techniques were
passed down through matrilineal lines, and daughters often remained
close to their mothers and grandmothers in adulthood to enjoy their
family tracts of land, to continue learning weaving techniques, and to
get elders' help with birth and child care.

I had experienced a similar intergenerational textile tradition. While my family had no Native heritage, I remember being enchanted by my mother working at a loom, weaving tapestries to decorate our home. I sensed that this was a powerful skill for me to learn, and I relished the afternoons that she spent teaching me about the warp and the weft. She also taught me how to sew—a skill she had learned from her mother. As a child, I wore many handmade dresses my grandmother and mother had sewn, and I then made my own babies their first garments. Across these generations, we were wrapping our daughters in love.

After the weekend workshop with the Parker family, I brought home a wobbly and uneven basket about the size of a cantaloupe. Julia told me that you are supposed to give away the first basket you make, and perhaps it will one day come back to you. I gifted mine to my kids and immediately set about teaching them how to make their own. We experimented with lots of different materials, from yarn and twist ties to blackberry canes (stripped of prickles) and pine needles. The projects we started were difficult for them to finish, so I stored away many half-done creations with the hope that they would pick them up again when their hand dexterity matured.

Inspired by my time with Julia and her family, several weeks later, I took my family to a reconstruction of a coastal Miwok village near Point Reyes National Seashore called Kule Loklo, or Bear Valley. On the short hike to the site, I pointed out the triple-leaf threat of poison oak so that we wouldn't get itchy later. The kids started to distinguish it from the similarly shaped, yet benign, blackberry vine. I gave the kids tastes of several edible plants, and my youngest made friends with a slug that she carried on her sleeve.

Once we arrived at the village, an interpretive sign informed us that the Miwok people were hunter-gatherers who created simple settlements across Northern California; George Lucas lived on their territory and used their history and redwood forest habitat as inspiration for the Ewoks in *Return of the Jedi*. My husband had agreed to join us, but while the kids and I explored the site's cone-shaped redwood bark shelters, gathering hall, and sweat lodge, he got an alert on his phone, so he had to retreat to a picnic bench to tap out the final edits to a legal brief. The girls and I turned over logs, tasted tender fir needles, scattered thistle seeds, and generally caused a positive disturbance to the quiet spot. We found some sturdy grasses and set about weaving quick, sloppy baskets. Even with these disheveled vessels, we connected to the traditionally female craft tradition, making round containers useful for gathering blackberries on our way back to the car. In my own way, I wanted to pass on this ancestral skill that I had initially learned at my mother's side, intertwining warp and weft.

While tradition assigns some tasks to one sex, it's liberating that today boundaries can be more flexible. Once I became a bit obsessed with basket weaving, I came across the work of Peter Michael Bauer, who is one of the most prominent popularizers of the craft in the rewilding scene today and who is a man. Reading through his blog posts and social media content about rewilding, I became convinced that he would be an ideal teacher for me, and I set up several meetings with him and traveled to attend the events he hosts each year.

Peter earned his first Boy Scout badge at age eleven for basket weaving. His enthusiasm for making useful objects with his hands and natural materials led him to drop out of high school to participate in backcountry wilderness programs. In his twenties, his attempt to live by practicing wild skills on the fringe of the city as a primitive hipster alter ego named Urban Scout—dressed only in a dumpster-dived loincloth—gained him some notoriety. His combination of handsome vigor, blunt countercultural messaging, and millennial media savvy made for a captivating online figure. After many experimental years of trying to propagate the seeds of rewilding through various online forums, he decided to focus on his local area and even learned to speak the Native trade language of his region, Chinook Wawa. In 2009, he launched the nonprofit Rewild Portland, which teaches wild skills and ecological restoration to kids and adults. The organization advocates studying how humans were able to maintain their ecological role on the planet for millions of years without wreaking havoc on the environment. Through classes, workshops, and two gatherings every year, Rewild Portland helps people discover "the ways in which civilization holds us captive and what we may do to break free," Peter said during a phone call. Allying with several Native groups in the Willamette Valley, Rewild Portland offers instruction in place-based traditional arts like basket making, wild food foraging, archery, natural dyeing, cordage making, hide tanning, and natural building. They hold free monthly classes and offer flexible pricing for events to make the skills more accessible.

Peter also inherited the leadership of a decades-old wild skills gathering every July called Echoes in Time, held on private land in the Willamette Valley. His work has shown thousands of people that by practicing the ancient skills of hunter-gatherers, they can reconnect to their healthiest selves while regaining a self-sufficient and non-destructive relationship with natural resources. The primary skill he teaches is basket weaving. "Basketry is an integral part of human connection to the local environment and goes back possibly forty thousand years," Peter told me. "It's nature-based and connects you to place because you keep returning to your harvesting sites and observing how you have affected the ecology there."

Ever the tinkerer, he's also found innovative ways to confront the invasive species that crowd out basket-making plants by harvesting exotics that can be woven. Fast-growing, tree-smothering English ivy is "the bane of every conservationist in the Northwest," he said. Ivy can smother habitat for native wildlife and matures into large, networked patches where no other plants can develop. As it reaches its tendrils out to climb trees, it damages bark, weakens branches, and then starves the forest floor of sunlight. Ivy-infested forest then becomes more susceptible to pests and disease. Portland's No Ivy League and the city parks department have made it their mission to try to eradicate the plant from public spaces using herbicides; like the Hydra's heads, the ivy grows back to continue its menace.

Yet characterizing the species as an interloper that needs to be eradicated offends Peter's sensibility. "Perhaps people will stop putting their hate into a plant and learn to respect it for the gifts that it has to offer us," he said, noting that he believes ivy, along with most invasives, like the prickly Himalayan blackberry that has also spread throughout the region, are probably here to stay. Eradication and extermination are not sustainable solutions, especially with toxic chemicals, but using their materials to decrease their spread is something people can meaningfully participate in. Helping the native species flourish is also an achievable strategy. His solution is clever, and ready for mass adoption. Peter once told a Portland magazine that his dream was for every resident in Portland to weave a grocery basket out of invasive species to reduce ivy, disposable paper, and plastic.

He said that the key is to disrupt the relationship between invasives and noninvasives by creating a new relationship between humans and the plants. The ecological context must also be considered; native plants are symbiotic with native pollinators and other insects that feed on them and spread their pollen. Invasive species haven't had the evolutionary timeline in the habitat of the Pacific Northwest, or many of the spots where they grow, to develop that give and take with other species. We need to develop this reciprocity too. "Deciding what plants get to live and which don't, that's not the role our ancestors played."

Domination of nature doesn't fit in with Peter's idea of weaving either. During one of his workshops that I attended at the Echoes in Time primitive skills gathering, he talked about how our ancestors were woven into their environment. He pointed out that all life is based on strands of molecules twisted into the double helix of DNA, which governs how other strands of proteins fold in on themselves in intricate loops. "Weaving is how things are held together, and it is a reflection of what you are made of," Peter said, further explaining that English ivy's scientific name, *Hedera helix*, references its spiraling growth pattern, weaving a carpet of the forest floor, which is itself knit together by the web of mycelium and microorganisms. "When I think about those connections, I honor it and think about it and weave my awe into the basket." [2]

While Julia is working to preserve her culture, Peter sees rewilding as a way to create a new culture using an ancient recipe. "It means returning to a more natural or wild state and reversing domestication," he wrote in his self-published book, *Rewild or Die*.[3] Rewilding is about learning to tend to the lives of what we eat and use so that we all can continue to live. He wrote that it ultimately requires abandoning industrial agriculture, which he called "a catastrophic practice to which we all act as slaves."

When I read *Rewild or Die*, I was struck by this extreme positioning, and I immediately judged his statements as adolescent—was he just misapplying punk rock fervor to ecology? Could he really believe that we could dismantle the entire system on which our modern lives now depend? Our cultural story tells us that agriculture brought us prosperity and continues to propel us forward on our never-ending journey of technological and cultural progress. I had never encountered anyone who didn't yearn to experience some of the finer aspects of modern society and technology in my limited fieldwork with rural Brazilian, Haitian, and Israeli communities. I've seen people's quality of life increase through simple improvements like electrification, irrigation, and the use of ATVs for hunting.

And how could Peter call humans domesticated when *we* had been the ones domesticating plants and animals for millennia? He seemed to perceive something I couldn't. When I met Peter, I was struck by his authentic emotional connection to the natural spaces near him. He talked about the land as if it were a cherished family member. We first connected at a time when a fifty-thousand-acre fire had just raged up the Columbia River Gorge. As he picked up the phone, he was nearly crying in shock. "These were sacred places," he told me, his voice breaking. Ignited by a teenager playing with prohibited fireworks, the conflagration was a touch point for Peter's sensitivity about how blind humans have become to the danger we pose to natural spaces.

Peter connected this human-caused disaster to agriculture. That didn't make sense to me. How was agriculture like a wildfire out of control? He explained that the clearing of fields, uprooting of existing plants, and tilling of the soil that are necessary to farm the land are similar to what happens after flooding, fires, volcanic eruptions, and earthquakes. Our mega farms keep simulating these catastrophes, year after year, on a much greater scale than anything "natural." The land never has time to recover, biodiversity is lost to monoculture, and water and erosion carry away the topsoil.[4] From the perspective of the earth, that teen playing with explosives and burning down innumerable acres of forests was just like any modern farmer.

But actually, agriculture was so much worse than a wildfire, because it had huge social ramifications. When it developed around ten thousand years ago, it led to more food security, but it also eventually caused never-before-seen warfare, slave labor, bureaucracy, environmental destruction, soil degradation, and subjugation of women over the ensuing centuries. This dramatic cause and effect also baffled me at first. Here's how Peter broke it down.

When food was no longer collected freely from the environment as it had been by human ancestors for millions of years, this changed how people related to each other. The food surpluses from large fields (mostly cereal grains that were less nutritious than wild foods) had to be protected, and some people had to become devoted solely to that task instead of gathering, hunting, or tending small plots. Not everyone got an equal share of the food, because some would hoard it, and conflict would break out over these scarce resources. Add to that the fact that early farmers endured much harder work, worse nutrition, and poorer health than their foraging ancestors until the last few hundred years. All the toiling and tilling did not yield a better diet or more free time, and most people were losing their ability to find food in nature. Clearly the benefits of a seasonal food harvest did not outweigh giving up the lifestyle of freely roaming the land in egalitarian bands, consuming hundreds of nutritious species of plants and animals. Yet after so many generations had passed, agriculturalists were stuck in farming settlements. Returning to hunting and gathering for most of their calories was no longer possible, and they had become dependent on cereal-based diets.

Fast-forward thousands of years, and now we, their descendants, are accustomed to processed, packaged foods and the extreme hierarchies of corporations and government that control their distribution. We're so disconnected from our original mode of eating that many school children today can no longer distinguish a potato from a tomato (as British chef Jamie Oliver once proved on TV). Small-scale horticulture doesn't have the same effect on society and would have been a better direction for humanity to pursue, but now most of the globe is dominated by one united industrial agricultural system.

This all made sense to me, as I had grown up traversing the never-ending corn fields of the Midwest, but it took a while for it to sink in. I had to realize that everything I had learned about human progress—that more streamlined production always led to a better quality of life—was wrong. And I didn't have a moment to catch my breath because there were more giant misconceptions that Peter wanted to help me dismantle.

When I asked him about how humans could be considered domesticated, he talked about recent research showing that there is a recognizable genetic signature of domestication in animals, a suite of traits known as "domestication syndrome." [5] The markers include a smaller overall size, decreased strength, shorter jaws, fewer physical differences between the sexes, more frequent ovulation cycles, juvenile behaviors that are retained into adulthood (such as prolonged play), and an increase in docile behaviors. These signs of animal domestication that are plain to see in any puppy also show up in modern humans but not in our extinct wild counterparts like Neanderthals and Denisovans. We all know that our brow ridges have gotten smaller since the time of our ancient forebears, but we also have smaller brains, shorter jaws (leading to more crowded and smaller teeth—to the delight of orthodontists everywhere), lower bone density and strength, and an extended juvenile period. Last I checked, most Americans hit eighteen and still need their parents' credit cards for another decade at least, whereas prehistoric teens were likely already rearing families of their own.

How did this happen? How did we lose strength, become more agreeable, lose gray matter, and start taking longer to mature? One theory suggests that humans self-domesticated through the sexual selection of less aggressive, more friendly mates. As *Homo sapiens* cooperated more and more, they bred out the bullies. Yet this kind of genetic selection occurs on an unconscious level, not with the same process of outright manipulation of plant and animal reproduction. Another theory states that domestication involves the biological changes brought about through living almost exclusively in enclosed houses and yards, which are artificial environments, akin to how animals live in a zoo. Yet there are some species that show signs of domestication, like our close relatives the bonobos, who have never altered their habitat.

Even if the biological aspects of domestication are still being sorted out by science, rewilders emphasize the fact that humans are utterly dependent on centralized production systems. Just as the dog, formerly a wild wolf, now expects its nightly kibble and soft bed, humans expect to get all their calories from the grocery store and snooze on a Tempur-Pedic mattress inside a home kept at a constant seventy degrees. Super domestic.

There were more changes that developed as a result of moving our habitat from the outdoors to the indoors. Now, with a barrier between us and nature, we started to lose what could be considered the religion of our nomadic hunter-gatherer ancestors, who saw spiritual and energetic connections between themselves and everything in the world. As Yuval Noah Harari wrote in the widely popular *Sapiens*, the rise of human civilization replaced a daily life based on the physical reality of the natural world with one based on imagined social constructs that only exist because we make them up. Once humans had amassed settled populations in communities greater than 150 individuals, recognized as the upper limit that facilitates stable reciprocal relationships, it was necessary to form impersonal bonds based on money, gods, empires, nations, and corporations. The institutions that formed around these constructs keep order through social hierarchies and maintain the top-down power structure with deadly force.

With Harari's explanation, I better understood how civilization accomplished the large-scale suppression of the forager way of life. It entailed the cooperation of hundreds, thousands, and now millions and billions of humans in a complex society that produces crafts and technology from specialized labor. It naturalized its authority by controlling and dominating humans and nature. Harari wrote that civilized people live in a dual reality, made up of, on the one hand, "the objective reality of rivers, trees, and lions; and on the other hand, the imagined reality of gods, nations, and corporations." [6] Yet the original and undeniable authority of nature and its self-governed processes has been overtaken by these imagined fictions. The survival of all life on earth is now thought to be determined by governments and various tech companies instead of by nature. What's more real? The American symbol of the bald eagle or the soaring bird hunting for prey?

Recognizing this, rewilders have become the new iconoclasts. Peter believes his work is a way of destroying the myths of corporate and national authority in order to bring us back into a reciprocal relationship with the land, to return to a life based on physical reality rather than made-up symbols.

When people ask Peter about simple things they can do to rewild, he said that his response generally annoys them, because he doesn't regurgitate advice common in liberal circles or prepper-style communities. "I don't say to them: invest in green technology, stockpile canned foods, arm yourself with guns and ammo, and ride your bike more," he said. Instead, he tells them to learn about native edible plants, practice wilderness skills, and try to form locally based social support networks. Anyone trying to make a buck off the rewilding movement is also suspect to him, because they don't understand that rewilding is about decreasing dependency on manufactured goods and centralized production. "If you've got a product you're selling, then you're not rewilding," he intoned.

This comment helped me modify my own habits because I realized that you can't buy your way into a wilder life. You must create, produce, and manifest wildness yourself or with your small group. Gone were my bottles of supplements, the exercise devices, and the apps that I used in an effort to come into alignment with my evolutionary environment. Instead of taking vitamin D, I could spend more time in the sun. Instead of running on a treadmill at the gym, burning gas to get there and wasting electricity through the machine, I could just run outside. To replace my meditation app, I could sit by a burbling stream. None of these solutions required an ecological, economic, or emotional price.

True, it's very hard to replace everything modern with something natural, and Peter displays the ironic choices he has made (that aren't particularly wild) to engage more people. One of his popular Facebook posts shows him clad entirely in buckskin, typing on his computer. The caption reads, "Nature leader spends all day inside on laptop, organizing rewilding activities."

His definition of rewilding has changed over the years. While he once quipped that rewilding was about "undoing domestication," the negative orientation of such a phrase didn't mesh with the creation of regenerative practices. The idea of restoration of the environment also plagued him. "What are we restoring ourselves and our land to?" he asked an audience at the rewilding conference he organized in 2018. Many conservationists have proposed aiming for reestablishing a lifestyle and environmental conditions that resemble the end of the Pleistocene era, after the most recent Ice Age, about 11,700 years ago. This would entail erasing the effects of any industrial action, farming, ranching, and permanent human settlement on the land. They advocate for reintroducing species into areas where they once lived before something—hunting, environmental degradation, extinction—drove them out.

Adding predators often restores ecosystems to the way they functioned before modern humans mucked them up. Reintroducing wolves to Yellowstone National Park in the 1990s after they'd been nearly hunted into extinction in the 1920s is the prime example, though it was bitterly fought by local ranchers who feared losing their livestock to hungry wild canines. Yet with the wolves back at the top of the food chain, the elk population stabilized, the grasslands and river areas they had overgrazed rebounded, and even the park's waterways were able to support more biodiversity as a result.

Many other species have been successfully rewilded into their original habitats, including bison in Montana, beavers in the Scottish Highlands, and elk in Marin, California. Each species initiated a cascade of positive effects through the food chain and more of a balance between every participant, improving the whole region.

But a restoration will not work across most areas of human settlement because we are living in a climate and ecosystem entirely transformed by people, a shift that prompted scientists to declare a new geological epoch called the Anthropocene Imagine: at the end of the last Ice Age, there were woolly mammoths roaming Portland's surrounds, and the megafauna that humans encountered in their first forays on the North American continent were abundant. Today, those species are extinct. The air, water, and soil are polluted, and we have added tens of thousands of synthesized compounds to the biosphere, in addition to billions of humans. Civilization itself has become an unstoppable force of nature. The best we can do, Peter said, is decrease our reliance on it. Eventually, he predicts, the disease of civilization will eat up everything within reach, and from there, it's only a matter of time before it can eat no more, and it will shrink and die out. Collapse of our economic system, our commercial infrastructure, and our power grid is inevitable, and Peter has been preparing for such catastrophes his whole life. What's most important is to try to adapt to our new, contaminated, and overbuilt environment by encouraging nature everywhere. So he's recently redefined rewilding as "increasing wildness."

I wasn't sure that it was an improved definition. The word *wild* is so overused in English to mean "extreme" that it would not be surprising to see Red Bull sponsor its entry in the dictionary. The origin of the word gives satisfying context, however. It comes from the Old Dutch word *wilde*, which means desire and want. In current English usage, it means untamed and not domesticated. For Peter, something untamed is subject to its own desires; it isn't controlled, and it doesn't seek to dominate. Relinquishing the urge to manage other things means to return to ways of life that seamlessly blend with the cycles of nature rather than launching a war to subdue them. Harvest and weave the ivy; don't spray it.

The beneficial aspects of rewilding are obvious to folks who start getting connected to nature and improving their health, and as people begin to explore the various entry points to rewilding, Peter often sees them become more uncompromising in their practices. "All paths lead to rewilding," he said. Say someone begins with a desire to quit working for a boss. Their quest for control over how they make their living might lead them to wonder why so many people sacrifice their autonomy for the security of a paycheck. Then they ask themselves, *Why work for money if what I really require is food and shelter?* Soon, the former cubicle dweller is learning to forage food and build an off-grid cabin. Another example: someone's interest in the Paleo diet leads them to buy local foods, which leads to foraging wild greens, which leads to exploring how their area's Native people tended wild gardens to ensure the supply year after year. That would soon happen to me.

"Then you realize that a lot of these foraging practices are illegal, and the knowledge about how to do it is disappearing because

Natives can't practice their traditions," he said. This, in turn, might lead to an understanding that because of laws, regulations, police forces, and taxation, there are enormous barriers in place that prevent anyone from fully rewilding. All the strands of a wild life eventually twine together into a cohesive whole in which the individual chooses more and more activities that are integrated with nature while civilization unravels. And the more dedicated rewilders following as much of a Paleolithic lifestyle as they can are best able to access and increase their wildness. They will become the ones leading the rest of us in the aftermath of apocalypse.

Peter's critics frequently allege that this way of being with nature simply isn't available or accessible anymore to most people. He hears the refrain of "we can't go back" as an attempt by domesticated profit seekers to silence the most obvious and free choice available to anyone. Living wild had *always* been available and had proved to be the most enduring and sustainable mode of existence on the planet. Hunter-gatherers were seamlessly woven into their environment and manifested that intertwining intelligence into everything they did, from basket weaving and social relationships to spirituality and inter-generational traditions.

I yearned to weave myself and my family back into the fabric of wildness, and I was grateful that I had found a guide. Peter hadn't given up on the possibility of splicing wildness into his urban life, and he knew dozens of folks who were out on rural land, trying to live without most of the constraints of civilization. I wanted to hear their stories and learn from them.

When Peter shared some of his contacts with me, I realized that each of them taught at primitive skills gatherings and had gotten their start with stints at wilderness survival schools. While all paths could conceivably lead to rewilding, these two routes seemed to offer a shortcut. The trail I was following suddenly became clearer. I knew where I had to go.

CHAPTER 3

Gathering

For spring break 2018, I rented a camper van with a folded double bed and kitchen supplies packed up inside, which made camping as a solo parent more manageable. Having set up a tent or two with a toddler underfoot in years past, I knew that my exhaustion usually set in long before the sleeping bags got rolled out and the source of my fatigue finally closed her eyes. In this kitted-out vehicle, we headed to the rolling hills outside Santa Barbara.

The Acorn Gathering, billed as a week of "natural living skills," took place on a twenty-eight-hundred-acre cattle ranch surrounded by hilly oak woodland. The event website was scrappy, not flashy, and had at first seemed amateur to my Silicon Valley eyes. But after further consideration, I thought it indicated that the gathering would be good because the leaders were living their outdoor skilled lives, not tinkering around with JavaScript. I hoped that by attending, I would get a full immersion in rewilding culture with my kids.

When I clicked on the photo galleries from previous years, I saw scenes from what might have been a Paleolithic Burning Man festival. Groups of long-haired folks sat in circles under the oak trees, working on crafts. Men of all ages linked arms in a boisterous dance. Women held babies while they smoothed out animal fur into felt for hats and bags. Young girls stretched out bows while squinting to gauge their arrow's target. Giant hides dried in the sun while kids climbed trees, *Maybe a little too high*, I thought.

The participants all looked really healthy: they had sunned skin, long hair, lush beards, bare feet, glowing smiles. They were quite fit, their muscles working visibly as they crafted. Babies and toddlers weren't trapped in strollers or carriers or car seats; they were naked and free, grabbing on to whomever wanted to play with them. Kids with tangled hair and unwashed hands played instruments, picked flowers, and ran wherever they wanted. This looked nothing like our life in the city and our highly scripted routines of going to school, the playground, and the grocery store, always strapped in, wiped clean, and smeared in sunscreen.

The signposts of this subculture were clear in their fashions. Handmade hats, well-worn leather boots and sandals, and unlaundered buckskin layers were the norm. The scenes looked like the work of set and costume designers for a PBS period drama, but the period was hybridized. Was this Paleolithic? Elizabethan? Nineteenth century Western homestead? Whatever the era, it seemed that these people were quietly slipping back into balance with themselves and the land. Looking at these images fed my desire for a more wild life. I needed to know: Who *were* they? Why hadn't I seen them around? How could I become more like them? Or at least follow them on social media?

My futile search to find "nature clothes" on the internet revealed just how little I knew about this "natural skills" lifestyle. Nevertheless, before we left, the girls and I took a trip to a thrift store to acquire some earth-toned cotton and wool clothes. I feared that our usual outdoor garb of synthetic, brightly dyed tops and athletic pants would make us stick out too much as newcomers. Yet I would soon learn that my focus on appearances was more indicative of my consumer mindset than the motives of people in this community.

Walking around on our first afternoon, we saw people practicing flint knapping, archery, basket weaving, wood carving, friction fire, buckskin sewing, hide tanning, and food preparation with only fire. In this village from the past, private campsites were set up around the main workshop areas. The central gathering space spread out across a few acres in a canyon, flanked by hills that we would climb to glimpse the sunset. A communal tipi stretched up to the sky in front of a long rectangular fire trench with a makeshift propane-fueled kitchen behind.

Despite first appearances, a gathering like Acorn isn't a hippie festival, nor is it a cult centered on a spiritual tradition. While there might be intoxicants discreetly going around, gatherings for ancestral skills are officially no-drugs, no-alcohol, and family-friendly events. The price for a ticket is comparably affordable for a week of camping in which attendees receive two meals a day and attend classes running from early morning to night. These are structured as choose your own adventure, with no guidance counselors to assist with course selection. Some classes last a few hours for a small project or presentation, but some last for days, and at the end, the participants take home a basket, a tanned hide, a fired pot, or a long bow.

At the opening circle, all the instructors, organizers, and participants crowded around to welcome each other. We received a traditional blessing from Tataucho Muhuawit, a Chumash man in his
late sixties who mentored Gabriel Kelly, Acorn's founder. The scent
of burning sage permeated the air as the sun cleared through the
clouds, sending us all searching for our hats, scarves, and sunglasses.

Over the next hour, every instructor got a chance to talk about
what they would be teaching over the week. Attendees had come
from Oaxaca, Mexico; Vancouver, Canada; and all over the West. I
was overwhelmed keeping track of the who, what, and where of the
upcoming day. The topics were a grab bag of toolmaking, crafting,
therapeutic and transformational practices, and skill development
that affirmed the attendees' views and attitudes toward the natural
world. They mixed Paleo, Native American, European medieval,
and American pioneer traditions.

There was salmon skin tanning up on the hill, a wild plant walk
meeting by the kitchen, Chumash legends and acorn processing at
the fire circle, leather pouch sewing by the women's tent, herbal
medicine at the medical tent, bow making down the road, and knife
skills at the children's tipi. "Just sink into the experience," coached
one instructor. "No devices. Let your batteries die. You'll find your
way to where you need to be. Don't worry about the photos; we
have a photographer." I appreciated those tips, but I also felt the
need to write everything down in my notebook and try to make a
schedule.

One spritely, older instructor, Myron Cretney, gave the crowd a
series of boisterous instructions that I found surprisingly charming.

Barefoot and dressed in buckskin shorts, a chunky knit sweater, and a woven cattail hat, he implored the attendees not to turn on their headlamps while walking back to the campsites in the dark. "It's like a dagger to your peepers!" he yelled as he drove his hands toward his squinched-up eyes and dramatically shrank backward and nearly fell on the ground. I thought of Oedipus and laughed at how he had turned a tragic image into comedy. "Instead," he said, getting up, "I want you to think about how much bigger the world is in the dark when we don't reduce it down to a beam. I invite you to experience...night!" Rather than hectoring us with a list of rules that might make us feel restrained and therefore rebellious, he pointed out how silly modern humans have separated ourselves from the once common experience of darkness. The need to illuminate everything all the time has its drawbacks—we have an addiction to flashlights. Why had we ignored the power of our dilated pupils in moonlight, causing other people headaches with our need to see every corner of the path?

The appeal to empathy rather than an insistence on rules typified the way things were run at Acorn. The head organizer, Gabriel, and his wife, Luna, who ran the kitchen operations, smoothly handled logistics for the group. With their crowd of lifelong, rugged, nature-focused pals, they have been bringing folks together at Acorn since 2008 with minimal rules for attendees. "The number one rule here is self-supervision," Gabriel informed the crowd with a smile. "And you are responsible for how you affect others, including the birds and the trees." They were adamant about regular hand washing and picking up trash. But they didn't care where or how you pitched your tent or whether children were closely supervised. The kids at Acorn carried knives and knew how to set fires, but this was not a big concern. There were classes teaching them exactly how to behave with these powerful forces. Everyone in the village was supposed to keep an eye out for danger.

Like his namesake, Gabriel had an angelic glow emanating off his golden curls. giving him the air of a surfer prophet. He grew up in the mountains and learned how to live off the land from infancy. He was such a perfect combination of Californian sun-kissed glamour and self-reliance that he'd been cast on the National Geographic reality television series *Live Free or Die* in 2014. Across ten episodes, he had demonstrated his optimistic approach to survival, tirelessly pursuing rodents and wild boar for his dinner, and finally returning to his tiny home with Luna after a three-month walkabout. I watched the series with my kids, and we laughed at the way network TV distorted his way of life by twisting mundane details into potential crises. In one episode, the show narrator emphasized how Gabriel had brought only one bottle of water on a hike. "He must find water before sundown, or he may expire from dehydration in this sizzling heat," we heard from an alarmist voice-over as Gabriel furrowed his eyebrows at the sunset horizon. Spoiler alert: he was fine, but these kinds of narrative exaggerations eventually led to his decision to drop out of the show.

I didn't know it at the time, but I learned later that Gabriel was part of a second generation of primitive skills practitioners, and he was building on over thirty years of gatherings to create a working framework for his event. About three dozen gatherings like Acorn happen across America over every season of the year, bringing together practitioners and students interested in rewilding. They began in the 1970s as opportunities for small groups of self-taught people (mostly men) to revive what they referred to as "primitive" skills.[1] Some of these men called themselves "experimental archaeologists," and many of them had working knowledge about the tools and habits of Paleolithic clans through the study of artifacts. Experimental archaeology attempts to test out hypotheses about ancient cultures by replicating objects from the past with the historically appropriate materials and tools in order to learn about how they could be made and used to perform specific tasks.[2] Through working with these replicas, experimenters might also reveal ways they could be done better with new scientific understanding.

They may also revive an ancient practice that no living human uses anymore, such as cooking food inside a ruminant's stomach over an open fire or throwing an atlatl dart. In the latter case, these long spear projectiles, which predate the bow and arrow, were first discovered by amateur archaeologists in the nineteenth century. The atlatl includes a throwing stick that has a socket on one end and a hand grip on the other. This construction takes advantage of the spear's leverage, allowing it to be launched with incredible speed and force, more than could be achieved by hand. As a result of experimental archaeologists' ongoing work, the sport of atlatl archery was established in the 1980s, and today there are state, regional, and international contests where throwers compete at increasingly difficult levels. Yet skeptics didn't believe Paleolithic humans used atlatls to kill big game until archaeologist George

Frison showed conclusively in 1989 that an arrowhead fashioned in the style of the Clovis people from thirteen thousand years ago could fatally wound an elephant.[3] Yes, he slayed that big game himself just to prove that the tool worked. Since then, many hunters have killed large mammals using this ancient weapon and continue to provide archaeologically relevant data about its performance.

However, early primitive skills enthusiasts weren't primarily interested in academic debates. They wanted to revive the use of artifacts and techniques for their own enjoyment, restore their connections to nature, and embody our collective legacy as tool-wielding primates. Their pursuit couldn't have come soon enough, because the existing cultures using Paleolithic tools were rapidly modernizing or dying out, and elders were not passing traditions on to the next generation. Plus, the decline of these communities meant there was a decrease in opportunities to observe how traditional tools were made and used, which had, for about one hundred years, provided reliable stand-ins for how these materials were used in prehistory. The experimental archaeologists of this era found that they were unintentionally keeping traditions alive that might have completely disappeared otherwise. Many of them sought out older Native Americans to learn traditional techniques from, initiating lasting relationships with reservation communities.

According to the first founders, the origins for skills gatherings were laid in the 1960s, when a stone-working hobbyist named Don Crabtree began publishing his findings about experiments with flint and his recreation of lithic artifacts. Despite his lack of academic credentials, Crabtree became a celebrated teacher and honorary scientist in the field, training many young men who went on to build up knowledge of stone tools, archery, atlatl technique, and primitive building. By the 1970s, a lively dialogue and exchange was going on across the country about flint knapping. People started coming together for informal camping excursions to rock hound and share skills at events called knap-ins.

It was one of Crabtree's students who organized the first big primitive skills gathering on the West Coast called Rabbitstick. Larry Dean Olsen was a wilderness skills instructor who also taught at Brigham Young University and frequently took young people out into the woods to practice survival. In 1969, he published the book *Outdoor Survival Skills*, which inspired a generation of readers and influenced the direction of prominent outdoor recreation schools like the National Outdoor Leadership School and Outward Bound toward survival-oriented instruction. Held in June 1978, Rabbitstick was an intensive, four-day immersion in the Paleolithic. Olsen sent out the announcement to the event as a sort of wild freak manifesto, declaring that it was "specially for under-snuck desert trekkers; for blanket-pack packin' packrat eaters and biscuit root gourmets; for all rabbit stick throwin', atlatl flingin' troubadours of the wilds—and any other good guys or gals brave enough to chance it!"[4]

If someone was familiar enough with the land to know that biscuit root is a forager's tasty treasure and that a rabbit stick is a Native hare-assassination device, then they had the bona fides to haul their beat-up Westfalia out to central Utah to be welcomed by the likes of woodsy mavericks Tom Brown Jr. and Jim Riggs. Brown had recently founded the first tracker school in New Jersey, claiming that he learned a wide array of primitive skills from Stalking Wolf, his Native "grandfather," although this account is widely questioned. Riggs was a buckskin-clad archaeologist deeply immersed in primitive skills who is best known for reviving the practice of brain tanning deer hide, in which a solution of the animal's brain was used to soften its skin. Showing off their skills by constructing tree-bark tents, weaving cattail mats, and carrying around their supplies in juniper-bark baskets, these two men did a lot of the heavy lifting for stoking wider interest in nature skills in the early days.

After some leadership changes and skipped years in the eighties, the Rabbitstick gathering was relaunched in 1988 by David Wescott, who had trained under Olsen and started his own wilderness training organization in Boulder, Utah, the Boulder Outdoor Survival School (BOSS). Looking for a way to gather teachers from across the country to better train his school's instructors, Wescott invited every primitive technologist he knew, ending up with forty-eight instructors at the event. The reinvigorated gathering took off, motivating Wescott and pals to form the Society for Primitive Technology, which, for the next twenty-five years, produced a journal cataloguing all the experiments and knowledge they were accumulating about prehistoric lifeways. For a young person who had aspirations to live like Robin Hood, Tarzan, or Ishi—the last member of the Native Californian Yahi tribe, who died in 1916—coming across a *Bulletin of the Society for Primitive Technology* promised a real, tested pathway to a more wild life. Publishing articles like "Making Grass Ropes," "Living with Scorpions in the Southwest Desert of Arizona," and "Mummy Varnish, Spruce Gum and Other

Sticky Stuff," the SPT offered a studious yet fun-loving resource, one of the only records of wild experimentation for a hungry audience. I too eagerly flipped through a set of them like I was a lucky seven-year-old gorging on issues of *Mad* magazine.

In the early days of the primitive skills revival in the sixties and seventies, there were very few teachers and only a handful of available manuals, so people had to use trial and error to find, for example, which trees made the best hand drills for friction fire, which rocks split the cleanest to create a blade, and how many hours a deer hide needed to be smoked to make it durable. The growing passion for learning these old skills started mostly as a Western American trend, which spread to the Pacific Northwest, the Midwest, the East Coast, the South, Canada, Europe, and Israel. Today the skills gatherings bring at least ten thousand people together at different times of the year to keep human ancestral knowledge and contemporary Indigenous traditions alive.[5] Many of these events still happened during COVID-19, often in defiance of local ordinances prohibiting large group gatherings.

I noticed that the participants were resistant to mainstream ways of life. Pinpointing how these folks fit within various subcultures and historical trends is somewhat counterintuitive to outside observers. Tim Smith, the founder of the Jack Mountain Bushcraft School in Maine, once stated that the ancestral skills movement "has no political agenda or worldview, isn't about preparing for the end of the world, and isn't an 'ism.' It is made up of people of all ages, ethnicities, and backgrounds who share a love for being active outdoors."[6] The community's activities draw from the history of self-sufficient Mormon pioneers and Oregon Trail land-claim immigrants as well as the simple, handmade traditions of the Shaker and arts and crafts artisans, who opposed the impersonal manufacture of mass-produced goods. Ernest Thompson Seton, who launched the early-twentieth-century woodcraft movement, is also considered a forefather of primitive skills. His educational efforts emphasized camping and outdoor skills and eventually led to the formation of the Boy Scouts of America.

Underlying all these predecessor movements was a moral directive to make things by hand, which is seen as a more meaningful relationship to the material world that allows an individual to acquire more knowledge than they would using industrial tools. The contemporary trend of "maker" culture expresses renewed interest in old-fashioned crafts like knitting, canning food, keeping bees, and woodworking, and it draws on similar morals as the primitive skills movement, virtuously incorporating environmental and economic concerns into everyday life. One has only to peruse the 2.5 million shops on Etsy, the e-commerce forum for artisans and antique collectors of all kinds, to see that consumer demand for nonindustrial goods has flourished since the site launched in 2005.

Yet for many practitioners, these age-old crafts are not amateur, though they decidedly are for me. As Alexander Langlands wrote in *Craeft* (2018), the Old English term *craeft*, from which the modern word "craft" is derived, signifies a profound knowledge of materials, resourcefulness, human relationships, and the land. Craft builds concentration, ingenuity, and character and requires more than simple instructions for assembly. After Langlands learned to thatch a roof with organic material, he wrote that the process "proved to me most forcefully that it's not that we have lost these ancient skills, it's worse than that. It's that we have lost the conception of those skills and what they can do for us." [7] At a skills gathering, this conception is being regained with each woven basket and tanned hide.

In addition to classes offered to all attendees, Acorn also offered a full day of programming for children, which was supposed to allow parents the liberty to attend classes and socialize. Yet since it was our first gathering and we didn't know anyone, my kids didn't feel comfortable joining, and they urged me to stay with them. I was torn because I longed to jump into the action. The conflict between nurturing them and fulfilling my own desires was made worse by not having my husband around to help. But by that point, I had been taking my two daughters on overnight excursions and long vacations alone for years because he stayed home to work. I didn't push him to come along because I knew he wouldn't enjoy most places I wanted to go. Given any free time, he'd prefer to unwind with a book or a movie or take a run on a paved surface. I figured I was saving myself from having to tend to and solve his discomfort, so I didn't mind terribly that he wasn't there, except for when I really needed help with the kids. As a solo-mom adaptation strategy, I let my days be guided by the kids' desires, perhaps to my own detriment. I was pleasantly surprised, however, at how the gathering allowed us all to get what we needed.

I took the girls over to a small group of folks sitting under some oaks learning from a striking woman named Madelyn in a goddess-styled dress who had mastered a method of sandal crafting derived from the Tarahumara Indians of Mexico's remote Copper Canyons. The Tarahumara are renowned for their extraordinary skill at endurance running over rough terrain wearing only rawhide or upcycled tire-tread sandals. She showed us several different designs we could attempt and displayed the materials we'd be using. Up until this workshop, my chief concern with footwear was how it looked and, when I was pregnant, how it felt. Sitting there, trying to understand how the sandal straps fit into the sole, I berated myself for my narrow point of view. This was the first time in my life I had ever thought about how shoes were made.

To create a sandal that feels and looks good on your foot, you need to first step onto the material for the sole. Each of my girls took a turn planting herself on standard paper-sized sheets of natural rubber while I outlined her feet, which was made difficult by some ticklish reactions to the pencil. After many restarts, I managed to complete the silhouette drawings I needed. From there, we had to figure out where to place the notches for the leather strap that would be strung around and through the sole to attach it to the foot. It was arduous to cut through the rubber with a knife and keep the edge smooth. The girls had fun seasoning their leather straps with oil and then threading them through the holes I had poked into the soles with an awl. A few fit adjustments ensued as I tried not to press or tug at their delicate feet. Despite some frustration and annoyance, at the end of the three-hour process, they each had new custom sandals, and I realized how quickly three hours flew by when we were immersed in a productive new project.

From there, we made our way over to Jim Langell's camp. A

brusque and no-frills guy in his sixties, Jim had run an Italian deli in San Francisco since the 1970s. On nights and weekends, he pursued his hobbies of making the materials needed for archery and hide tanning by hand. Extraordinarily generous, he'd announced at the morning circle that he was giving away bows and arrows to every kid at the gathering if they would just complete the final touches of sanding the bow and curing it with genuine bear fat at his camp. When we arrived, we saw that he had extended a canopy from the back of his truck, suspended on poles strung with animal pelts that everyone could browse: lynx, beaver, badger, and several different kinds of fox. He was also selling arrows, quivers, and gourds in the only official shop of the gathering. Jim's place functioned as the central watering hole for the community, and he liked to chat people up as they came to inspect his wares.

My girls and I spent a long time feeling the furs, learning to identify the markings of each species, comparing their softness, and holding the fuzzy pelts up to our cheeks. Yet in the back of my mind were some moral questions. I had always taken the concerns of vegetarians and vegans seriously: the subjective experience of animals was an essential consideration for consumers. From this perspective, hunting and trapping for pelts was cruel. And tanning them with chemical agents was polluting and toxic. I saw my older daughter falling in love with a white fluff ball from an arctic fox. She had it around her neck and was cooing at it. I glanced at the $200 price tag and told her that she had plenty of stuffed animals at home. To distract her, I encouraged her and her sister to start sanding their new bows so we could visit the archery zone for target practice. It worked, and I was relieved that I could maintain my self-image as a "conscious consumer." In half an hour, they were pulling the bowstrings back toward their cheeks, solidifying their powerful poses and triumphantly releasing their arrows like little Artemises.

Jim also sold hard-shelled bottle gourds, *Lagenaria siceraria*, one of the earliest cultivated species in history. The gourds still make durable, beautiful containers, and we selected a few to turn into bowls. We cut them open, cleaned out the dried seeds and dust inside, and used sandpaper to smooth out their insides. To be able to eat from these and reuse them, we'd have to soak them in a tanning solution to prevent rot. We remembered that another camp had piles of acorns, which contain some of the strongest tannins around. We brought our gourds over there and made a soaking solution out of the nuts. While there, the kids got involved with a small group of girls pounding nut meat with stone mortars.

Our string of five days at the gathering continued like this: we would walk around and discover a captivating project, try it out, finish it or abandon it, and then join some other activity. To my delight, the girls befriended another set of sisters and took to running around with them for hours at a time. Unleashed on the land, the kids were free to explore and play screen-free, imitating their heroes from *Island of the Blue Dolphins* and *The Jungle Book*. This allowed me some time to visit the flint-knapping pit, which looked a little too dangerous to bring them into.

There, I discovered that smashing rocks does much to arouse the primal instinct. All over the world, beginning perhaps 3.3 million years ago, early humans found similar ways to hit a glassy rock—like

obsidian, chert, or flint—with a harder rock so that it would predict-
ably flake off into a sharp-edged tool that could be used to cut wood
and animal parts.[8] The cutting tool could be further refined and ser-
rated through a process of pressure flaking to form an arrowhead or
knife blade that could be attached, or hafted, to a handle. The phys-
ics of fracture points and pressures now explains how this occurs,
but early humans figured it out through experimentation.

I found it magical to hit upon the exact angle that would break
my obsidian core into sharper and sharper edges. At the knapping
pit, I heard the outlandish idea that these blades are so microscop-
ically smooth that they can split molecules. That might be an exag-
geration, but it is definitely true that some surgeons prefer to work
with them over metal scalpels, and Jim Riggs once provided his surgeon with a handmade blade for a procedure.

After half an hour of clacking, I had a pile of shards at my feet,
dust all over my clothes, and a few crude hand axes known as
bifaces, because they are shaped on both sides of the rock. Creating
such sharp edges quickly meant that our ancestors didn't need to
transport their weapons with them on their nomadic journeys.
They just needed to know where to source the right type of rocks
whenever they needed to cut into something. To this day, the shards
that flake off the central core of the tool, called lithic scatter, can be
found across the American West in undisturbed locations. Unlike
glamorous arrowheads and spearpoints, these signs of former
Paleo inhabitants usually go unrecognized by the casual day hiker
charging over a path, yet they can reveal just as much about the
people and societies that created them.

Looking around at my own lithic scatter and admiring the bifaces, gourd bowls, and sandals that I had made gave me a satisfying feeling. I had exercised a creative urge uncommon in modern life—I was using the original "digital" technology. Like most of my peers, I grew up having almost everything I needed bought for me, and—except for some sewing and weaving projects with my mother—I never had to make any of my essential items. I don't understand materials, how things are made, or how to fix them. The muscle memory in my hands doesn't go beyond pressing keys, opening cans, and doing up buttons. But my hands *evolved* to make tools. They derive their unique form and function from the environmental pressures our ancestors encountered. It felt right to put them to their adapted use for the first time, to transform myself into a maker. I also felt so much more appreciation for the determination and intelligence of our ancestors, having attempted some of their tasks.

By Thursday of the weeklong gathering, we had settled in, and I had ceased thinking about anything but what was happening at Acorn. Our new friends urged us to attend that night's group event: the trade blanket. It started at "dark thirty," so we just watched out for when people started crowding around Jim's tent and headed over. Jim had placed a huge tarp on the ground, and on top of that was a simple muslin blanket held down by lanterns on the corners. He welcomed the large crowd to the trade blanket, which was based on a custom from nineteenth-century fur-trading days when trappers, fur traders, and Native Americans would exchange goods at festive events called "mountain rendezvous."

Jim explained the strict protocol. An offerer presents an item, describes its origin, how it was made, how it was acquired, and what it can be used for, and sets it down in the center of the blanket. Anyone who wants to trade for it sets their own item(s) out on the blanket. The offerer goes around and inspects all corners of the blanket, and if they find something they like, they shake hands with the owner and execute the exchange. If nothing satisfies the offerer, they can announce that they "respectfully decline to trade." Goods must be either handmade or very high quality, and they have to have been legally acquired. All items with animal parts on them have to be ethically sourced—no birds of prey or endangered species. Money is discouraged to trade with, but if it is offered, it is called a "frogskin" by the officiant so as to avoid taxes and other legal restrictions for anyone involved.

The girls and I had assumed we were just going to an open-air market, but after we saw how everyone interacted, we understood that the trade blanket was an excuse for people to show off, practice stand-up comedy, roast their friends, and party. The trades were often surprising, and we spent the evening rapt and laughing. An antique sword was exchanged for twenty pounds of dried apples. A thrift store vintage leather purse went for a pile of abalone shells and some homemade jam. A gorgeous, tanned buckskin proved too precious for its owner to give up, even after he was offered a tomahawk, a case of homemade wine, and a leather-bound journal. If shoes or clothing were offered on the blanket, the trader modeled them playfully for the crowd. Some folks never gave up the dream that they might be able to offload their mediocre junk for a treasure, putting it out repeatedly despite lack of interest, which became a running joke. Most of the offered goods were prized for their craftsmanship but not necessarily aesthetics. People claiming trades off the blanket were more concerned about the functionality and durability of what they had acquired, reflecting a philosophy in opposition to mainstream consumer culture, in which novelty and design take priority over longevity.

When the air grew colder, the crowd trickled away and my youngest collapsed onto my lap. We gathered up our stuff and I hauled her sleepy, limp form back to our camper in the unilluminated dark, recalling what Myron had told us about the power of night vision.

The flashlight was an example of the ever-present duality of technology for people at the gathering, which I also struggled with. I heard many discussions about the unfortunate necessity of cell phones, computers, cars, and electronic devices of convenience and the difficulty of rejecting technology. One mother I spent time with there told me about how she crocheted her dish rags while watching TV in her RV home, but she wished she could just be content with singing while crafting. A teacher who instructed fish-skin tanning said that he would never give up his passion for landscape photography. Myron Cretney got by with only a landline in his mobile home and was much more comfortable with a bow drill kit than a Wi-Fi router. He found a balance of only using chainsaws when necessary, preferring hand tools to do his forestry work and prepare for teaching skills classes.

These choices about technology seemed entirely driven by

individual preference rather than through a community-enforced set of rules like Amish communities have. Many adopt the wildest option possible while still participating in the essential technologies of our time, a practice that's been called "making a buckskin laptop case."[9] I would go on to experiment with this hybrid approach many times; for instance, I once created business cards by carving my name into the bark from a young fir tree.

The resistant attitude to technology was accompanied by other, perhaps more rebellious, influences that I picked up by observing a wide array of T-shirts proclaiming punk-rock anarchy, libertarianism, and prepper wisdom. It seemed that many folks were attracted to learning skills and reviving community because they were fiercely opposed to a liberal, regulated state dominated by mainstream capitalist culture. An attempt to describe this mishmash of subcultures might best be done on a coordinate grid. Imagine the X axis spanning a continuum of attitudes about the role of technology and violence. On one end of the X, there are permaculture enthusiasts, herbalists, and Waldorf school affiliates—they're gentle and optimistic about prosocial human qualities and the cooperative aspects of nature, perhaps to a fault. On the other end are ex-military members, survival-skills experts, self-designated "rednecks," and doomsday preppers who don't hesitate to acquire what they need to stay alive and maintain it by force. The overlap can be odd: I encountered a backcountry hunter living out of a double-wide trailer stocked with guns at the same buckskin-tanning session as an organic-farm-hopping, pot-growing #vanlifer. They had a lot in common to discuss. On the up-and-down Y axis, denoting cultural sophistication, there are fashionable woke hipsters on one end and homeschooled nature lovers who moonlight at Renaissance fairs on the other. The sweet spot in the middle of both these spectrums—if I may sociologically diagnose coordinate 0,0—is what we would call a humble, down-to-earth badass

The coordinate grid needs to expand three-dimensionally, however, because there's also a generational divide between the older practitioners, who see their craft as a way to replicate artifacts and learn from the past, and the younger folks, who believe that practicing skills will bring about physical, social, and spiritual transformation for them and their communities. Those who are focused on craft view the gatherings as opportunities to sharpen their skills, but others view them as temporary village retreats outside civilization that minimize modern technology.

I also met plenty of hobbyists as well as some people who call themselves amateur historians and heritage educators focused on prehistoric eras. Some take the lifestyle very seriously, living in the woods without modern conveniences, while others just attend a gathering or two each year and occasionally dabble with skills at home. A common misconception is that they are "cosplay" reenactors who don a period costume for the fun of it. It's not just about the entertainment. There's also a crossover with academia, with professional archaeologists and anthropologists learning alongside highly skilled but nonpedigreed practitioners. By and large, attendees see the value of Paleolithic technology in their modern or not-so-modern lives, and many accrue prestige in their community for doing so to the furthest extent possible.

It was hard to miss that the participants and instructors skewed heavily toward white, heterosexual people with European ancestry. This has been the case since the movement got underway in the 1970s; in recent years, the leaders of gatherings have been struggling to diversify the demographics. The Firefly skills gathering near Asheville, North Carolina, has very deliberately done outreach to nearby communities of color, recruited minority staff, formed a council of elders made up of half people of color, offered classes in Spanish, and spent time understanding the obstacles that keep people who have experienced racism from feeling welcome at gatherings.

In 2019, when I spoke with the executive director, Chloe Tipton Chisholm, she explained that Firefly views the collection of ancestral skills as a way to help under-resourced groups increase their opportunity. "When we say that all of us can live closer to the land but in a healthier, more self-sufficient way, that is counter to this cycle of needing money to have access to opportunity," she said. "These skills sidestep that whole biased system, where anyone can say, 'If I know what to look for, I can have a bountiful harvest from the woods whenever I want. I can do my own preventive health care with herbs and a healthy lifestyle and avoid interfacing with the medical system so much.'" But it's still a hard sell to get some people who, for example, grew up poor or descend from slaves to want to kill chickens, pick wild greens, make their own clothes, or build their own shelters. "If that's what you come from, you have this really deep desire to get away from those skills because those are tied to a deep, painful history of oppression. Why would I want to learn those things? We spent so much time getting away from that. So these skills get painted as a white person's hobby," she explained.

Not only that, it appears that going camping or spending extended time in nature is a disproportionately white affair, as noted by the comic website Stuff White People Like, which posted this gem: "If you find yourself trapped in the middle of the woods without electricity, running water, or a car you would likely describe that situation as a 'nightmare' or 'a worst-case scenario like after plane crash or something.' White people refer to it as 'camping.'" [10]

Other gatherings offer affinity discussion groups to address racial and cultural issues that crop up, and many have followed Firefly in offering discounted rates to Black, Indigenous, and other people of color (BIPOC). There are also opportunities for non-BIPOC attendees to understand how racial privilege determines who feels comfortable practicing wild skills and convening in nature in order to raise awareness and make all wild spaces more comfortable for everyone.

Addressing the heteronormativity of the survival skills world, Pinar and So Sinopoulos-Lloyd founded Queer Nature, a small nonprofit out of Washington and Oregon offering wild skills instruction for BIPOC and LGBTQ2+ folks. Since the queer community has historically gathered in urban places like bars and clubs, the wilderness has not necessarily been a welcoming place, and Queer Nature seeks to change that. Furthermore, many in their community didn't have opportunities to gain nature knowledge because they didn't relate to or were excluded from hunting, Boy Scouts, or the military. They were also impeded from expressing their full identity in many institutional contexts growing up. "As queer folks, we have many reasons for already being used to 'taking a step back' and assessing our prospective safety, resources, and threats when we enter social and public spaces," they write on the group's website.[11] Yet their perspective is that these skills, borne out of persecution, can be turned into an asset. "This disposition to hyperawareness of our social and political environment can be beautifully leveraged in the arts and sciences of stealthcraft," it reads, noting that blending into surroundings, going unnoticed, and collecting strategic information about the environment is useful for camouflage, concealment, evasion, and tracking. The goal of the group's courses in stealthcraft and survival skills is to help folks feel well-resourced, wherever they are.

Natalie Bogwalker, who founded Firefly, also emphasized the need to address the gender imbalance in leadership positions. She once informally surveyed teachers at Firefly and estimated that 80 percent were male. "I try to bring in skilled instructors, and there are definitely more men who have been doing this stuff longer. But I think it's so important to change that. I definitely give some preference to female teachers," she said in an interview.[12]

While many of the activities do line up along traditional gender lines, there is no protocol for who does what. Men dominate skills like flint knapping, bow making, and animal processing, but a number of women regularly offer workshops in these topics and others like basket weaving, leather sewing, and felting. There are occasionally female-specific classes and separate learning spaces meant to reduce the possible intimidation women without experience with tools might feel in the presence of highly skilled men. One such workshop I attended focused on how women can leverage their strength when using an axe to chop wood, requiring different approaches than men usually employ. Some gatherings also now offer men's circles to discuss issues of masculinity and feminism, and others provide space to discuss queer issues in rewilding, along with forums for people who have endured the pervasive effects of racism. Some of the events, such as Echoes in Time in Oregon and Saskatoon Circle in Washington, make a point to invite local Native teachers and offer scholarships for Native participants and people from disadvantaged backgrounds.

In decades past, the role of Native Americans in the primitive skills community was not as mindfully and respectfully considered as it might have been. While the American Indian Movement was gaining political victories in the 1970s, the issue of Indigenous sovereignty was not something primitive skills practitioners were pushed to engage with. The old-timers in the skills community considered basic human survival skills the legacy of all humans, practiced across the globe. While that may be true, this outlook failed to acknowledge that when non-Native people develop a relationship with their bioregion and learn how to process acorns or fashion baskets out of tule, this sets up a drastic inequality. Existing Native communities in the area whose ancestors were violently expelled from their territory by European settlers are now no longer able to gather, for instance, acorns or tule.[13] One Native attendee at the Colorado Wild Roots gathering put words to this dynamic, remarking, "I don't understand how all of these white people can run into the forest making up and practicing their rituals when we can't even go into our sacred forest and practice our rituals." [14]

Yet the most recent generation of rewilders has begun to engage seriously with these issues. Peter Michael Bauer of Rewild Portland has made Native and non-Native relations a priority of the events he hosts. He noted that Americans from originally immigrant backgrounds may build a deep connection to the lands they live on, but they don't have the cultural connection going back millennia that Native communities do. Acknowledging that colonialism confers benefits to people of European descent living in America, he stated that it is also important to recognize that, similar to Native people, it is impossible for those descendants of immigrants to return to their ancestral homelands. "We must grow roots wherever we have landed, and we must do this with respect to the Native cultures here so that we don't just end up as neocolonialists," he said.

Teasing out how to do this with respect to Native cultures has become a hot-button issue for many of the gatherings and practitioners. Taking interest in Native concerns would become my approach to sorting out how my engagement with nature skills could impact Native communities and their rights to ancestral lands. I had to fumble through missteps and misunderstandings that would occasionally lead to shared vision and a course of action for rectifying past wrongs for Native communities. I would meet many Native folks who would encourage me to learn parts of their traditions and who would echo the sentiments of the early primitive skills leaders, saying that the original skills of subsistence belong to all humans.

At Acorn, I'd learned how to make sandals, tan a gourd, and

sharpen an obsidian blade, but as we prepared to leave the camp on the final day, I realized that one of the best parts of the week had been living communally and getting to know the other attendees. While we were doing projects, we met all sorts of people who shared their stories of embracing nature and living with more wild intention. Then we'd see them over and over again, passing on a trail, coming out of the latrine, or headed to mealtime, where we'd restart our conversations. By the end of the week, I felt like I had met everyone. The only other time I'd ever felt that way was while living in my college dorm. This was a community of people with shared values and goals who were passionate about honoring the land and practicing skills to survive and thrive. Many attendees had developed deep trust and excellent communication with each other based on a lifetime of shared experience that reignited at each meeting. For that week, I could fulfill my longing for an intact, connected, nourishing village.

Many of my interactions in the city had recently become fraught with tension as a result of my shift toward nature and away from technology and consumerism. For instance, my neighbor and I fought over whether he could spray the carcinogenic herbicide Roundup on the sidewalk next to my house where my kids drew with chalk. I had to regularly remind my daughter's teachers not to show videos when the students actually needed more playtime outside. Biking around the city with my girls in tow, I physically fought for a safe space to ride in the street, sometimes nearly getting sideswiped by angry drivers. The daily uphill climb to maintain a full-time workload while raising kids demanded warrior energy.

Waging a one-woman war every day exhausted me. At Acorn, I didn't have to fight anyone. I also didn't have to work so hard to make sure my girls were fed, clothed, educated, and entertained because of the group activities throughout the day. While it might take days of back-and-forth texts and emails to arrange a single playdate for my children after school, it was laughable how easy it was to find kids to play with here—no calendars required. As a result of this ease of living, my stress melted away. My kids and I could belong and feel supported by the social group, exactly as hominids had been doing for millions of years. I wondered: *Were skills gatherings the real Kule Loklo—that recreated Native village where I had played with my kids? The place where we could all belong with each other and with nature?* If so, I wanted to visit as many as I could.

CHAPTER 4

Survivaling

If I had learned anything from the Acorn gathering, it was that I really *can* do a lot for myself. So when my daughter fell in love with the Arctic fox pelt at Jim's shop and then we just happened to find a roadkill fox, I knew what I wanted to do. If I could just get the fur off that beautiful animal, my daughter could have what she wanted. We wouldn't have to pay anyone else for it, I would hone a new skill, and I would have honored the life of the dead animal. Win-win-win-win!

Of course, it didn't work out that way. I mangled it because I was unskilled with the knife and had little knowledge of the animal's anatomy. I was only able to get scraps of the pelt, which reeked of skunk. I did have more nature knowledge and understanding of the importance of making my own things, but I still had little wild experience. I continued to look for ways to fit wild skills into my family life and intense work schedule. Because my husband's job as an attorney required demanding hours in his office, I didn't know how I could leave my girls for an extended time to get training. We didn't have any other dependable help.

I daydreamed about enrolling in a crash course in survival

skills and even found one that looked suitable with the Wilderness Awareness School (WAS) in Duvall, Washington, outside Seattle. The founder, Jon Young, had been tutored in plant identification, animal observation, and tracking as a youth by Tracker School founder Tom Brown Jr. Young then cut his teeth at Brown's school before launching his own school. The two have become quite influential in the field of wilderness survival and naturalist training, but their adherence to Indigenous knowledge distinguishes their methods. Other courses I had looked into had the typical domesticated outlook on wild spaces, which had to be protected and left alone to flourish without human input. However, if our ancestors had left nature "alone" for the past thousand generations, we wouldn't be here. I knew that there were important reasons that we were told to leave no trace, because if modern people were to suddenly start utilizing wild resources en masse, these places would be destroyed. People today don't understand how to live reciprocally and regeneratively with our environment, but Brown and Young were teaching just this type of relationship with nature.

Both Brown and Young advocate developing heightened perceptual awareness: learning how wildlife communicates and spending long periods of observation in the same spot. They help students develop powerful links with the species around them that begin to awaken students' instinctual senses and the spiritual side of nature connection. Some of these inexplicable understandings—invisible strings tied between all beings—that influence our knowledge of ourselves and the world cannot be rationally explained. Several times, I've been ruminating on a problem outside when a powerful animal will appear to spur a new insight or confirm my intuition. The hawk hovering on a thermal, the mother deer staring out from a garden, and the squirrel chattering in a tree—and even one particular fox—have all brought me messages I would not have picked up on otherwise. Other people have told me how their experiences with lightning storms, cedar trees at dawn, and the mysterious murmuration of birds provoked life-changing insights. Generation after generation, humans have been compelled to talk to the trees and howl with the wolves in a communion greater than themselves. These occurrences have no place in current scientific teaching.

Students who have studied extensively with Brown or Young report becoming conscious of where animals are hiding without receiving sensory clues. They begin to sense the thoughts and feelings of the people around them without speaking to them. They walk in directions without knowing why, only to find themselves witness to some startling event: eagles feasting on a carcass, the red flash at sunset, or a wolf pack on the prowl. They say that they feel what it's like to be rewoven into the web connecting all beings, the fabric of the real world.

The WAS offers a self-study course in natural history that aims to help students acquire these "native eyes" (which may sound a bit unwoke in the present climate—the course was launched in the 1990s). As he was developing his curriculum, Young made presentations about local nature to area public schools. Hundreds of kids he spoke to were unable to identify the animals and plants they lived around by sight or sound—not even a robin. The aim of his naturalist study program, then, was to transform these kids from tourists in their neighborhoods to "natives" with an intimate connection to the ferns and frogs around them.

The test to qualify as a neighborhood native is hard. I sent away for the first volume of his naturalist course and was flabbergasted at the level of detail necessary to complete it properly. Some examples of the prompts:

» Describe the odor of red fox urine.
» If the wind is blowing from the southeast, what will the weather be like tomorrow morning?
» What type of caterpillar feeds on cherry?
» How are willow catkins pollinated?
» What types of rock in your area can be used for making durable arrowheads?
» Name seven poisonous plants in your vicinity.[1]

Answering these questions requires more than a Google search and would take hours and hours of field study and observation to get right for most of us. However, if you grew up wild, you'd likely know these answers without having to consult sources.

I tried to do the first part of the course when I first quit my office job. The curriculum asked that I choose a "sit spot," which is one rather secluded place to return to every day to observe for at least twenty minutes. Spending hours outside alone would not happen as long as I had to make sure small, vulnerable people had their needs attended to. Plus, the magic of being mentored was missing from this scheme. The program was all self-discipline and lonely inquiry—not a communal experience. Yet community was what I had found most valuable about attending the Acorn gathering and what I needed.

I checked in with Peter Michael Bauer to get his advice about my next steps toward wild proficiency, since the solo-study course wasn't working. We discussed how he was unable to build a viable rewilding community outside Portland. When he spent extended periods gathering wild food, weaving baskets, and making friction fires in the woods, he missed his friends acutely, making him realize that his most urgent primal need was for social contact. That's ultimately why he focused his efforts on urban rewilding, where he could be with people. Along these lines, he urged me to look into the work of Martín Prechtel. The spiritual leader of a Mayan village in Guatemala, Prechtel grew up on a Pueblo Indian reservation with half-Native ancestry. He's written several books about Indigenous spirituality and regularly trains non-Native folks in this wisdom. I would later meet several people who revered him for helping them participate in the more-than-human world. In an interview with Derrick Jensen in *The Sun* magazine, Prechtel addressed my struggle while trying to learn skills alone. "Our culture emphasizes individual freedom, but such freedom can be enjoyed only when there is a waiting village of open-armed, laughing elders who...catch us, keep us grounded, and protect us from ourselves," he said.[2] Prechtel was lamenting the loss of multigenerational communities where people knew one another well and shared the ups and downs of everyday life while minding everyone's well-being.

Peter and I agreed that the role of the elders in the life of the community has been replaced by vigorous internet searching and YouTube watching. When I have a question about a practical, ethical, or spiritual matter, I hop online first. Again—Alexa: *What's the meaning of life?* While the sources I encounter may answer my questions, the impersonal website authors do not know my specific situation, nor do they offer life experience, wisdom, or a nurturing perspective that will help me grow. They can't protect me from myself, as Prechtel said. There is no feedback loop keeping me from making harmful mistakes. Yet an "open-armed, laughing elder" would presumably follow my progress with further suggestions and would be invested in my success. Later, I would likely reciprocate their care with a kind gift or visit.

Such relationships have decreased quite rapidly in developed countries in the span of a generation or two. Even though most people still live somewhat close to their parents (the typical American is within eighteen miles of their mother), the lack of supportive elders in my life is indicative of a growing trend. Studies show that the more education and economic success an individual achieves, the more likely they are to live far away from their family of origin.[3]

When I seek in-person community or the advice of more experienced people, I usually have to pay for it, whether it's through membership at a gym, museum, or synagogue or through buying therapy sessions and midwifery care. Prechtel insists this freedom to choose and pay for community is not an adequate substitute for the supportive village. The community that is bought can disappear as soon as the membership or service ends, whereas community based on reciprocal relationships tends to endure. I recalled that when my mother died, I was unable to get a meeting with the rabbi at a synagogue I no longer belonged to, which left me feeling further abandoned.

Peter did cautiously endorse the WAS, telling me that he'd had the same issues with the self-study Kamana naturalist course as I'd had. The sit spot, in particular, was problematic for him because it had very little to do with nomadic hunter-gatherer life and was predicated on a sedentary lifestyle in which one had the leisure to visit one place repeatedly over the seasons. He thought self-study was more about cultivating "nerdy loners" than wild community. But since I was interested in enrolling in a weeklong wilderness survival skills immersion course, he said that would give me much more group support. Do it, he encouraged me.

I liked that the WAS survival skills course description began with the question I had been asking myself: *What would it be like to relate to the earth without the conveniences of our modern world?* The wilderness survival immersion offered a stepping stone to partici-pants who wanted to build a deeper connection with nature through primitive living skills like making friction fire, finding food and water, building shelter, surviving with minimal supplies, and expe-riencing the forest in an ancient and meaningful way. The program's marketing copy promised precisely what I was looking for: "Feel the freedom of surviving off the land and learn to trust the earth to provide for all of your needs." I was skeptical that this could be achieved in seven days, and the warning that we would be uncom-fortable and without food for long periods of time frightened me

a bit, but I had heard wonderful feedback about WAS from other
acquaintances besides Peter. If I could gain these skills, I would be
well-equipped to bring my kids into the woods for extended adventures. As a long-distance runner, I knew I could handle discomfort, and having suffered through the Jewish holiday of Yom Kippur
annually (which requires not eating for twenty-four hours), I figured I'd get through the hard parts (with some beating of my chest).

Coincidentally, around the same time in spring 2019, my filmmaker pal Saul unwittingly walked into his own survival experience. He got lost on a forest trail on Lopez Island at sunset, and
after spending an hour walking in circles, he had to call to be rescued by the fire department. He was fine, but his mishap could have
been much worse. When I told Saul about the survival course I had
my eye on, he immediately and enthusiastically proposed that we
do it together. "I'll be your wilderness doula!" he announced.

This wasn't as odd a suggestion as it may seem. Saul had trained
as a doula to assist women in labor. He did this out of his own
interest but also to prepare to make a riveting documentary about
one woman's home birth. It was the first time anyone filmed every
moment of a baby's emergence for general audiences, giving them
the chance to witness a birthing mother's strength and suffering as
she gave herself over to new life. After screenings, men would tell
Saul about the emotional journey they had gone on during his film,
how they had no idea how strong women could be because birth
had previously been hidden from their view.

I liked the idea of having his supportive presence along with
me as I entered a new world. And he thought he'd benefit from

gaining survival skills that would prevent another emergency rescue. Once we agreed to do the course together, my brother and his wife volunteered to take care of my girls for the week at their home in Seattle.

The packing supply list we received was cryptic. In addition to our personal toiletries and very minimal clothing, we were told to bring duct tape wrapped around a pen, a utility knife, a rain poncho with grommets, a belt, a heavy-duty kitchen garbage bag, and fifteen feet of paracord. We could only bring one snack; no other food or electronic devices were permitted. No tent or sleeping bag. Not even a watch.

We were almost late for the opening program because I had to reassure my kids over and over that I would be fine and they would be in good hands. It was the longest time I had spent away from them, and they couldn't let go. When Saul and I arrived, we seated ourselves around a campfire with two head instructors, two assistants, and twelve other participants. There, it dawned on me that I had just left everything critically important in my life—my children, my phone, my bed, even food and bathrooms—for a week. I tried to dampen my anxiety with humor. When we each shared why we were there, I joked that I had enrolled because I'd heard the weight loss results were incredible. (We had been warned we could lose up to five pounds.) People laughed nervously.

The instructors handed each of us fixed steel-blade Mora knives in plastic sheaths that we were to keep on us at all times. The handles held a slot for a ferro rod, which produces quick sparks when struck with the back of the knife blade. We were told that the knife was our key to survival: with it, we could harvest all sorts of materials, make fire, and defend ourselves. Then we dove into preparations for the week: chopping pieces of wood (for eventually making friction fires), sewing a foraging satchel from an old pillowcase, and getting our backpacks thoroughly inspected. That was more intimidating than a preflight TSA pat down, and most everyone was visibly riled up by having their belongings scrutinized and occasionally rejected. The assistant instructor interrogated me about why I was bringing five pairs of underwear for the week—two more than suggested. She questioned my choice of boots. Then there was a big hullabaloo about the fact that I'd forgotten a belt. She consulted with the lead instructor, who said I could use my paracord if necessary, but for what, I had no idea, since none of my pants had belt loops.

Before we left the meetup location, the lead female instructor explained that the six women in our group needed to carry large packs of pink plastic tampons and pads. "Stressful situations can bring on your period, and we know from experience that even if you're not expecting your cycle, you might get it this week," she said. I had brought my own (plain, organic, unobtrusive) supplies, so I declined to carry the standard issue. It bothered me that she was insisting on a specific way of handling female biology, even out in the forest, far away from the reproductive industrial complex. I had recently read an Environmental Working Group report that many widely available menstrual products contain known reproductive carcinogens, so I was surprised that they were required.[4] Using pads and tampons also seemed antithetical to the course experience, which had promised on the website: "You will experience the simplicity and abundance of nature as you sink into a wild place with minimal gear. You will have the opportunity to learn how to flow with natural processes as you rely upon nature's bounty for food, water, and shelter." Menstruation clearly wasn't the natural process they wanted us to flow with. I was even further surprised when my refusal was not accepted.

"You have to take them," the instructor insisted, thrusting the pack toward me.

"But I don't need them," I said, pointing to my own stash.

"You're also carrying them for someone else who might need more," she said, appealing to my superego. But I wouldn't budge.

Luckily Saul stepped in to save me. "I'll carry them!" he chirped, performing his first duty as my doula.

Despite this taxing start, the course promised that I'd learn skills, which was my main goal in life at the time. I felt protected because someone I trusted was with me and we were looking out for each other. The other folks looked scared, but Saul and I were jovial, cracking jokes performatively to ease their tension. It was almost a certainty that a grueling experience would cement some new bonds between us all.

We were then driven out to the campsite, two hours east, deep in the North Cascade mountain range by the Sauk-Suiattle River. We arrived at 9:30 p.m. and walked single file through the drizzly cold night to stay together. For the first mile, we trudged on a flat path, but then we headed up into steep wooded terrain that required climbing uphill over logs and branches, some very precarious, in the total dripping dark, for maybe an hour. Dread and wonder flooded my mind: *Where are they taking us? How long will we be scrambling like this?*

The drizzle became rain. We were holding the hands of the people in front of us to get through some patches where vines snaked across branches on the ground or we needed to navigate sinkholes. The man behind me, a Zen priest in training named Daishin, was toting a giant, cumbersome cooking pot that he'd pass to me while he scrambled over slippery logs. Then I'd painstakingly place it back into his wet hands. Of course, the pot wasn't cooperative, and we fumbled around, clanging the lid and dropping the whole thing a few times. Daishin was a wiry, bald, blue-eyed dear of a man, sincere and thoughtful, who seemed much older than his thirty-three years, and I could sense how his deep mindfulness training was keeping him centered during this bizarre quest.

Our beleaguered crew had just reached a spot where most of us had a bit of even, solid ground under foot when the instructors abruptly said, "G'night! We'll see you in the morning!" No further instructions. This was supposed to be our simulated "crash landing moment," when the surviving really began. Not knowing the time or the location, we had to operate on assumptions.

As my fellow campers quieted down, my mind fell back on all that I'd left behind, wondering what my kids were up to and how many texts and emails I was missing. But I quickly realized I wasn't in a productive thought pattern. Nostalgia for comfort is not a survival skill. I snapped back to the present moment of disorientation and the night ahead in an unknown, cold, wet forest. Probably there weren't any predators about? Hopefully we weren't in a patch of creepy-crawly things? Perhaps we'd be okay until the sun rose? Someone came up with the bright idea that we should stay within earshot of each other. Saul and I bedded down close on top of our packs to conserve warmth. The ground was cold, and the trees were leaking on us all night. I would pass out for a stretch of time and then wake up to recall that it was the weirdest night of my life—I had willingly chosen to sleep on top of a garbage bag out in the elements. At least I was finally having a wilderness adventure.

We got up the next day to find that we were inside an old-growth cedar and hemlock forest draped with stringy lichens and carpeted with ferns. As our group reconstituted itself, tired and disheveled and strewn with leaves, the instructors rejoined us, and we embarked on another hike to the riverside. I was busy gathering plants I knew I could eat, since I had a feeling it would be a while until we were presented with a meal. I plucked sour Oregon grapes and their young, almost fluorescent green leaves, chewed on turkey tail mushrooms, and every so often found a juicy salmon berry. The field guide we had been required to obtain prior to the week, *Plants of the Pacific Northwest Coast* by Jim Pojar and Andy MacKinnon (referred to simply as "the Pojar"), contained helpful ethnographic notes about how the Native people of the area had subsisted on foods like these.[5]

By midafternoon, the group was feeling exhausted, but we were tasked with building shelters before we could nap. Saul and I were teamed with another man in his midthirties, Matt, who thankfully found our sibling-style bickering amusing instead of annoying. The three of us combed over the forest floor for an hour, collecting sturdy sticks and an enormous amount of dried-up sword ferns, a species that requires significant hand strength to uproot. We carried heaping stacks of dry fronds, piled them into a three-person-wide mattress-sized area, and then took turns flopping on them. We joked that these were "fronds with benefits." But before we could continue building our dream home, the assistant instructor Gabe nixed our chosen site. I'd chosen a spot under a giant cedar where two felled logs crisscrossed, forming half of a bed frame. I thought I had come up with a clever strategy for economizing with existing materials, but Gabe was horrified. The risk for huge dead branches to fall on us from above was too great. It took us another two tries to secure a site he approved of that wouldn't endanger our slumber party with what he called "a widow maker."

Gabe intrigued me, and not only because he was the epitome of a handsome mountain man. Living in a wall tent on a permaculture farm, he spent the GI Bill money from his four years of military service in Afghanistan on wilderness training programs. He had already spent two years training with WAS and was just beginning to take on instructor positions with the school. When he taught, in a very soft voice, he'd sit back on his heels and close his eyes as if remembering something he'd memorized. Over the week, he'd tell us the various ways to source clean water by leaving out tarps overnight, digging seep holes, and creating DIY water filters from charcoal. He also led us on an excursion tracking an elusive bear through a nearby streambed, though I had to stick close by his side to hear what he was explaining. What he lacked in charismatic authority he made up for in personal conviction. He said he only ate meat he slaughtered himself and spent his free time studying field guides and tracking animals along riverbeds. He wore just one pair of all-weather pants, and a leather-sheathed, hand-forged knife never left his scruffy, bearded neck. I found him shyly humorous and thoughtful, and over the next few days, we enjoyed geeking out together about botanical identification. One time, we came across a species of geranium called herb Robert. This pink-flowering plant spreads out indiscriminately and can be identified by its mildewy stench. He caught my eye and announced, "Jessica, I'd like you to meet Stinky Bob!"

While I had known that the course specifics wouldn't be revealed to us ahead of time, I found this uncertainty frustrating. I didn't like that other people were in charge of my schedule and that I couldn't anticipate what would happen next. Though we were not allowed in their camp area, the instructors clearly had food and shelter that we didn't, which made me feel like we were their captives. I started resenting the format of the course. The leaders counseled us to expect strong reactions to being underfed and underslept and dealing with the unknowns of the woods. All that was fine with me, but it was the unspoken psychological mind game going on that irked me. I didn't feel that it provided an accurate setup for a survival situation. While the circumstances were intended to replicate the feeling of being at the mercy of the wilderness, the effect was more to test how we dealt with having other people totally in control. Could we relax and stay alert? Or would we freak out? I felt like I was becoming friends with Gabe, so I tried to approach him with my questions about the setup.

"So where do you instructors sleep?" I asked him, but his face suddenly went ashen.

"I can't tell you," he said.

"And are you all eating meals?" I pushed.

"I'm not supposed to say anything, I'm so sorry." He briefly glanced at me and then stared ahead. I saw how he defaulted to his military training, which seemed so out of place in this peaceful forest.

On our second day without food, we were so hungry that we followed the instructors' suggestion to search for grubs and insects inside the bark of dead trees. I crushed a handful of ants into a micro burger and dutifully swallowed this "needed protein." Others were grimacing and chewing small white larvae. The mood was grim. An instructor suggested looking for a forgotten cache of stored food left by an animal preparing for winter, and Gabe, now making a point to keep me more informed, told me to follow him to where Daishin was peeling back the shredded fibers of a cedar log. Laughter and cheers rang out among our famished group as he revealed several bananas and pineapples hidden in the log. Certainly these were the sweetest and most nourishing fruits I had ever eaten, and I even chewed on the peels, but the artifice of finding tropical grocery store fare in the woods left a sour taste in my mouth. Saul and I began referring to our activities as "survivaling," because of the con-trived circumstances.

June in the North Cascades offered abundant rain, so our goal every day was to stay as dry and warm as possible. Inevitably, we would get soaked and have to scramble around looking for dry wood to make a fire to sit around and air our stuff out. Matt, Saul, and I rigged up our ponchos (with the grommets) using the paracord (no longer a mystery) to protect our sleeping space. To that end, the instructors told us that it would make a great deal of sense if we all snuggled up tight at night. I set about making a "comforter" from our three trash bags, filling them with giant piles of soft lichen and old leaves and securing the edges with the duct tape I had handily wrapped around the prescribed pen.

I thought the highly suggested snuggling might be awkward, but my bed partners and I would joke late into the night before making like the spoon slot in the silverware drawer as the temperature plummeted and the rain pattered on our poncho roof. In the morning, we'd rib each other about who kicked whom during the night. I was the champion, since they let me sleep in the middle. We did stay warm and dry (with just a few slipped discs in the neck).

In the morning, I approximated bathing in a stream by the river. We had mini classes throughout the day showing us how to forage edibles, stay alert to predators, and deal with other common hazards of wilderness living. I struggled with the skill of friction fire, which required twisting a spindle with a bow on a notched board until the spindle started smoking and flammable shavings dropped to the ground underneath it. It took precise timing to know when to transfer these shavings into a pile of grass and slowly blow on them to nurture a flame. Regrettably, I never set a fire, but a few men did.

The second night, we drank only a broth made from nettles we had collected. It was so delicious—like spinach and miso soup. As an instructor said: hunger is the best condiment. By the third night, they served us some lentils and quinoa that were magically aggrandized by our meager state into umami magnificence. Breakfast was bits of flour-and-water dough cooked in the ashes of a fire. Just to lighten the low-cal mood, I would periodically ask Saul if I had chocolate on my face.

Despite the artificial scenario and my qualms about the power dynamics, I was enjoying spending all my time outside and away from technology. I hadn't grown up camping and outdoor adventuring, so this was one of my first weeks alfresco. For many folks in our society, this kind of nature immersion is a pretty exclusive activity. The forests, streams, and wetlands of this country have been greatly diminished, and those that still exist are far from where most people live in cities and suburbs. It takes resources and know-how to access it. If no one in your community regularly ventures out into nonhuman spaces, you are unlikely to want to do it. Your nature is whatever you can find on the windowsill, in the yard, or at local parks. It's usually planted, contained, and controlled. People of color, families with children, and low-income groups are the most likely to lack access to nature and the benefits that come with it. I was lucky that I did know people, including my own brother, who had spent significant time in wilderness and were able to give me tips and encouragement.

One morning, midweek, we were sent out for the infamous sit-spot practice. The instructor told us to focus on whatever came into view and resist the urge to sink into thought for twenty minutes. This was to prepare us to go tracking, which requires paying close attention to animal signs. Sitting on a dry creek bed, I watched how ants determined their paths through the terrain of tiny sand grains, reacting to obstacles with gyrating antennae and rapid legs. I saw that the patterns in the sand they crawled on were guided by a previous flow of water. Like the insects, I was also slowly bending and adjusting to the physical matter around me, looking up at noisy birds, scanning the branches of trees as the wind ruffled their leaves. When I lay back on the sand, my weight flattened the hills and ridges. The ants poured into the valleys I had created. There were ants still careening through my digestive system from the micro burger of the day before. I was becoming embedded in the landscape, my presence affecting the creatures around me, just as they signaled me to respond and perhaps consume. Becoming aware of these reciprocal interactions, my senses enlivened.

Studying another species of insect that had colonized a nearby cottonwood sprout, I followed the trails they had chewed through the leaves, noting that they only consumed the most tender sections. If I had normally been walking on a path through this spot, I never would have stopped to study these minuscule beings. Made to sit without stimulation in a waiting room, I would have retreated to my inner world or my phone to avoid boredom. But in that slow moment at my sit spot, I learned that I could be fascinated by what I trained my focus on. It dawned on me that I was feeling happy and relaxed, an unfamiliar state. I was experiencing what environmental psychologists Stephen and Rachel Kaplan called "attention restoration." They studied how time away from urban environments and the cognitively fatiguing tasks of modern life allows people to recover the capacity to pay attention and become fascinated by their surroundings.[6] Still feeling content, I returned to the group circle and shared my riveting experience among the insects.

Later that day, we were summoned into a remote part of the woods, away from the comfort zone of our temporary shelters. Sam, a new instructor, arrived to lead a class that remained a mystery until we heard strange bleats from across a small meadow. He announced that the sheep and goat we heard in the distance were going to be our dinner. I looked around at the group and saw raised eyebrows, open mouths, and a few shy grins. My pulse quickened, and I took a deep breath to steady myself. At the Acorn gathering, I had been introduced to animal harvesting and had processed a few game birds, though my oldest daughter was much braver than me when it came to dispatching them. Would we have to witness the pain and suffering of the animals? Would I be able to contain my gut reactions and keep my focus on the task? Wilderness survival training usually entails learning how to hunt or trap wild animals, but this was beyond the scope of the WAS program, so they brought in domesticated animals. Sam told us that we would learn the method for "giving death" to the animals, a term the school used to parallel the phrase "giving birth" and lessen the triggering impact of a word like "killing."

Emotional preparation was necessary. We sat in a circle in the sunlit meadow for an hour sharing feelings and perspectives about eating meat. Daishin spoke in even tones about how he honored the sanctity of all life, calling on his Buddhist tradition. A schoolteacher from Japan spoke about how he had grown up fishing, though he didn't eat any other animals. He felt that fish were not as evolved an organism as the mammals we were going to consume, so their suffering was less when they were killed. He said he might just watch us. One woman cried, admitting that she was shocked to be asked to kill a living creature. She had always been a vegetarian for animal rights reasons and also declined to commit to the process. An accomplished hunter implored us all to open up to the opportunity because, he said, it probably wasn't as scary as we might think. He had been butchering animals his whole life, having learned from his father, who learned from his father. A guy in his early twenties was raised on Texas barbecue and always wondered what it would be like to kill his own. I talked about my desire to always buy precut meat and how I yearned to become less squeamish. Sam then explained how much meaning he derived from stewarding animals humanely on a small farm instead of purchasing factory-farmed meat from an exploitive and polluting industrial system. Raising and slaughtering his own livestock was the only way he said he could ensure that the food he was eating was ethically treated.

We were rehashing the common arguments about meat eating today—ones that rest on the fact that Homo sapiens is an omnivorous species that has always shown a preference and demonstrated a nutritional need for animal protein's essential B vitamins, which are almost negligent in any other food source.[7] Yet as our agricultural populations expanded across the globe, producing the vast quantity of meat that consumers desired has led to three chief problems. First, raising meat is expensive because it demands massive energy and resource consumption, which means that it is available mostly for the global wealthy.[8] Second, it causes severe and widespread environmental degradation. Tropical forests across the globe have been extensively converted to animal pastures, and enormous swathes of land are cultivated for grain to feed the animals. Further impacts to water and land are created by the fertilizers and pesticides applied to crop fields and by the solid and gas emissions from livestock. Yes, cow farts make global warming worse. Finally, industrial meat production uses concentrated facilities that create unnatural, stressful, and painful conditions for the animals. Given these realities, eating meat today is inherently destructive to the environment and nothing but bad for animal welfare. But our lead instructor brought us back to the most primal perspective, the one that we had all chosen to focus on during the week: survival.

"Beyond all this discussion," he stated, "is the fact that in a survival situation, if you were given a choice of starvation or killing an animal for food, you should know what you are choosing and why. Our ancient ancestors survived by eating meat, and we may owe our intelligence to their hunting skill." He was referring to the idea that human brain size, which is the largest among primates, began to increase big time only when a few species of our hominin ancestors began scavenging and hunting animals around 2.6 million years ago.[9] Evidence shows that all early humans ate some quantity of meat, and our digestive systems evolved to accommodate animal protein. The nutrients that animals provided were previously unavailable from plant sources and could have fueled the growth and evolution of our intellectual capacity to what it is today.[10] The process of cooking with fire, which emerged some 1.8 million years ago, is responsible for a second major boost in brain size.[11] Furthermore, the planning and coordination necessary to pursue, kill, and butcher large game communally might be a key driver in the development of language, which might have emerged to coordinate hunting strategies.[12]

Sam was telling us that, basically, we couldn't be fully human without eating meat. We certainly couldn't be wild without it. Our group was about to embark on the ancient cooperative task that had made us who we were by collectively harvesting and consuming these two animals that he had raised. He said it was time to set aside emotions and global issues and get started so we could finish before sundown. This was our one chance to eat well during the week, and as the edge of hunger grated on us, we sprang into action. Two people would make the fatal cuts, while four would hold each of the animals down. Skinning and gutting would be done by anyone interested, while several people would construct the wood tripods to hoist the animals for processing.

As we went around the circle expressing our desired roles, I urged Saul to volunteer to kill the goat. "You know you have to," I pleaded, half teasing, half channeling my inner Jedi master. I thought a powerful act could restore some of the confidence he had lost because of his emergency rescue. He laughed but accepted the challenge.

To everyone's surprise, Daishin, the dharma student, said he wanted to kill the sheep, even though the Buddhist tradition usually prohibits the killing and eating of animals, and he most certainly had taken a vow to this effect. Saul later told me that because Daishin volunteered for the slaughter, it made it easier for him. "If an aspiring Zen master can do it, this nebbish should be able to slaughter a goat," he said.

The day also allowed me to rid myself of another sacrificial lamb—I cut down a tree for the first time. Inspired by stories like *The Lorax*, I had been speaking for trees I never met my whole life, protesting deforestation and highway on-ramps with the best of the ecowarriors. But we needed six small trees to create tripods. And Gabe told me that the forest needed to be thinned to prevent severe forest fires. In one moment, my view shifted because of what he said. *Cutting a tree down isn't always a bad thing!*

Gripping Gabe's handsaw, I combed the forest for a Douglas fir tree of the proper diameter. I passed over several before I found the right one. I said a thanksgiving prayer before edging my blade diagonally into the lower trunk. Shoving the saw forward and forcefully pulling it back, I heaved and cut until my arm gave out. Then I discovered that I could push my arm forward with my bent knee. My strokes were slower but more powerful, and the tree finally fell gently on some ferns. Resting for a moment, I sawed off its small branches with more satisfying exertions and hauled the twelve-foot trunk back to our site, breathing heavily. My broad smile gave away my exhilaration. Saul congratulated me for cutting down a tree by myself. "Here's the ladybeast!" he cheered at me. I was glad he thought I was getting to be pretty badass, but a *ladybeast*? That was a hilarious mischaracterization of me, as someone who had dropped out of my college rugby team after one day, to the dismay of my football-playing mother. I was eighteen, and I just remember thinking: *I don't want to wake up sore for months.*

I spent some time hanging out with the one-year-old goat and feeling its aliveness radiate into me. I tried to hug it to give it some maternal nurturing, but it kept backing away from me and plunging its head toward the ground as if sending me away. Was it scared? I walked away from it and burst into tears. This goat was about the size of my own precious little six-year-old kid, and looking into its warm, wet eyes and feeling it breathe was too similar for comfort. This was a lost babe, severed from its mama, and I couldn't console it. Over my decade of mothering, I had grown accustomed to being able to soothe my children. My intimate bond with them meant that I empathically experienced their upset; by calming them, I could calm myself. Making sure my babies were all right was my primal motivation, so this exchange with the baby goat left me unsettled.

A few minutes later, we all gathered to help with the big moment of "giving death." Daishin was assigned to the sheep, which was held down, two people to a leg, to keep it from kicking in distress. As his knife plunged into the animal's neck, we all felt the violent shock as blood gushed from the wound and deep maroon rivulets slowly seeped into the earth. The animal gasped and shuddered and attempted to kick and wrestle, but we held fast. We could hear a strange suction noise, and it seemed like the animal was still getting some air, even though its throat was severed. This went on, everyone fixated on the sheep's head and open eyes. I held tight to its back legs until it started to get awkward. Was this how it was supposed to be? I avoided looking at anyone. Time seemed to pass in slow motion. Wasn't it going to...die?

After an eternity, Gabe quietly consulted with Sam, and they determined that the first cut was not sufficient. Daishin had to make another cut that would go through the neck vertebra to ensure the jugular vein and carotid artery were disconnected. He did it, his hand shaking. More convulsions from the sheep, more blood gushing out, and finally, the peace that we had all been awaiting descended on the animal. She was gone. It had taken about thirteen minutes of witnessing the sheep suffering.

Without cleaning up or taking a break, Gabe quickly asked Saul to dispatch the goat. I wondered if Saul could go through with it. He wouldn't look at me. Instead, he stared upward, and then with quick, strong decisiveness, he jammed the knife near the vertebra of the goat's neck and pulled the blade toward himself through its throat.

I knew that killing the goat would resonate with Saul because of our shared knowledge of Jewish tradition. The holiday of Yom Kippur, a powerful day of prayerful atonement (and hunger), had once involved a ritual goat slaughter. One goat was offered as a payment to God that accounted for the people's sins—this was a sacrifice. The other goat was released or allowed to escape, giving rise to the term "scapegoat." This animal fled into the wilderness where it symbolically carried the sins of the Jewish people on its back. The goats were innocent, but their suffering was understood to release the Jews from theirs. They could wake up the next day feeling renewed because they had been absolved and could live another year. Animal sacrifice like this had been a key practice for Jews for possibly thousands of years until the rituals of prayer were established after the destruction of the Second Temple in 70 CE.

It wasn't that Saul was religious, nor did he feel he had any sins to cast off. But he did yearn for a path to strength and certainty. Like many cultural groups living in a twenty-first-century melting pot of diversity, some Jews like Saul are seeking a powerful alignment with their heritage, a feeling of communal connection, and a deeper understanding of their ancestors' world that can guide them even today.

His cut was effective. The animal bleated and then went silent; within seconds, it disappeared from consciousness. In the kosher tradition, this is the kind of slaughter the rabbis advised because they believed it was painless and swift and did not permit the animal to suffer or become conscious of its demise, though this is now contested. As we continued to watch the goat, suspended in the intensity, the sky opened up with warm rain.

Later I asked Saul what that moment was like for him. "I was kneeling, it was raining, and in the washed-out coloring, I was channeling what it feels like to be the diminished figure of a goat. I felt the opposite of desensitized," he said. I thought it sounded like a moment of empowerment.

My adrenaline surged the rest of the afternoon as we learned how to tie the animals up on the tree poles and get them ready to cook. I wanted to skin the goat, making the first incisions into the hide with my Mora knife and then pulling with all my weight in one long motion to disconnect it from the underlying fascia. As my ear passed over the body, I heard the unsuctioning sound of loosening skin that had been tightly bound to flesh. Gabe taught us about the animal's anatomy and digestive biology and demonstrated knife techniques for working difficult parts, like the tendons around the carpal joints. He showed us how tendons could be peeled off, dried, and fashioned into a tough cord for hafting weapons.

The light rain continued until we were back at our camp, hastily building a fire and chopping the meat for the evening feast. We whittled skewer sticks from cedar branches while Gabe crafted a primitive rotisserie mounted over coals. He spiced and salted small pieces of meat and roasted them to perfection on rotating rods.

As we ate, we discussed how the day had gone. I was hopeful that this meal would feel like an immediate-return food-sharing feast after a successful hunt—a staple scene of the ethnographic literature, an occasion full of ritual significance. Since the dawn of humanity, people have loved a good barbecue, and the choice parts of meat are presented to people of honor. But here, given the previously stated concerns about eating meat, the scene was interspersed with expressions of grief and sadness. What might have been a joyful celebration was more like an extended therapy session. Most had not witnessed killing before; they had not been forced to confront the back end of the grocery store deli department. Hamburgers came in plastic packages that you dumped into a hot, oiled pan. They didn't bleat, cry, and bleed or call for hours of hacking and slicing. It was understandable that some participants couldn't celebrate like an immediate-return band; they had to first understand how our culture had never given them the emotional tools to embrace the end of life. Death was hidden from sight, as Saul lamented to the group during his sharing time. I, however, felt the processing day was invigorating and perhaps essential for meat eaters to experience.

In what was maybe an overwrought gesture, I carefully seared and then served Saul a piece of goat heart on a stick to honor his contribution. I had been eating organ meat for years, but this offering pushed him over the edge emotionally, since he rarely ate meat. I'm not sure how he was able to get it down. But with that bite, he fully embraced the story of his heroism that we had written that day. The goat, which represented his fragility, had been slaughtered. He had gained a real survival skill. We slept soundly that night.

I woke up wanting to laze around by the river, but the course was designed with the intensity of Class V whitewater rapids, and our deeply moving animal processing day was followed by getting ready for a solo quest. Despite the staff trying to keep everything under wraps, we had been expecting this, because solos are a staple of wilderness training programs. Since the 1970s, outdoor education outfits had been offering programs loosely based on a specific rite of passage from Plains and Paiute Native American traditions. Guided by elders, young men would leave the community for four days of fasting in a remote, sacred location. During their "vision quests," the young men might receive inspiration from other realms for their role in society as young warriors. It was an extraordinary, singular event that was meant to advance them into full maturity—the culmination of a lifetime lived in one place with one group of people.

Today, as a result of the popularization of vision quests, many individuals find that fasting and contemplating alone in nature promotes spiritual transformation, but I was less convinced that the practice, which might be considered cultural appropriation, fit

well with the aim of learning wilderness skills. The offer of a supportive "village" led by surrogate "elders" of the kind that Martín
Prechtel said were needed to protect us from ourselves becomes
available only to those who can pay the price, for a short time. If
these programs are something that we must pay for and experience as individuals, then they are inextricably part of a capitalist
framework—the same one that disconnects us from our communities and requires that we consume to survive.

    I also questioned the prominence of a quest originally centered
on males in the larger ethnographic context. Not even half of the
world's traditional cultures practice initiation ceremonies, and of
those that do, the majority are for girls when they first menstruate
and enter into womanhood.[13] Yet within Western culture, and especially in wilderness programs, there is a persistent idea that boys
become men by braving the elements alone and returning with an
elevated consciousness or a trophy animal.[14] Furthermore, the lone
adventurer is perceived as admirable and heroic, despite the fact
that long-term solitude contradicts how most people live and have
ever lived.

    From Jesus and Thoreau to the hero in The Revenant and Into the
Wild's Christopher McCandless (who walked off into the Alaskan
wild only to die in a bus from poisoning and starvation), the lone
man in the wilderness has provided persistent fascination for the
Western mind. It's easy to call up the image of a rugged fellow
surviving by wits and brawn, battling predators and the demons
in his own head, from any number of films, books, and TV programs. He may be okay for a while, but there's a reason that solitary

confinement is a type of punishment. We are social primates, and when we are deprived of supportive social contact, we suffer. (I don't take being alone for an extended period of time lightly—it should come with a surgeon general's warning.) Social isolation has been shown to have negative effects on physical health comparable to smoking cigarettes, and loneliness is a major risk factor for most psychological issues, including depression.[15] This makes evolutionary sense, because for most of human history, those who didn't maintain close relationships were less likely to survive in a moment of need. Paleolithic life was intensely social, and it would be rare for an individual (especially a woman) to voluntarily spend extended periods alone unless they were watching behind a hunting blind or guarding a camp at night.

With all this in mind, I wasn't pleased when the instructors told us we would spend a night alone during which we weren't allowed to leave our spot or communicate with anyone. Was it truly a fundamental wilderness skill to trust yourself alone in nature, or was this activity inspired by the myth of the lone man? I wanted to believe that an authentic wilderness experience would include strengthening relationships among the group members instead of more isolation. That was why I had recruited a friend to join me.

I muddled through the night alone but didn't glimpse any spiritual fireworks. I built a basic shelter against a cedar tree, collected some nettles and berries for the night, and gorged on a stash of nuts that was supposed to last me the next day and a half. When the mosquitoes came to torment me, I left the area and rebelliously jogged along the river. I felt cranky and irritable. Why did I have to be alone? When I returned to my little lean-to, I lay down and watched the sky darken, just a fingernail moon waning. Then, the unexpected: wetness, cramps, an impending tide. I had gotten my period.

There's a powerful evolutionary argument for why menstruation often coincides with the new moon. Early African hominids in a savannah environment rife with nocturnal predators would not want to travel out on dark nights. Yet when there is bright moonlight in the sky, it's much safer to seek sex, according to evolutionary anthropologist Camilla Power. Females whose ovulation lined up with the full moon would gain a reproductive advantage. Two weeks later, during the new moon, if they weren't pregnant, they would bleed and start the cycle again.[16]

This blood became a pivoting signal in human symbolic culture, she asserted, proposing that the very first forms of ritual in human life were likely focused on a bloodred celebration of fertility. "When young, fertile women have their periods, they signify to men that they are not pregnant, but they soon could be. Therefore, menstruation gains primacy and power in human band societies," she said.[17]

Other primate species show obvious signs of ovulation, but it's concealed for humans—even from the woman herself—which makes menstruation the only obvious sign of fertility. Hidden fertility allows the woman to receive more investment from a man, because he doesn't know precisely when she can get pregnant. Because human infants require breastfeeding and intensive care for months after birth, a mother is usually unable to secure her own food and shelter alone. She needs a committed provider and a larger group to survive postpartum. Not knowing the timing of her ovulation induces her mate to stick around and offer assistance, most likely because he gets more opportunities to reproduce and be certain that the offspring belong to him. The moon, the egg, and the man's behavior are woven into a delicate balance to create a mother.

My blood had come a bit earlier than I expected, but it was just one of about four hundred periods I will have in my lifetime. My experience as a Western, educated woman is quite different from typical menstruation throughout *Homo sapiens'* history. A hunter-gatherer woman might only tally 180 cycles in her lifetime. Studies of these populations have shown that these women get their periods later in their teen years, have more pregnancies, and breastfeed for much longer periods—up to seven years—which halts ovulation most of the time.[18] Unlike in agricultural societies, nomadic hunter-gatherer families are not very large. When you have to carry your young kids from place to place, it makes life easier if you have fewer children. Our culture is also quite deviant from the human norm in that we make great attempts to hide menses rather than celebrating it and using it to our advantage to guide male behavior.

Power, the anthropologist, has noted that humans began symbolically expressing fertility through applying red ochre as a cosmetic on their bodies and faces. Red ochre is a commonly found iron oxide clay pigment used in these celebrations across Asia, the Americas, and Africa. Its use continues today, most notably among the Himba women in Namibia, who spread butter mixed with red ochre on their skin every day as a beauty routine.[19] Power explained that fertility rituals consist of reproductive-age women painting

themselves red and performing a dramatic display while only some
of them were on their cycles, which supposedly confused men about
who was biologically receptive to sexual advances.[20] Older, more
experienced females who understood the necessity of extended
male investment for family survival would initiate newly cycling
females into these rituals. In this way, female coalitions, led by
mothers, would band together to discourage dominant males from
abandoning newly pregnant or nursing mothers in favor of other
fertile females. Red ochre cosmetics, therefore, enabled women to
seize control over their reproductive signals. If true, Power's theory
overturns the long-held idea that symbolic culture, or art, only
began with cave paintings about forty thousand years ago.[21] Caches
of red ochre used by humans date back one hundred thousand to
two hundred thousand years, possibly indicating that the first "art"
was instead made by women on their periods.

Recalling all these insights while lying under that nearly new
moon, I realized that I was a woman of reproductive age who was
sleeping alone in the woods, without my children, my mate, or any
kind of female coalition. Was this yet another evolutionary mismatch? And if so, what could I do to come back into alignment?

The next morning, I followed the sound of the instructors' coyote
calls and wandered back through the woods, seeing the ground with
new eyes. Along the path, I could see patches of disturbance where,
mixed in with the soil, red clay grabbed my eye. I gathered some in
my pockets and then rubbed my fingertips on my cheeks for my own
quiet, cosmetic observance of fertility.

Back with the group, Saul approached me. "You look weird," he said. "What's on your face?" The instructor glared at him and told him to maintain silence until we got back to camp. I whispered back to Saul: "Chocolate."

We hiked back to our fire circle where we were warmly greeted with a song from the other instructors, who wanted to honor us for making it through the solo night. As we shared our experiences, I found commonality with some of the other women. Three other mothers were in our group of twelve woodsy wannabes—not a typical weekend warrior crew. Two of them had endured serious emotional upset during the week, triggered by missing their children, but they both had stuck it out. During the group sharing time, we moms came to an interesting insight that we pursued in a conversation afterward. Each of us admitted that we had enrolled in the course because we wanted to prove to ourselves that we could survive in the wild. Yet we all agreed that nothing we had yet experienced during the survival week challenged us as much as caring for our kids. Going hungry, killing animals, sleeping in the rain, and spending a night alone in the forest—these experiences didn't approach the level of difficulty of giving birth and endlessly, exhaustively nurturing little humans for years and years. Being a mom was much harder than survivaling. And even amid our daily heroics, we four still felt that we needed to take it up a notch and prove our mettle as survivalists. Why? We had already been through the hazing and boot camp of maternity; after that, nothing would ever prove as difficult. In light of that understanding, I raised this question: Why is it that a rugged man braving the wilderness alone is seen as more heroic than a mother raising children?

Sitting around the campfire with these other supermom, we became a makeshift support group. We told our war stories. The time a mom and both her kids got stomach flu, Dad was traveling, the babysitter canceled, and she had to nurse everyone while running to the bathroom every hour. The time the older kid broke her arm while the younger one was in the hospital for major surgery. The time a mom stayed up all night to finish a work project and was expected to host a big family gathering the next day. When one mom took a flight with her baby and toddler, the man in the adjacent seat swore at her the whole flight and refused to get up when she needed to take them to the bathroom. Yet we got through it all.

No one observing us had any idea how trying it actually was or how much planning it all took. Our achievements weren't celebrated in films and TV series and bestselling books. Nor did we feel appreciated by the men in this group for the nurturing we offered during the week. One woman lamented that she had diligently collected everyone's wet socks several times when gusts of wind knocked them from the tree they were drying in. We each only had two pairs for the week, so this act likely ended up saving our feet for the day, and none of us knew what she had done. But the whole group cheered when a man was able to blow his bow-drill coal into a raging fire.

I expressed my difficulty with not knowing what was going to happen each day and feeling like a captive. I felt like so much of my mom life had to be executed with military-like precision, so the loss of control was hitting me hard. "It's good we have this week to just look after ourselves," said Tricia, a sweet woman who had earlier told me that she was just starting a draining divorce process. "That's what

I've been missing in my family life and what I need a lot more of." She didn't mind not being in charge. "Maybe you could try to let go a little more, because soon you're going to be back in the thick of it," she advised.

Those words stayed with me as we concluded the survival week with another, unexpected solo night challenge to walk two miles through the woods back to the WAS base camp, navigating only by glow sticks that Gabe had strung up along an overgrown trail. After a cozy night sleeping in a wood cabin around a fire pit, we went around the circle, reflecting on our lives moving forward. Most everyone else was looking forward to hot showers, fresh coffee, and returning to normalcy, but I wanted to find a way to make wilderness immersion my new normal. Gabe gave me a huge grin and a thumbs-up after we shared a strangely long and tight embrace. I thought to myself: *I gotta see this guy again.*

Leaving the other mothers in a poignant group hug, we encouraged each other to "stay badass." Saul and I returned to Seattle, forever bonded in friendship by the goat episode and our nights on the ferns. I was proud that my kids had endured their own rite of passage, surviving the week without their mom just fine.

Later on that summer, I had the chance to get some perspective on my experience by talking with Laurel Holding, a master wilderness survival skills instructor for the Boulder Outdoor Survival School, the one founded by David Wescott. BOSS was the first school to offer the type of wilderness training week I had done with WAS. Both programs had a simulated impact event, in which participants were left in the woods at night. Both used the power of fasting and sleep deprivation to challenge participants to come up with stored reserves of energy. The peak experience of animal processing was followed by a reflective solo quest.

Laurel explained that survival challenges are not intended to replicate hunter-gatherer society, despite all the phrasing about Native traditions in the marketing materials and my own false expectations of what the course would be. Rather, these courses help cultivate the participants' resilience for any possible hardship in life. "The likelihood that any of us will be a lost hiker or survive a plane crash where you need to know these hard skills is vanishingly unlikely," she said. "But the mental skills that we gain from a course like that can help us when someone we love dies, we lose a job, or we get cancer," she explained.

But most importantly, she told me that mothers always do really well on these types of courses. "They have something to 'compare down to,' which is the phrase we use to explain how they excel. Moms, attorneys, and doctors are all in roles where they don't blink in the face of sleep deprivation. Their work is so grueling that they have developed a deep reservoir to suffer and keep going. They are the top-performing participants we get," she said.

I finally felt recognized. It was satisfying to hear her champion the tough mothers, and I better understood the aims of these hardcore wilderness programs. But I still thought they reinforced some core contradiction about how we think about being wild. Rather than focusing on an individual's quest, how could we emphasize that living outside the safety net of civilization is more about community, collectivity, and band-level survival? When I reflected on the week, I saw that, like Joseph Campbell's typical hero, my quest to gain something—wilderness skills—gave me the unexpected opportunity to appreciate what I already had: mother power.

CHAPTER 5

Subsistence

When I returned home from my survivaling week, I made a point of continuing to carry around my Mora knife every day and trying to eat wild food to stay connected to foraging—my favorite wild skill. Whenever I stepped outside, I was on the hunt for edible plants. I was fairly confident in my identification skills and my harvesting methods, but these were sometimes questionable. One week, my kids decided to call me "apricot thief" instead of Mommy, which drove that point home. In my defense, I frequently asked for permission to take fruit, but sometimes people aren't home, and their trees are dripping with treasures I can't ignore, but it's likely the owners will. My kids were therefore sworn to secrecy about some of our adventures in procuring wild food.

We sampled wild plums, countless herbs, wild artichoke, wild radish, nasturtiums, seaweed, sea rocket, pickle weed, huckleberry, salal berry, magnolia leaves, redwood shoots, chanterelles, and a grocery aisle's worth of edible greens. I've made medicinal tinctures from Oregon grape, turkey tail mushrooms, and the netted lichen called usnea, or old-man's beard. We experimented with making acorn flour, elderberry syrup, bay nut truffles, and mushroom soup with the help of foraging and wildcrafting guides. Our favorite wild food is only a flavoring—the candy cap mushroom, which is a sweet-scented member of the fungi kingdom. When dried, this species, known to scientists as *Lactarius rubidus,* produces an aroma similar to maple syrup that can perfume the entire room. And if you grind it into a powder and blend into delicious handmade ice cream, you'll never go back to maple or vanilla.

I reached out to a neighbor who I'd heard hadn't bought greens from a grocery store in seven years because he gathered them all from our neighborhood. Philip Stark is a statistics professor at UC Berkeley and has taken a scientific interest in foraging, founding Berkeley Open Source Food, which conducts experiments on the benefits of snagging veggies from the vacant lot next door. His research team works to make it easier and more acceptable for city slickers to collect the plants in the urban ecosystem, most of them considered weeds. He's shown that foraged greens can have a much higher nutritional content than store-bought produce and has demonstrated reassuringly that a simple tap-water rinse is all that's necessary to remove any contaminants.[1] Removing any plant that's not on your own private property violates city codes, so his activities are currently illegal, but he's also working with the city government to try to rectify that. His most compelling argument is that these are free, abundant, nutritious foods available to everyone, which could go a long way for "food desert" communities where produce is expensive or hard to get. It's going to take more than public service announcements to get most people to eat what they consider to be weeds though.

Philip and I became pals and went on foraging walks through the Berkeley hills, collecting peppery vetch, sow thistle stems, coyote mint, and all sorts of edible greens. When I scored a huge haul, I'd leave some on his doorstep—figs, coffee berries, holly-leaf cherries. He shared his concoctions, things like pickled magnolia leaves (they taste like ginger) and bay-leaf infused vodka. When the acorns began to fall a bit early in the season onto his front deck, he texted me for advice. I said: Wait until the second drop—these first green ones are not the goodies.

He had dabbled in some primitive skills, whipping around a slingshot in his backyard and making his own sandals that he wears when running ultramarathons. He told me about the time he tried to go persistence hunting for antelope in Wyoming with a group of well-known ultrarunners and Paleo enthusiasts. It was an occasion to celebrate his fiftieth birthday and also, he admits, to see if he was still a useful participant in the hunt. Persistence hunting means stalking a herd over miles and miles and finally chasing one animal down, using the fundamentally human advantage of endurance over the animal's short-spurt metabolism.[2] As people keep running with their efficient cooling systems, the antelope is forced to rest to regain its equilibrium and cool down, eventually—after many, many miles—making itself an easy target. Nevertheless, it's a practice best honed over decades of training in a tribal context; Philip's party was not successful, but not solely because of his age.

I've been running since age twelve, so I guess I could say that's one of the only survival skills I mastered at a young age. Long after I outgrew school sports, I kept going because I thrived on the endorphins. While I've been running for three decades, our evo-lutionary line has been running for two million years in order to outlast the faster but quicker-to-tire prey that we pursued. I wasn't hunting, but there were other benefits to strutting along rhythmi-cally on two feet. Clearing my mind and working out my tension on a trail allowed me to stir up insights and come to decisions faster than I could while sitting still or staring at a blinking cursor. Scientists have found that tasks involving mental executive func-tioning improve with as little as ten minutes a day of brisk activ-ity like that.[3] Speeding through a forested park or along a rushing stream didn't leave me much time to carefully observe what was living there, however. The scenery formed a backdrop for my inner explorations. While this was healthy—and often profoundly spir-itual—I had little awareness of the incredible ecocomplexity that surrounded me. So I was glad I was getting a taste of that in midlife.

To encourage this for myself and Philip, I invited him and his girlfriend with me on Labor Day weekend 2019 to do some tracking with a terrific naturalist named Marley Peifer whom I'd met at the Acorn gathering. Marley had spent weeks with the Hadza tribe in Tanzania, the same people who inspired James Woodburn's ideas about immediate-return societies. The Hadza are still practicing their eons-old hunting and gathering traditions in their territory bordering the Serengeti plains, one of the oldest human habitats on earth, even though they are now surrounded by pastoralists and farmers in close proximity and, even more recently, have become a well-known stop for a hardier brand of tourists.

When I met Marley at Acorn, he was taking small groups on

morning tracking runs before the camp stirred to life. Running barefoot, pointing out animal sign with a quiet gesture, he'd huddle us all
together and whisper about what he was noticing and give us tips
to discern what the animals had been up to in the night and where
they might be now. Sometimes he'd offer an episode from his Hadza
journey. Twice he had traveled alone to spend extended time observing and journaling their daily life, which included tracking baboons,
crafting arrows from birds they'd shot, and harvesting honey from
high up in a baobab tree. There were also many, many dull hours.

Marley expressed his angst about whether he should even be
there. He witnessed tourists visiting at the same time and saw how
those Europeans and urban Tanzanians expected the Hadza to
cater to them and put on a show so they could have a proper campfire in the bush. Marley asked himself how he was any different.
While he was there for a different purpose, to document hunting
and gathering, his very presence altered how the Hadza behaved,
and he introduced more money and goods into their community.[4]

For our local adventure, Marley proposed that we meet near
Point Reyes National Seashore to track river otters near a waterway that feeds into the Pacific Ocean, surrounded by sand dunes
and hills of chaparral. To my amazement, Philip pulled up in a
camper van with Daphne Miller, a doctor who had influenced my
passion for wild food. In one of my moments of utter breakdown
and burnout while working in tech, I had visited her medical practice. She told me to ditch all my untested biohacking supplements
and source all my nutrition from real food, and she shared that wild
food was best. I never had the chance to thank her for that good

advice. But now, here she was, a few years later, wearing the same handmade sandals Philip wore, getting ready to go out for hours in search of tiny animal signs in the sand. I told her how much she had impacted my path toward wildness. She might have been used to this praise. After their first marriages had dissolved, she and Philip started working together in pursuit of better food and better health, collaborating on the research and education about foraged foods and sharing their knowledge with the public.

We joined up with Marley and my friend Raven and her eleven-year-old, homeschooled son, Zac, whom I'd met at Rewild Portland's skills gathering in Oregon. Raven is a British experimental archaeologist and naturalist who was even more devoted to the skills scene than I was, regularly packing her son and their dog into her SUV to drive fifteen or more hours to Utah, Arizona, and Idaho to attend gatherings. Her home was like a curiosity cabinet filled with incredible artifacts she had made or collected, including hides of all kinds, fishing trap baskets, animal skulls, fertility sculptures, and tanned salmon skins. We shared an instant bond as moms traveling alone with our children, and I was delighted to find out that we were on the same intellectual journey, looking at ethnographic and archaeological sources to piece together a modern, healthy, rewilded life that centered on giving our kids time in nature. A single mom with an absent ex-husband, she had previously hired Marley to guide her son, who had learning disabilities, on tracking adventures that allowed Zac to gain the type of nature knowledge he'd never get in school. I could see that Zac had superior observation and navigation skills, which we were about to put to use.

Our clan for the day started out poring over the surface of the ground, trying to see who had been there before us. Over the morning, we discovered the deceptive qualities of large ground holes (most of the time, nothing is living in them, and they are likely just used for temporary hideaways), followed the tracks of ravens on sand and mused about what they had been doing, and broke open crustacean-shell clusters of otter scat to find out how recently they had been left.

Tracking is akin to learning to read in a new language. Instead of traversing the landscape appreciating beauty, identifying species, or simply spacing out, the environment becomes a rich field of clues for figuring out what happened, where, and who did it. A tracking tale might go something like this: First the turkeys stopped under this tree, fed on some grass, and then crossed the sandy path and left some scat. From their erratic toe prints, it looks like they may have been scared by something and quickly ran away through that field, where their trail is evident by the bent blades of grass. To read tracks accurately, it's necessary to invent a sequence of events for how they appeared. For this reason, many posit that tracking is the origin of the human ability to tell stories.

Trackers look for the smallest details to indicate decisions the animal made. When Laurens van der Post observed the immediate-return San people in the 1950s, he marveled at how their understanding of the animals in their environment seemed almost supernatural. "For instance, they seemed to know what it actually felt like to be an elephant, a lion, an antelope, a steenbuck, a lizard, a striped mouse, mantis, baobab tree, yellow-crested cobra or starry-eyed amaryllis, to mention only a few of the brilliant multitudes through which they moved," he wrote.[5] Sometimes their tracking skills could not be explained with scientific understanding of human cognition, but they were found to be accurate and beneficial for hunting, foraging, and medicine making. Often there is nothing but a vague erosion pattern to indicate the recent presence of a target, yet trackers can effectively pursue the animal and return home with it. Any twelve-year-old boy in this group can reproduce the tracks of dozens of surrounding mammals by drawing its likeness in the sand.[6]

These techniques were developed to assist the hunting process, but they are also instrumental for sharpening powers of observation and understanding what has transpired in the environment. Sand patterns, leaf debris, bent branches, water flows, wind prevalence, and the weather can all give indications of activity. Of particular interest is the point where two paths meet, because animals often make their presence known at the crossroads, where scat shows up as a territorial marker. Even the direction in which the scat is pointing should be noted, along with its relative age, condition, and contents.

Marley was very practiced. He was alert to tiny gradations in the sand that he said could be the work of the Western tiger beetle. He showed us how to look on the underside of signposts for praying mantis eggs and how to poke at bird droppings to find undigested caterpillar skin. The biggest gift of the training was our expanded perception—we were dismantling our touristic mode of viewing the land around the trail as one big picture window for our aesthetic pleasure. Instead, we saw millions of stories written in everything. Dramas large and small played out in front of us in the grand theater of creation. Tracking also prompts attention to the ground you walk on, the tracks you make, the disturbance you create in the environment.

Philip and Daphne were super curious and ready to jump, run, and crawl on the ground in pursuit of some information that would help us understand an animal more fully. Although they were both probably fifteen years older than me, I found their energy something to aspire to, and their partnership was powerful. Together they have educated so many people and continued to explore.

Marley didn't yield to our initial inclination to name what we observed and kept us guessing while we honed our ability to observe more closely. There is so much more to know about a creature besides pinning down that you've just seen a *Buteo lineatus* (red-shouldered hawk). If you move on to naming the next species, you will miss out on what else can be learned from this raptor. For instance, this creature is certainly one of nature's original angry birds, as it is frequently caught in food-related combat with crows and even great horned owls. Driving my car in the hills of San Francisco one afternoon, my daughter and I spotted a red-shouldered hawk with its telltale black-and-white-striped tail feathers duking it out with two American crows right above the intersection we were headed toward. As we pulled to a stop, the crows smacked down onto my hood, scuffled for a split second, and then flew off as if shot from a catapult. We'll never forget that encounter, and we watch for this behavior anytime we see those birds.

Only aiming for a correct ID is a narrowing of our perception, which is already restricted to the screens or walls we sit in front of for most of the day. By contrast, wild creatures rely on their awareness for survival; all their senses need to be activated to zero in on resources and stay alert to threats. They scan the sky and the land and listen to other creatures for clues about what the weather will be, where resources might reside, and what predators are doing. Birds, in particular, can be harbingers in a survival situation if you learn their language of territorial, mating, and alarm calls. For instance, a honking goose will indicate nearby water. If ground-dwelling songbirds are leaping up into trees and sounding their alarms, a predator is likely close. Paying attention to where the birds are feeding can also help with finding food sources. Favoring identification over the relational aspects of nature observation obscures how humans are fully integrated participants in the environment; we are not just eyeballs.

After several hours, we grew tired and were heading back to our cars when Zac spotted two river otters in the water. They were toying with the carcass of a pelican. We watched silently as they dipped playfully around the dismantled bird and seemed to be communicating with each other. Their muscular tails propelled them on graceful long underwater glides, and then they'd land on their webbed feet and slide into the muddy bank. We were lucky newbie trackers because we'd found what we'd been looking for.

I brought my daughters back to Abbotts Lagoon a couple of times during visits to Raven, but we never saw the otters again. But those weekends were valuable for observing how Raven and Zac knew every wild corner of their home territory of Point Reyes. They took us to secluded swimming holes where we'd jump off short cliffs into tule reed patches, showed us choice spots for picking huckleberries, and taught us to listen for the call of endangered spotted owls around her campfire at night. She and I would gossip about the rewilders we knew, the ones who were appearing on sensational reality TV shows like *Alone*, which we both were asked to audition for by a show producer who admitted to needing to scout female contestants. Neither of us felt aligned with the premise of the show, which reinforced the individualistic pursuit of a single person—80 percent of them male—surviving in harsh environments in a way that no human ever would have. Yet the chance to demonstrate wild skills and make some money doing it was appealing, and we both spent hours filming ourselves and submitting videos until realizing that we couldn't bear to be away from our kids for a season. It was clear to me that Raven would have done much better than me, as her father had raised her to hunt and fish, while I could barely make a simple deadfall trap for a rat.

Despite gaining more footing in my new direction, my increasing forays away from home started to take a toll on my marriage. I was searching for a different way of life that centered on nature and community, and each time I returned home to urban nuclear family life, my dissatisfaction grew. At the same time, my husband was embedding himself deeper into a highly structured, inordinately demanding profession; he never knew when he would need to respond to a legal brief or offer corrections on someone else's last-minute filing. I didn't feel the need to push him out of his comfort zone, but as I delved into more wild opportunities, he didn't get curious about the changes

I was making. The first night the kids and I made a friction fire in our backyard, he watched it from his bubbly seat in a new hot tub several meters away. I knew better than to tell him that I'd been experimenting with roadkill squirrel in our kitchen and stretching a goat hide on our back deck stairs. I'd offer him greens I'd foraged, but he'd decline and chow down on prewashed spinach from Trader Joe's.

He referred to my rewilding activities as a midlife crisis (I'm sure he was right), and he was patiently waiting for me to get over it and settle into our old domestic routines again. Who could blame him? What the hell happened to his wife who made him peanut butter and jelly sandwiches in the morning before he ran to catch the bus, happily soothed cranky kids, RSVP'd for birthday parties and Jewish holiday celebrations, and joyously danced to seventies jazz in the living room while he played along on the sax? Sadly, she was gone, and he missed her. Now he lived with a rebellious madwoman who kept running away to the forest and coming back with radical ideas like: *Let's homeschool the kids! Can we get chickens? I don't want to fly to see your family because...greenhouse gas emissions!* My newly feral nature was a lot to handle. When we stood under the chuppah at our wedding and made lifelong promises to each other, I couldn't have foreseen how much I would relish the eventual unraveling of my domestication.

Yet it wasn't all a loss for the family's harmony. I found that rewilding took some of the pressure off the difficult parts of modern parenting: the nagging, cajoling, and scolding to get my daughters to do things for the benefit of social conventions. I had accepted that these guiding behaviors were a reality of parenting in our society, but then I read more about how Indigenous children are raised, noting that kids rarely conflict with parents and elders. With ethnographic comparison ever present in my mind, I didn't see much point in making my kids change their clothes daily unless they wanted to. I was used to expending lots of energy to get them to bathe regularly, but then I realized that they have a much better time swimming, whether at a pool or a lake. They would take a shower when they knew that was the fastest way to warm up afterward.

I was pleased that my invention of feral dinner saved me a lot of trouble. The girls would scare up some flat bark for plates, carve rudimentary spoons from thick sticks, and squat around our backyard firepit for coal-baked potatoes and roasted banana. Ash cakes proved to be almost as enticing as doughnuts, because they could make them by themselves, and they were fresh and warm when they came out, once all the ash was dusted off. We would challenge one another to eat apple cores, broccoli stalks, and strawberry tops—all edible parts of food that we usually waste. For those meals, I didn't have to do the dishes or take out the trash.

But for all the relief I felt on these fun occasions, as I integrated old ideas about humans and nature, the more uncomfortable interactions I had with people unfamiliar with rewilding. My husband wasn't the only one getting suspicious about what I was up to with the kids. I got some raised eyebrows from my old Bay Area pals when I talked about my adventures picking up roadkill, making knives from rock and sinew, and settling down to sleep alfresco on a bed of ferns. When I taught my kids to discreetly pee outside in a way that feeds the plants instead of wasting their excess nitrogen in porta-potties or plumbed toilets, one of their friend's parents was not amused.

I got a harsh dressing-down from my neuroscientist mom friend when I advocated for unstructured time in nature as a viable treatment for kids with ADHD. "How could you possibly get doctors to prescribe visits to the woods?" she questioned. "You're crazy." She didn't know that doctors are already writing scripts for nature time, spurred on by the burgeoning field of ecotherapy, which treats psychological and stress-related disorders with regimented time outside. Some evolutionary biologists think that kids with ADHD would have been useful in an immediate-return environment where alertness to changes (or what we call distractibility) is an adaptive advantage that should not be medicated away.

The more this went on, the more I got worried about getting called out on social media or showing up in tabloid headlines. *"Wild Mom" says germs are good for you, so don't wash your hands before mealtime!*

What a distortion! What I really say is: "What mealtime? Kids, you gotta fast for a few days like your Paleolithic ancestors!"

I once took my girls for a weekend camping trip organized by a San Francisco social club that included an evening pig roast. We were walking the trails by the kitchen when we saw the pig getting prepped, apple in its mouth and all. I got excited to show the kids what we would be eating that night and have them plainly see that it came from a living creature. But as we approached the scene, the cooks warned me that I might not want the girls to witness what they were doing, it might traumatize them...you know, Peppa Pig is dinner. I laughed. With everything we've done, my girls are more traumatized when they're taken to a fast-food joint, because they know how *those* animals have lived and died. And they still adore Peppa.

The girls had heard my stories about processing animals during my survival week, and they were eager to help me make something out of the goat skin that I had brought home. We decided that we wanted to make a drum with it. My mom's most beloved cousin, Judy, was a drummer who had taught me traditional rhythms on the djembe as a teen. The most moving moment of my mom's memorial service was when Judy played an improvised series of rhythms dedicated to my mom's free spirit. This was a skill worth passing on.

First, we had to scrape all the hair off, smooth out the skin texture, and then cut it and mount the skin on a circular frame. Despite the fact that this was a relatively easy process, I still procrastinated for months, not wanting to mess this hide up. This time, I had plenty of folks to consult about the way to do it. I had brought home some drinking gourds from a gathering, and I cut one on two sides to get a curved hoop. Once the hide had been soaked and dehaired, we perforated the edges of it, threaded buckskin lacing through the holes, stretched the hide tightly across the frame, and secured the lacing across the bottom of the drum, making a handle. The next day, it had dried, and we threw ourselves a dance party, taking turns banging on our new instrument.

I had the chance to tell some of these tales when I attended the Rewilding Conference in Portland, Oregon, the winter of 2019. This is a gathering of about 150 people who are interested in the wide spectrum of rewilding. There are folks with urban permaculture gardens coming to learn more about native plants, Indigenous activists, herbal healers, punk crafters who sell jewelry on Etsy, and tech-bashing anarchists, among others. There is no unity about the approach to rewilding, and at the helm of it all is Peter Michael Bauer, who gathers people twice a year to push the movement forward. In the summer, he hosts the Echoes in Time skills gathering that he inherited from some legendary 1970s-era flint knappers, and in the winter, he spearheads this indoor, ideas-focused conference. Peter invited me to host a discussion about rewilding and parenting, which was an underrepresented topic for this community.

At my session, about twenty people gathered to talk about how parents could replace their kids' screen time with "green time." In the golden years of childhood, from age eight to twelve, kids are spending an average of six hours a day in front of digital media.[7] As a result, these children are more likely to develop obesity, anxiety, self-esteem issues, a decrease in cognitive ability, and other behavioral problems.[8] They also have much less playtime outside, which has led to a huge decrease in their nature connection compared to previous generations.[9] What could be done?

One participant brought up the theories of psychologist and addiction expert Gabor Maté, who contends that all addictions are rooted in childhood trauma or emotional loss, including compulsions to check social media and play video games.[10] Our culture's pervasive emotional loss from lack of nature connection might be what motivates our screen addiction. According to Maté's theory, to eliminate an addiction, it must be replaced by something equally compelling.

Several of the people at my discussion were nature educators, and they testified that face-to-face free play in nature was the solution and the antidote to all the screen time. Just two hours a week of

immersive nature time has been shown to improve well-being sig-
nificantly by improving concentration, mood, self-esteem, cooperation, memory, and immune system functioning.[11] We talked about
the rise of hundreds of nature-based education programs across
the country in the past fifteen years, like Rewild Portland, along
with a rapid increase in the number of "forest schools"—an enduring Scandinavian tradition in which most learning takes place outside. Even if the parents don't try to acquire any nature knowledge,
many kids are getting it, and their ability to identify plants, shoot
with a bow and arrow, start fires, and sharpen knives will positively
impact them for the rest of their lives.

Furthermore, through these schools, camps, and after-school
and weekend programs, it might be possible to recreate the village
conditions of childhood from a previous era when kids could roam
through the woods, fording creeks, climbing trees, and catching
frogs—a time when they were an integrated component of healthy
community life and their existence did not require a totally separate succession of institutions, meals, and programming, each at a
high cost to parents. The true meaning of "it takes a village to raise
a child" isn't only that there are always watchful eyes on the kids. A
village guarantees enough kids to pal around with.

One woman summed up what we wanted to achieve: "Ideally,
kids get to run around freely, all day every day, with a pack of mixed
ages they've known all their life. They can learn as they choose from
adults who are doing useful activities in the community. They're all
supported by tradition and story and elders." But several people
brought up the fact that programs that mimicked this vision mostly

served the educated elite, while what we really needed was integration of two hours a day of free-play nature time among kids of different ages in every public school system. I challenged this idea, though, saying that a vision of rewilding based on our hunter-gatherer heritage was less about reforming institutions and more about empowering small, local groups of people and individual families to create regular nature opportunities for kids.

What could the twenty of us here do to unite around a shared vision? The most urgent need seemed to be for the dissemination of ideas about how drastically children's culture had changed in just a few generations. If more parents knew that the now-common norms of all-day structured activity, restrictions and rules on play and learning, and keeping kids only in similar-age groups was doing more harm than good, might we start to see change? I had to admit that I had wanted more concrete answers from this discussion, since the older my kids got, the less influence I thought I would have on them. But I had been able to get them to switch off *Minecraft* and start foraging, a skill they would have for life. I just had to have faith in our path forward.

I left my session and found some books to browse at a table set up by Black and Green Press, an anti-civilization publisher founded by radical writer Kevin Tucker. His book, *For Wildness and Anarchy*, had first pushed me to connect how the structures of civilization have eroded our connection to our nature-embedded life in nomadic hunter-gatherer bands. I'd reached out to Kevin and his partner Natasha and, finding that we were equally passionate about rewilding, we'd had hours of calls and text marathons about anthropology and history, debating whether we should engage the wider world with these ideas on corporate social media or bow out of the system entirely. They were giving a talk on how to deal with the trauma of civilization while their merch table was overseen by a guy named Jaime Van Lanen. He and I started chatting, and he offered me some grizzly bear sausage that he'd made from a bear he'd hunted. He told me to chew it slowly; this wasn't just a breakfast link. This was spirit power and a chance for me to feel the wild infuse me. I was impressed. He had a surfer bro demeanor and a boyish look, though he was approaching his late forties. I was drawn to his vigor and forthright statements about how important it was to eat wild meat. Later on, sitting next to him in open conference sessions like "Animism in the Anthropocene" and "Rebellion and Compliance in the Educational Industrial Complex," he kept offering treats from his bag, like moose jerky and smoked salmon dipped in bear fat, to people around him. I felt compelled to give him some of my nuts and dried fruit. We were sharing food we had each gotten ourselves, little case studies in self-sufficiency.

I realized I had read his writing before, in the Black and Green journal called *Wild Resistance,* where he used the moniker "Four Legged Human," which is the English translation of "bear" in a Native Alaskan language. He didn't want to use his real name because it wouldn't have looked wonderful for a government employee to write regularly for an anarchist journal. Jaime has a master's degree in anthropology and worked for government wildlife agencies in Alaska since 2008. He owns property there with multiple cabins, access to salmon fishing in the river, and hunting grounds for bear, moose, caribou, and sheep. He's also got a spot of land outside Yellowstone National Park and spends time at an inherited family home in eastern Wyoming. He was already twenty years into his rewilding quest and had a lot to share, which he did in a group session about hunting and the "feral return" that I made sure to attend.

There, he talked severely and directly to a group of about ten folks, emphasizing that we all needed to be preparing for difficult environmental conditions. He warned us that the years ahead would call for hard work, discomfort, pain, danger, and risk if we wanted to become self-sufficient on the land. We had all been softened by domestication, he said, and we needed not only to gain wild skills but also acquire the mental and physical toughness that would only come through rigorous outdoor physical training. For emphasis, he jumped up from his seat onto a waist-high stage behind him. When he saw some of the women in the group looking intimidated, he said, "This is not a macho thing. It is a human thing." Climbing down, he told us to take every chance we could to swim, climb, jump, run, travel long distances on foot, carry heavy weights, and practice self-defense. "You need to be ready to kill something," he urged. Climate change was going to unleash massive earth forces, and we couldn't panic or imagine that institutions would save us. Becoming focused and resolved in our self-sufficiency and learning to provide for our own transportation, food, shelter, and medical needs was the best strategy in the face of wildfires, hurricanes, and supply chain shortages.

Like house cats who leave their owners and resume hunting

mice for survival, we could also imagine ourselves going feral. Plus, all this would ultimately lead to better health and a more fulfilling life, he said. "We can't avoid the harsh physical and psychological realities which accompany a feral return," he said. "Hard work, discomfort, pain, danger, risk... I hold no illusions regarding what befalls us. I say this all with a deep humility based on my own feeble attempts at rewilding, experiences which have often left me retreating back into the comforts of civilization. Going feral requires physical and mental toughness."

Jaime's perspective reminded me of another piece of advice from the Russian writer Dmitry Orlov, who witnessed the fall of the USSR and has become somewhat of an expert on societal collapse. Orlov cautioned readers to spare themselves the lengthy process of earning credentials to qualify for jobs that will no longer exist and instead invest in "acquiring useful skills that can make you self-sufficient in building and maintaining shelter, finding food, taking care of your medical needs, providing for your defense and security, and much more." Forget college, kids. Soon, your degrees won't be worth anything, he seemed to be saying. Orlov wrote that people who are accustomed to technological and political assistance become panicked and unsure during catastrophic situations, waiting for rescue. Transforming into someone who is "focused, resolved, and engaged in forging a new path must involve some amount of pain," he wrote.[12] But nobody wants to hear this, as was evidenced by how the crowd reacted to Jaime's similar statements. Wide eyes, open mouths.

One woman raised her hand to timidly ask what he thought of

urban permaculture. Wouldn't it be wise for us to stay in our cities and make *them* more subsistence-based? A few others nodded, wondering if Jaime could make an allowance in our calamitous future for a utopian vision of city roof gardens and strip mall medians full of chin-high corn.

"People should stop looking to half measures like urban permaculture," he said. "You need to know that you can live on wild food predominantly." He explained that people who can continue to rely on wild resources in the least developed places were the ones who would protect those wild spaces for all of us in the future. He was referring both to Indigenous groups who have fiercely defended their territories and foraging lifeways amid the onslaught of missionaries, colonizers, and industrialists as well as the folks like him who had chosen to experiment with hunting and gathering, which is admittedly much easier to do in Alaska, where there are millions of acres of wilderness and more lenient foraging laws.

He continued musing on why promoting domesticated agriculture inside cities was wrongheaded and then touched on a hotbutton issue. The boom in the homeless population is a good sign in some ways, he said, because some of the people who take to the streets because they reject a domesticated lifestyle, for whatever reason, are more equipped to fend for themselves. They have more survival skills than most anyone with an address. They're excellent scavengers, doing exactly what we evolved to do—make the best use of available resources in an area. Furthermore, they band together in small groups that look out for one another, often with more loyalty than anyone would find at the average workplace.

"Our insistence on domestic urban living is a crutch toward our future survival," he announced, looking at the group and offering this challenge: "If you're not in charge of getting your food in some way, then what are you doing?" Fittingly, the theme of that year's conference, emblazoned on the organic cotton T-shirts for sale, was "subsistence is resistance." I took that to mean that getting your own food could be a powerful, rebellious act against systemic control that would empower you in the coming era of possible collapse. It was a simple, basic, human drive that could overturn the dominating hierarchies of capitalism.

Months after the conference, Jaime's question still rang out in my mind. "If you're not getting food, what are you doing?" I started calling him for inspiration and got further interested in his life and research and drawn into his fantastic survival stories. His job was to document the traditional subsistence practices of Native people across the state. In Alaska, anyone is allowed to subsist off the land without cumbersome regulations dictating how much an individual can harvest. Over a decade, he gained the skills necessary to live out in harsh conditions and take moose, caribou, sheep, bear, and fish to provide for himself. Not all his skills were physical either. "Primitive longbow hunting helped me get meditative consciousness," he admitted. "Sitting by myself for up to five hours waiting, I would actually lose my thought in the intense observation."

He once hunted a moose with a longbow. "Moose are the hardest to hunt. They're like ghosts," he told me. He had been taught a method for enticing a nearby moose into range by some Gwich'in Athabaskans, and one time it worked for him in a spot where he found some fresh scat pellets. Because the males often rub their giant racks vigorously against trees, making a cacophonous sound, he had a moose scapula with him that he beat against some wood, which he learned from the Gwich'in perfectly imitates the noise made by the moose. If an aggressive male moose was nearby, it would likely grow curious and move toward what it heard. "That's what happened, and I barely had time to shoot it with the longbow as it charged toward me," he said.

Jaime carried it out of the forest in hundred-pound chunks and made an incredible coat from the hide, good for subzero temperatures. It took him years. He carried the hide around in the back of his truck, waiting to meet up with someone who would help him tan it. He had written about this: "A man without community, alone with a moose, brought despair, the loneliest I've ever been. Now when my wanderings gift me flesh, fur, fat, bones I share. Wildness is sharing rather than hoarding." [13]

We started calling one another regularly, sharing videos about hunter-gatherer anthropology, holding long-distance book discussions, slowly working through our favorite authors, and plotting an upcoming trip to practice experimental archaeology. The most important validation I got from Jaime was his belief that within anthropology lies the map to the maze of modern life. He studies ethnographies and archaeological reports of hunter-gatherers like they are field guides. The nuances of the anthropological record—particularly of immediate-return band societies—can show us "exactly where we're going, how we got ourselves on this path, and how we can get ourselves out of it," he said. "The record gives us evidence for these cultures that never were on our trajectory and that maintained authentically sustainable ways of life for probably hundreds of thousands of years."

Jaime has done academic anthropological fieldwork on four continents in addition to his Native Alaskan ethnography. Unlike the academic mainstream, he doesn't hesitate to criticize the modes by which Native people can be seduced into a dependent life in civilization. Their subsistence methods were being annihilated by contact with industrial goods, he believed. When I asked him about how tribal communities could receive assistance to maintain their lifeways, he was not enthusiastic and noted that when the government offers what it considers to be helpful, their efforts destroy the people's remaining subsistence activities. "Engaging with Native economic realities today means promoting economic development that perpetuates their dependency on cash and technology," he said. Instead, Jaime has focused his professional efforts on broadening tribal hunting rights and access to ancestral lands and preserving the knowledge of elders about hunting and gathering techniques.

For example, he pointed out that as hunters become accustomed to using fossil fuel–based vehicles and guns to hunt with, they gradually lose the skills to make their own weapons from local materials and track animals by foot. Within a generation, no one hunts without these industrial machines. Even though the hunters are still surviving off the land, they have no choice but to also find a way to make money to buy their machines, fuel, and guns. Slowly they get drawn into the global economy, never to return to their autonomous lifestyle. This drive toward complete dependence on industrial goods is viewed as positive "progress" according to mid-twentieth-century modernization theory.[14]

He also saw how the hallmark qualities of Indigenous hunting societies, like sharing meat across the community and deriving their materials from local sources, began to disappear. In his discussions with Native elders around Alaska, many of them remarked on the loss of skill and awareness that came from slower-paced traditional hunting methods, which are no longer practiced. They remembered that their villages were more resilient and autonomous before they started importing global goods.

Fueled by these insights, when his agency proposed giving iPads to Native community members so they could map and track game on their territories, Jaime fought it hard within his department. Just as iPhones have taken away much of our ability to remember phone numbers, navigate through unfamiliar neighborhoods, or just sit without doing anything, he thought the introduction of this technology would soon deprive the Indigenous groups of their skillful orienteering by natural cues. Jaime didn't heed anyone's arguments about how denying technology to a poor community was paternalistic, which it may be. He knew that what was at stake was their one sustainable way of life, and somebody had to stand up for it and back the elders in the community who were more wary of drastic change.

According to him, new technology introduced a slippery slope toward total domestication, which he identified in almost every encounter between Indigenous folks and the more technologically dependent societies throughout history. The heroic holdouts in this conflict were the small foraging and forest gardening bands of the Amazon rain forest and islands of the Andaman Sea who had deliberately isolated themselves and consistently resisted contact with the surrounding society in order to maintain their way of life. Jaime postulated that these groups had consciously chosen to live in isolation and evade interaction because they still carried trauma from how their ancestors' and neighboring Indigenous groups' way of life was destroyed when they became civilized.[15]

His observations sparked my research, and every time we talked, he had more papers and books to recommend from anthropologists and anti-civilization writers. I'd read them, and we'd discuss, conducting an informal seminar that drew us deeper into a relationship, the nature of which was growing a bit muddled. I admit I did wonder if he would someday become the wild antidote to my domesticated husband.

When Jaime invited me to visit him the following fall at one of his outposts in Wyoming, I knew I had to go and see him in action. By this point, my kids were getting used to my research trips, so I felt all right leaving them with my highly capable husband for a few days, confident in their growing security without me. But I wasn't sure that I had that security with my mate. We barely connected anymore. When we did, it was mostly to discuss logistics about the house or the kids. I knew that I felt more free when I wasn't in our house with him; the truth was that my trips were also a way for me to test how I felt as an independent woman, able to engage with anyone, anywhere.

———

Over decades of visiting Wyoming, Jaime had learned how the land was used by the first inhabitants and had explored many similar sites, identifying untold amounts of prehistoric artifacts from the hunter-gatherers who once roamed these mountains and plains, from twelve thousand to eight thousand years ago. On my visit, we were planning to check out an area he had always wanted to scout. It was the first time we had seen each other since meeting at the Rewild Portland conference the previous winter. He had invited me to stay at what used to be his grandparents' house in the small town of Torrington, where he spent some of the winter and housed a lot of his stone, bone, and hunting materials. Impressive mounts of caribou and elk antlers hung in the room he used for his library. He had also redesigned a two-story gymnasium that his grandfather had first used for boxing training that was adjacent to an in-house Swedish sauna. He kept up a rigorous fitness routine of weights, sprints, boxing moves, and CrossFit exercises and regularly spent more time in the sauna than any medical authority would find advisable.

I set up a desk to work my way through some of his book collection, and we had hours-long conversations about his research on immediate-return societies and his thoughts about the controversial "sheep eaters," or local Tukudika people, who are believed to be a group of holdout Mountain Shoshone who never adopted guns or horses and maintained a pedestrian lifestyle quite close to immediate return. They allegedly lived year-round in what is now Yellowstone National Park up until the late nineteenth century; many wild sheep corrals had been found that suggested they had camped there. Jaime also thought that the artifacts he kept finding on open land were from an earlier people that the Tukudika may have descended from.

We would take breaks to work out in his gym, and he enjoyed endlessly challenging me with timed planks, punching drills, and basketball games (which I did win one time). I seemed to meet his fitness expectations, but I bristled at his competitive drive. "These seem like male exercises; they're so competitive," I said.

He resisted that idea. "No, you gotta work your big muscle groups," he countered.

"Yes, but as a woman, I'm also concerned about flexibility and cooperation," I said as I crouched in a squat and then lunged into a yoga move known as cobra. He didn't follow my lead. Later, I failed his sauna contest. After twenty minutes of Death-Valley-in-summer torture, I ran out gasping. I could hear him taunting me from inside, where he stayed for another fifteen minutes chanting and yelling to purge himself of deep-seated rage, but I no longer cared to compete. My time with him was punctuated by these kinds of endurance challenges, most of which I willingly accepted but ultimately found to be based on his ideas about masculine strength. I started making a point to show him where he could broaden his thinking with a feminine perspective. But the competitive dynamic between us cooled any hint of romance for me. What he and I shared was more valuable than some kind of fling that would have made me feel guilty and compromised. We had passion for the wild. He had a lot to teach me, and perhaps I could teach him something too.

I was thrilled when, on my third day there, we finally went out into the field to witness ancient encampments firsthand. "This is the environment of nomadic hunter-gatherers," Jaime announced emphatically as we looked out at a vast sun-faded view of Laramie Peak from a sparsely forested ridge we were exploring on public land in eastern Wyoming. He led me toward a drop-off into a ravine that he said would have made the perfect hunting spot for Paleo-Indians tracking antelope. He pointed into the distance at some cows grazing and told me to imagine that they were buffalo. "See how easily you could aim for them without them sensing anything?" he asked. "Imagine a guy knapping a chopper tool or sharpening an arrowhead right here, knocking off flakes and then taking off," he said as I interjected, "Or maybe it was a woman?" He smiled and subtly acknowledged this idea, which I researched and discovered was plausible. He later wrote about that possibility in an anarchist journal, crediting my insight. Women also had to make their own stone tools because they were usually the hide tanners and clothing makers in need of scrapers and cutting blades.

Acting on well-honed intuition, Jaime started scanning the exposed dirt on the ground. "Here it is. Lithic scatter!" he shouted. We could see dozens of small, flat stone chips of red and yellow chert embedded in the surface of the soil. We scrutinized them, overturning each one and examining their edges for the telltale signs of pressure flaking by human hands. Indeed, we found several stone tools amid the scatter. They were all created through the process of hammering away at a larger stone to produce a piece with a sharpened edge for scraping or a half-circle notch for straightening arrows. We marveled that these artifacts remained exactly where they had been left by their makers so that we could stumble on them so many millennia later.

Later on that day, as the wind picked up and the air started to cool, he identified several shelter rings—circles of heavy stones left from a period of settlement that were used to weigh down the hides that formed the tipi. The wind was fierce, our noses were dripping, and our hands were going numb and tight as we thumbed through the gravel surrounding each ring, inspecting every bright jewellike piece. Jaime found a nearly intact spearpoint that filled him with boyish glee. Several times, we found hand-size chopper tools that were used for breaking bones, and he demonstrated how to split open a deer tibia to get at the marrow, which would have been one of the most valuable nutrients that this group had access to. "Archaeology is tracking humans, wherever and whenever they exist," Jaime said. "Every rewilder needs to learn this skill, to be able to read the land and know how it was once used by our ancestors. It can show you where a good camp location would be and where the most productive hunting can happen," he said.

At one point, we found a pristine chopper sitting just a foot away from a discarded small-device circuit board—two technological artifacts separated by millennia. While one was returned seamlessly to the environment and could still be used, the other would never fully decompose or be functional again. I thought about the differences between the two societies that had produced these objects. At that moment, I belonged to both of those human legacies and had to find a way to reconcile my dependence on the polluting consequences of the circuit board with my desire to pick up that chopper again. "We will never live in an immediate-return society," I said to Jaime.

"No," he agreed, "but our grandkids might. Don't give up on them." This was a very sore point for Jaime, as he was currently working out a difficult custody situation for his one-year-old daughter, who lived with her mom on the Olympic Peninsula. At that point, it wasn't clear to Jaime whether he'd ever be able to parent his child, let alone know her children in the future.

We stayed out at the site past the time we should have left and had to hike the two miles back to his car in the dark. This gave him the opportunity to show me how to navigate by using the stars and the shadows of the surrounding mountains. That night, he served me tender roadkill caribou steak for dinner that he had found on his way to the Anchorage airport and just managed to get into his freezer in Wyoming before it started going off.

Jaime continually encouraged me to go hunting with him. I knew that getting food was what life has always been centered on. It's the core meaning of "immediate return," and it's the basic need that drove the development of agricultural civilization. While I had intended for my tracking education with Marley to lead to hunting experience in the field and I had learned about the varieties of primitive snares and traps, even securing a state hunting license, I could never pull the trigger, so to speak. I didn't feel innately that I was a hunter. I was drawn to the ease of picking up roadkill and the way it made sense in our global industrial system of waste. If I could become a scavenger, I felt like I could keep the world more wild. I wouldn't have to take a life if so much was already waiting for me everywhere I drove.

Soon after I returned from Wyoming, I was presented with a perfect opportunity to scavenge while taking a retreat in California Gold Country. My kids and I had been gathering juicy fat acorns and wild grapes—collecting them in big baskets that were piling up in the cabin I had rented. Deer were common in the area, as were turkeys, so I was always alert to the fact that I was missing out on abundant protein opportunities.

One night after the kids were back at home and I stayed on for a few days, I spotted a young buck conspicuously propped up along the right shoulder of Highway 108 when I drove by. I vowed that I would retrieve it the next morning if it was still there. Arising at dawn, I packed my knife and a handkerchief into my shabby Toyota Corolla and returned to the site to find the animal perfectly intact. I parked my car in a pullout adjacent to the spot across the two-lane highway and furtively crossed the road to inspect the animal. With the handkerchief in my hands, I grasped its hind legs and waited for a break in traffic. When the time came, I used all my strength to haul it across to my car. I judged that it might have been about 120 pounds—a weight that I knew had me at the edge of my strength, as it was the size of my two daughters combined. They were just at the point where I could only hold them up, one in each arm, for a few seconds before my muscles gave out.

Attempting to hoist the buck into my trunk went disastrously. There was no way for me to manage its bulk. I dragged it toward

my back seat, ever alert for a passing cop on the road. It took perhaps half an hour of continuous effort and many initial failures to
place it fully inside, and I ended up using my daughter's swimsuit
and my handkerchief as pulleys to leverage its upper body into
the seat, where it slumped ungracefully. At the beginning, I was
hesitant to touch it, but it didn't take long before I was forcefully
grasping at its fur and handling its limbs as if it were a child having
a tantrum. I blocked the windows with cardboard and then drove
home like a wildlife Uber, nervously anticipating what would
become an entire day of work. Lugging it to a secluded spot, I
surveyed the gorgeous creature whose life had ended the night
before. I knew that because its antlers were stubby, it was in its
first year of life. Its cloudy eyes and desiccating lips still retained a
regal presence, and I said a short statement of gratitude for its life
that would become my nourishment.

I called Jaime, who laid out a plan for me: Skin it, gut it if possible, retrieve the tenderloin from deep inside, and then work
assiduously to cut out the prized backstrap and the sinew that
supported it. This sinew was perhaps the most valuable inedible
part, as it could be used to make cordage and durable fasteners
for weapons, containers, and clothing. He was going on and on
about how to make the cuts and the important things that I had to
do in order to prove that I could butcher properly, but I was overwhelmed by his intensity, so I cut him off short to make my own
plan. He couldn't understand the difference between his body and
mine, but I knew I'd find other ways to work with the deer that a
female could handle alone.

For example, I couldn't hoist the deer up on a tripod, so I had to process one side at a time. The plan worked until I discovered how bloated its belly was and found the impact injury on its back haunch. I wasn't going to gut it and risk contaminating the meat with what was certainly an inner cavity flowing with dangerous bile. The tenderloin would just have to rot. Hundreds of flies joined me in taking advantage of the flesh, and the sun moved in with ferocity until I was drenched in sweat. My initial repulsion to the flies gave way as I realized that they were just an annoyance that I didn't have time to pay attention to.

Just an hour into processing the buck, my hands were aching and slow, and I didn't know how I would persist, given the fatigue. It was a reminder that my hands were likely underused and I would benefit from more activities like this that would build my grip strength and dexterity. As midafternoon approached, I had a dozen plastic bags filled with fresh meat, an intact hide, and a couple of strings of sinew that were drying in the sun. Making proper European butchering cuts was beyond my capability at that point; I just hacked at the muscle meat to get it off the bones. By the end, the messy process had coated the meat with fur and blood, so I went down to a stream to wash every piece.

When I finally relaxed for the first time that day, sitting on the stream bank rocks, lazily rinsing my free food, I realized that I had just guaranteed my subsistence for several weeks, if not months, since my plan was to freeze the fifty to sixty pounds that I'd been able to cut away. My younger daughter and I had gone to look at the crawdads in the creek and learn about their behavior the previous week, and I noticed that these small arthropods were starting to emerge and capture the small pieces of flesh that had floated down to the creek bed. *I'm feeding them too*, I thought, in addition to the bacteria, fungi, and scavengers that would decompose the remaining carcass.

I looked up at the pine tree above me, perfectly bisecting the blasting sunshine on a seventy-five-degree day, and shouted out, "This is my life!" I knew I could rely on myself. Plus, I had a full deerskin that I could properly tan now. I envisioned the moccasins I wanted to make for my kids out of it. I didn't want to be anywhere else doing anything else but this, listening to the bird calls around me.

That night, I cooked up part of the backstrap, adding garden greens and figs I had picked. It was the wildest meal I'd ever made, and I felt rich. My girls got accustomed to eating venison stew, and I was happy to share the meat with guests intrigued by eating roadkill for the first time. We enjoyed it all winter.

CHAPTER 6

Birthright

Thousands and thousands of years ago, we all used to know how to make tools to process animals, skins, and plants for our daily needs. Today, very few people know how. For those of us who desire to be trained in Paleolithic skills, we must take time off work, travel some distance, and pay a fee to learn them from a stranger. Some folks now make their living teaching just these skills, meager as the earnings are. Learning to be a nonindustrial self-reliant *Homo sapiens* requires a significant amount of money and—in the modern-day context—privilege. Even those with recent Native ancestry—perhaps especially those with ties to Native community—don't find these skills easy to acquire, even though as humans, it is our birthright to learn what it takes to survive on this planet. This fact came into high relief for me the more gatherings I attended. It was sometimes a source of humor, sometimes a source of shame, and always a big reason to keep learning.

At the second gathering I attended, I left my kids at home so I could wear my research cap more tightly. At a workshop about bone tools, the young woman leading it expressed grief at having to charge us money to teach us what she thought was our birthright. "We shouldn't have to pay to learn what we all used to be taught by our people," she lamented. She showed us her collection of bones and antlers that could be used to make a variety of useful things: awls, buttons, belt buckles, toothpicks, combs, knives. These objects were completely novel to me, and I tried to imagine myself as a hunter-gatherer adolescent learning about them from my elders. What came to mind was my Jewish grandmother—who had been raised in Queens, New York— taking a break from sautéing chicken and listening to NPR to squat down with me in her perfectly pressed white slacks and hammer at some elk femurs to extract the marrow and maybe fashion a button or two. The idea was so absurd that I almost laughed out loud. My birthright was a set of encyclopedias and a membership to MoMA. But I knew that way back down my ancestral line, there was a femur-hammering grandma.

These contradictions strike many people as funny. At the Acorn gathering, I remembered how Tataucho, a Chumash elder, opened the event by burning sage to bless a mostly white crowd. "I don't know how all you strike a fire with only sticks," he said. "I gotta use a lighter." As the crowd laughed, he pulled one out of a plastic lunch box and ignited the sage bundle, allowing him to begin the prayer.

In a perfect inversion of that message, I later encountered a bearded guy in his thirties leading a friction fire workshop who opined for over an hour about the process of gathering the right kind of dry wood scraps, stringy lichen, and grass filaments for a tinder fire starter. "We can flick a BIC," he said, "which makes it so easy, but then we miss out on the coal-making and tinder process and no longer have the connection to nature." It was hard to square his message of making an "authentic" fire with the image of Tataucho holding up the smoking sage. Was one better than the other? Who was administering the purity test here? I would need to seek my own answers about the moral questions that vexed rewilding, as everyone must do, absent of an intact culture rooted in the earth.

I had to abandon my previous conceptions of who does what with Paleolithic tools, and what I observed erased every pop-culture stereotype about Indians, cavemen, and survivalists I had ever witnessed. I have seen Native people learning to tan a buffalo hide from a white woman. I've seen a bunch of kids, including my own, weaving tiny textiles with traditional Zapotecan wool from a man whose ancestry in Oaxaca goes back many thousands of years to the beginning of his people's calendar. I learned a traditional method for making cedar bark hats from a Native family who lives on Squamish tribal land in Vancouver, Canada. Their kids were taking classes on rabbit fur processing and bow making, learning for the first time the skills that their great-great-great-grandparents used to survive in the Pacific Northwest.

I appreciated that the gatherings were inclusive of so many knowledgeable people and that we could all share what we knew respectfully. But I noticed that the skills dealing with subsistence were usually taught by non-Natives, even though it was Native people who used them most recently in history, and in the case of West Coast populations, sometimes only a century ago. Through genocide and persecution under colonization, their way of life was outlawed, and their land was stolen.

Today it is hard for most Native descendants to practice any subsistence skills because their ancestral land base is gone, and their communities have acculturated into contemporary civilization. In many examples, even if communities have lost their capacity to practice land-based subsistence, they retain cultural beliefs, spiritual rituals, stories, and art and craft traditions. But more often than not, parts of these traditions are also misappropriated by settler culture for new money-making contexts. It's hard to ignore the sports team mascots, the corporate logos, the fashion statements, and the New Age fads that all derive from pieces of Native culture ripped crudely from their original web of meaning. Native cultural advocates have been calling for an end to this kind of blatant disrespect for decades, yet it persists. It's clear that the process of colonization didn't stop once the (notoriously ineffective) treaties were signed with Native American tribes in the nineteenth and twentieth centuries, because the extraction and appropriation of Native ways is ongoing and invasive.

Since wild skills gatherings are settings for reviving traditions and skills, they inevitably bring these complex cultural dynamics into play. It's impossible to rectify centuries of colonial abuse, genocide, and the massive theft of land from Native stewardship. When I hear land acknowledgments before events, which name the Native groups who once lived in the vicinity, it does little to provide clarity on these complex issues and seems a bit silly at best. I think: *If we are noting that the land we're on was stolen, why don't we just give it back?*

It's not easy to seek approval from an appropriate authority about what is or isn't okay to say about or do with Native cultures, because within Indigenous communities, structures of authority are so different from those within settler society, not to mention the fact that most of them didn't carry the same notions about ownership of territory that our culture does. Plus, many of these Native authority structures have been disrupted by colonialism, making it even harder to receive "permission." No one is the official judge of whether it's okay to participate in a Native American sweat lodge ritual if you have no Native ancestry. Or if you have Native ancestry but little training in traditional skills, who can say if it would be acceptable to learn how to tan hides from a blond-haired, blue-eyed surfer?

Defying all expectations, one of the foremost instructors of Paleolithic skills is actually a fiftysomething former punk rocker from the UK named Lynx Vilden. Since 2001, she has been operating a program called Living Wild, which invites people to spend a season preparing traditional supplies like buckskin clothing, stone weapons, and dried wild foods in order to take a big supply pack up into the mountains of Eastern Washington and survive as a group of hunter-gatherers for a month or so. She also runs workshops across Norway and France and moved her classes there during the COVID-19 lockdowns. She was trained at BOSS in Utah, and she's schooled many of the instructors who now teach across the Western skills gatherings. At these events, most everyone has heard of Lynx, making her a bit of a legend for folks who have never met her and an esteemed mentor for those who have. Still, some have criticisms of her extreme project.

I had fallen for her image of Living Wild, though, and I thought she was the most badass woman I could imagine. On days when

I felt the need to escape my family routine, I'd click through her website, showing her riding off into the sunset on her palomino steed, her fur coat glinting in the light. I felt like she was writing to me when I read her website's questions. "Do you feel called to live a wilder life? To be in community, learning with and from the land? Would you like to explore rock, stick, bone, and water? Be in connection with feather, fur, and fin? Create ceremony and feel belonging with the ancestors and the more-than-human world?" Hallelujah, yes, I do![1]

Lynx posed with her students from each of her programs, and clicking through these feral class photos showed me that there were dozens, maybe over one hundred people, who were willing to give up absolutely everything modern, don an entirely buckskin wardrobe, and learn to rely on their handiwork to replace those store-bought items that I thought everyone needed: trail mix, socks, sunscreen, even Band-Aids (also made of buckskin). I met several of her former students and saw how they treasured the items they made under her tutelage, like a brain-tanned buffalo hide that could keep a sleeper warm in subzero temperatures and a natural clay drinking pot hung on nettle cordage for easy access on the hunt. I didn't care that she allegedly enjoyed lots of modern creature comforts when she wasn't off with students or that she would try to use her cougar powers to seduce young men. Her work sustained a dream for me and so many others, particularly Peter Michael Bauer.

He wrote about his experience with Living Wild, claiming that her program was the most effective way to learn primitive skills because students had to use them to live day by day. He described useful techniques like the technique for lifting a handmade clay pot from hot coals with sticks and how to fix rawhide sandals with a bone awl in the moonlight. Yet he lamented that the temporary, unintegrated nature of the program meant that he didn't learn how people could function through cooperative group dynamics and regenerative land management. "Sure, we were hunting and gathering," he wrote, "but not like hunter-gatherers. This was my one caveat with the program: looking wild is not the same thing as living wild." That said, he admitted, even looking wild is a necessary step on the path to rewilding. Considering the issue more deeply, he noted that the imagery of mostly white people who appear indigenous in ways that don't steal from Native culture is powerfully inspirational. They were living in a style that predated Native American migration to North America, and their aesthetic belongs to every human who descended from Paleolithic ancestors. "Beyond what Lynx's program does for creating proficiency in her students, the imagery she creates does an amazing job of giving us back a modern, visual, Indigenous identity," he wrote.[2]

It's kind of a cop-out, though, to be satisfied with just looking wild. Truly living wild requires reclaiming the birthright of connected community living in nature. The vast majority of humans have lost this. Yet we still live on land that is full of the history of this human legacy. The people I met who have grappled with these issues much longer than I have—Native and non-Native folks—kept telling me that it is crucial to know about the Native people of my home area and about their current struggles. How did they live before colonization, and how do they live today? Understanding their ways of life provides a field guide for living on the land in a beneficial way while paying attention to the context in which we do so.

Learning with and from today's Native people can be a humble act of honoring painful histories. At the Rewilding Conference I attended, Chumash educator Deana Dartt provided the mostly non-Native audience with some actionable advice for understanding their place on stolen land. "Know your own settler history. Know the history of the land and recognize the inherent grief and trauma there. Recognize your privilege. Become familiar with contemporary Native issues," she intoned. Dartt also cautioned rewilders about the potential harm their activities could do to existing Native communities. She said that rewilders tend to value only the historic, ethnographic information about Native people, because they view Natives as casino operators who don't have sophisticated communities and ways of life.

Dartt believes that many practices of well-intended non-Native people such as those at Rainbow Gatherings, attendees at Burning Man, and New Age mystics are another level of extraction from and an erasure of Native people. "Don't call yourself a tribe, and don't choose a spirit animal," she warned, noting that adopting these cultural practices was offensive to her. "Even rewilding, if it is done with entitlement and a lack of humility, still erases Indigenous history and presence."

Dartt proposed principles for becoming a good guest on the land that Native people once lived on. "Who are the best guests?" she asked. "They ask for permission; they ask to be invited to the table. They're humble and they bring a gift." She was not saying that

Native communities wanted settlers to leave but to join with them to elevate Native voices and respond humbly to their concerns. For Dartt, the idea of decolonizing, which has become a popular idea in leftist circles, is insidious because it assumes that it is possible to reverse the impacts of colonization. Rather, she advises focusing on "reindigenizing," in which the goal is to recognize the worldview of Indigenous knowledge and perspectives and to "incorporate Indigenous ways of knowing and doing." These include centering Native people's goals related to self-determination and sovereignty while strengthening family and community networks, reciprocity to the land and people, healing the land, and living in gratitude. She said that if we are really doing the work, it is going to feel hard and uncomfortable.

Reflecting on Dartt's presentation, I knew I had to try to walk this talk. The old 1970s primitive skills attitude that everyone on earth is equally entitled to regain our birthright as *Homo sapiens* didn't account for the privileges that made it much easier for, say, an educated, middle-class Jewish woman to rewild than most others.

Where I live in the San Francisco Bay Area, there was a human population of thousands of people before the Spanish arrived in the eighteenth century. Native people were living off the abundant wild resources in a mild climate with diverse marine and land species. Exploring the local Native cultures became a preoccupation of mine, especially during my naturalist studies. I had always been interested in Indigenous culture as an anthropology major in college and then as a graduate student. But I hadn't ever considered how I could be personally connected to those ways of living or how I could ever participate in them. The implication from most guidebooks and scholarly texts was that those cultures had been destroyed, along with most of the Indigenous people. The assumed role of early anthropology was to document these cultures before they completely disappeared, a practice known as "salvage ethnography."[3] While documenting the histories, languages, and cultures of Indigenous people, anthropologists reinforced a belief that Native American societies were inevitably disappearing. Of course, the main aim of colonialism has always been to disappear Indigenous people, and this was very much the intent of colonizers in the United States. But their efforts ultimately failed. Today in California, there is a vast network of tribal descendants, working hard to preserve, restore, and propagate language, culture, food, and the arts of these communities. The more I looked, the more I found.

Near me lived people who are now called the Ohlone—a collection of about forty separate small tribelets of complex hunter-gatherers who were lumped together for the convenience of colonizing missionaries. According to Malcolm Margolin, who wrote one of the most vivid reconstructions of their culture in the historical fiction account *The Ohlone Way* (1978), they participated in an intertribal network of feasting, trading, gift giving, and ceremony, and they were linked by marriage and traditional collecting rights on their different territories. He described how they didn't have many possessions, but they highly valued generosity. They lived seminomadically, following seasonal cycles of game and plant harvest times. They enjoyed acorns, quail, salmon, deer, and a wide variety of native plants and berries, along with mussels, clams, and oysters from the sea. They never developed any agriculture, though they tended patches of plants and practiced controlled burning to groom the land for deer and elk to feed on annual grasses.

The importance of acorns to these people can't be overstated, which seems obvious each fall when I mark the annual acorn drop, which scatters millions of powerhouse seeds across nearby open spaces and leafy backyards. Ethnographic reports state that the Ohlone oriented their understanding of time based on the oak trees. The annual cycle began with a great fall acorn-collecting fes-tival, when neighboring tribelets would gather to harvest enough acorns to make it through the coming winter, trade various items, and party late into the night wearing costumes of feathers and the potent original cosmetic of red ochre body paint. Young men and women would pair off, sometimes finding their lifelong mates. All year, the people would look forward to this celebration. If the acorns were plentiful, they could relax in the joyous atmosphere of tasty food. If the nuts were scarce, they'd collect buckeyes, which was, I heard from an Ohlone man, like settling for rice cakes when you're craving doughnuts. The best that could be said about buck-eyes, according to him, was that you wouldn't starve if you could get them.

Yet the Native people weren't just leaving the acorn harvest up to chance. Evidence from early Spanish explorers along with the memories of elders and anthropological accounts showed that they engaged in many activities meant to increase yields and improve the quality of the materials they were getting from the oaks.[4] The ground underneath the oaks was regularly swept clean of excess brush so that if a fire came through, it wouldn't ladder up to the crown of the tree. They'd also prune branches, weed out less hardy sprouts, and regularly set fire to some groves, which influenced the species growing there and promoted fertility of the soil.

When the Spanish arrived, they attempted to convert the Native Californians to Catholicism. They destroyed their abundant oak groves in order to establish farms and ranches as part of the mission system, which built twenty-one religious settlements along the Pacific coast over the turn of the nineteenth century. Decimated by European viruses and denied their modes of subsistence, the Native population declined 95 percent. During the ensuing gold rush of the mid-nineteenth century, the California governor declared a war of extermination on the Native people, offering significant bounties to promote their massacre.

While the genocidal history is now acknowledged and taught in schools and the state of California has delivered an official apology to Native residents, there are more than forty Native California groups, including the Ohlone, that are not recognized by the federal government. They receive no resources or reparations. Many of these groups are taking up their own initiatives to restore traditions that were lost for the past few generations; this is an area in which many welcome allies and contributions.

One outstanding champion, Vincent Medina, is a thirty-something Ohlone advocate who is reviving his tribe's food traditions and serving Native-inspired meals at a café inside a Berkeley bookstore every week and even infusing the experience with Native stories and games. I brought my kids there, and we sampled tea made from yerba buena and mint and ate hazelnut cookies and chia pudding, all inspired by what people were eating on this land two hundred years ago and further back in history.

Vincent spoke to our riveted, intimate crowd about his family's decimation and how Ohlone culture survived decades of oppression. Showing poignant pictures of his family members, his face beamed with pride and determination. My eyes misted up. It was a real triumph for him to be here and to be sharing so openly this story of trauma and reconciliation. "We are still here, and we continue our culture," he said forcefully to our receptive group. And then he brought the fun, pumped up his stereo with the sounds of A Tribe Called Red, and showed us a traditional Indian gambling game that we all tried, tossing sticks, throwing walnut shells, and laughing at the chaos on the table in front of us.

The Native American connection to gambling long predates the arrival of reservation casinos. They played games of chance, not to profit but to experience the same inexplicable force that seemed to influence the weather, fertility, and the success of a hunt. Playing games allowed them to try to appease the universal force that governed the cycle of life. When I looked into it, I found that the moral stigma we now associate with gambling is a symptom of civilized life, promulgated by the Roman Empire.

People tend to become distressed when things are unpredictable if their society is rarely upended by the forces of nature. They develop fear rather than resilience in the face of the unknown. The rise of agriculture triggered a mass psychological shift from embracing wild randomness to needing reliability of the harvest, year after year. The widespread use of gambling and games of chance among hunter-gatherer groups is their way of getting used to uncertainty and lessening their need for control. You know that you always get another chance.

After the games had ended and the crowd started to disperse, I told Vincent about my time learning the natural history of Mount Diablo, the highest mountain peak in our area visible from any spot on the major freeways. His smile faded. "My people don't go up to the top of Mount Diablo," he said solemnly. "It is too sacred. We call it Tuyshtak, which means 'at the dawn of time,' and it is the center of our story of creation, where we came from."

I looked down at the ground, prolonging an awkward moment. Had I done something wrong? I couldn't figure out how to respond appropriately. I tried to stand in his shoes. What if the situation were reversed, and I was giving a presentation about Jewish culture and what had happened to my ancestors over centuries of persecution? If someone had told me they enjoyed rock climbing on Jerusalem's Western Wall, the holiest Jewish site in the universe, would I be able to keep my calm?

I didn't know how to reconcile my desire to honor his culture (plus the traditions of the other twenty-five tribelets that also told powerful stories about the spiritual importance of this peak) with the elation I had felt when I brought my girls up to the top of Mount Diablo on a clear day in autumn. We leaned against a barricade at the very edge of the summit, and I held them both across the middle and we yelled out into the rippling canyons and hills of oaks and gray pine that faded into the sandy horizon hundreds of miles away. The wind whipped our hair and we said that we could see the whole world. Then we collected a few of the biggest canyon live oak acorns we had ever seen, as if the spirits of the place had blessed us with abundance, and we took them home to smash and grind up for a little wild treat. So, dream sequence fading, I told Vincent, "It is indeed a very powerful place."

All I could do was recall some arguments from anthropology that all of human history is like a bazaar. We've been stealing, trading, inheriting, improving, and passing along resources and technology between groups and individuals forever. Culture is not a fixed, pure entity. What is sacred to one might be ordinary to another. That said, it's important to understand the broader contexts for activities and to engage in them through living relationships when possible. I was grateful to Vincent and the other Ohlone, Miwok, and Pomo folks who were generous and open with their cultural traditions when I attended their events with my daughters so that we all could better understand the gifts of the land we were now on. But I didn't think that our lack of Native ancestry prohibited us altogether from harvesting the acorns around us (only the park regulations did) or making baskets from tule reed or creating friction fire kits from the California buckeye tree. If it was our industrial, civilized lifestyle that was responsible for cultural and natural destruction, then trying to return to wild ways seemed to be the least offensive direction we could go in. But I still needed more direction and guidance.

At the June 2019 Saskatoon Circle primitive skills gathering in Twisp, Washington, on the eastern side of the Cascade Mountains in the Methow Valley, my kids and I met several individuals who

had their own ways of following and contributing to Native traditions. I also got the unexpected chance to reconnect with my survivaling instructor Gabe, whom I spotted at a distance at the event's
opening circle. I finally found him just at sunset after my kids had
gone to bed. He was drinking whisky out of a canteen, perched
on a log under a tree. His sleeping bag was laid out under a tarp
connected to the tree. He had the same rugged pack he had toted
around during our week in the Cascades and the same pants. It
looked like he had been studying a field guide, since it was splayed
open next to his bed.

Sitting next to him, I felt that focused energy he'd had on the day
that we had processed the goat—quietly confident on his path to wildness. I started asking him about the skills he was going to work on at
the gathering. He wanted to learn more about hide tanning, because
he had been processing so many animals at the permaculture farm
he lived at and was finally able to give up on industrial meat sources.
I knew that his goal was eventually to get off any kind of reliance on
mass industrial production. We chatted about the practicalities for a
bit, what the ideal wild tool kit consists of, and whether he could live
with just a knife, an axe, a steel water bottle, and a dutch oven for
the rest of his life. "These are things that would last my lifetime and
that I could probably even pass on when I'm done," he said. "I can't
live in a fully Stone Age way because of the rainy, cold climate I'm in
and the fact that I don't have a community around me." With that last
comment, I was glad to hear that he didn't subscribe to the myth of
the lone man in the wilderness, though he could certainly attract the
attention of an adventure movie casting agent.

Accepting his offer of the whiskey canteen, I asked, "Out of all the basic human skills, which one is the priority?" I asked.

He waited awhile before answering, "People growing up in an intact culture, they follow their passion and that becomes what they do. They learn all the skills in their community that they need to know; it's not like one is more important than another. So it's kind of an artificial construct to ask that."

His reply showed that he was deeply embedded in the wild way of thought. Even though he taught at a nature school, had served four years in the army, and was clearly a product of industrial civilization, he could recognize the flaws of these systems. We were no longer what we used to be. As uprooted, dissociated, disconnected beings, we had to start somewhere, though, if we were going to regain our birthright. I made that point, which led him to speculate a bit more.

"After shelter, fire, and water, food is the last and hardest skill to attain in the wild. I'm still there trying to figure that out," he said. "Getting food involves so many skills—it is the longest of the journeys," he explained. "I live without complicated systems for energy. I just use fire and the sun. In my forested rainy environment, fire is more important than shelter. Just be safe and dry. Knowing how to do that is a priority."

He claimed that fire is the easiest skill to get instant feedback on. If you're not getting a spark, you keep adjusting your method. And since using fire to boil and purify water is the safest way to hydrate in the wild, making fire comes before finding water in order of priority. But with foraging food, there are longer and bigger considerations. If you harvest something, will it grow back the next year? How many annual cycles does it take for you to understand how much you can sustainably take? There's no instant feedback, and learning all the skills to successfully find food takes about twelve years in forager culture. Grown men and women don't reach their peak productivity in terms of hunting or gathering until their twenties and sometimes their forties. He thinks he'll be working on wild food for a decade before he feels totally confident.

I asked Gabe how he felt about the gathering. He wasn't so happy because he had left a bunch of projects in process at his home site, and he felt like he needed to stop traveling. The people here were having fun, he told me. He didn't need fun at that moment. He wanted to be rooted in his place and use his skills to live day to day. His seriousness of purpose was such a contrast to the culture of millennials I was used to, like the obnoxious Americans depicted in Judd Apatow movies.

Night had fallen and I had to get back to my sleeping girls in the dark, so he helped me navigate the campsite trails. As we got closer to our spot, he let out an audible gasp as he saw the tree we had chosen to sleep under—a widow maker! No, I assured him, I checked it out. The organizers removed the dead limb. It'd be okay. I had learned my lesson from him, and we both laughed at the full circle our paths had made together. Gabe left the next day to get back to his life. We would fall out of touch. I had hoped that I could be part of his tribe, learn from him, and share outdoor aliveness, but he wasn't inviting.

During the next few days at the gathering, my girls got involved with a project with a couple of Native instructors. Samuel and Tiśina (Ti-sheena) were helping them weave tiny woolen rugs in the traditional Oaxacan style of Samuel's Zapotec family, who have been creating them since time immemorial. They created simple looms from light pieces of wood and stretched cotton thread. With their nimble little fingers, the girls were pulling strand by strand of naturally dyed yarn into the warp and weft, creating simpler versions of the vibrant serpents, diamonds, and corn symbols that form both the decoration of the rugs and the cosmology of his millennia-old culture. Samuel helps operate his family's farm and rug business in Oaxaca, and he also has a PhD from Oxford University in sustainable product design. I'd seen him at a few of the gatherings, but this time I got to know him a bit and heard about how he's actively bridging Native and non-Native worlds, the ancient past with the future. His girlfriend, Tiśina, was on hand to help the kids figure out their patterns, and I found out that she was from the Bay Area and needed a ride back to Seattle to catch a flight home.

When the gathering ended, Tiśina came with us in our rented camper van back to Seattle. The journey was four hours of incredible vistas winding through the Northern Cascades. During the ride, she mentioned her family background, and my jaw fell open. Her grandmother was Julia Parker, who had led the basket-making workshop I had done two years before. Tiśina had grown up around the legendary artisans of Pomo, Miwok, and Paiute heritage. I couldn't believe the coincidence, especially because we were so far from the Bay Area. She, her family, her boyfriend, his family—they were all literally weaving and woven together out of Native history.

They came from different traditions, but what they were doing was essentially the same: twining and twisting the world into beauty despite centuries of conquistadors and colonizers. As we sailed through some of the most beautiful mountainous terrain I'd ever seen, she dispelled some of the romantic ideas I had conjured about her family and painted a much more complex picture of the practice of ancestral skills.

Tiśina is strongly bonded to the three tribal groups in the Yosemite area from which she descended, and she now works for an Indigenous arts group and volunteers her time for a few other Native activist groups. Following her family tradition, she pursued textile and fashion design at one of the Bay Area's top art colleges and incorporated Native materials into her final project for her degree. "I got very interested in creating tribal ceremonial regalia and learned to brain tan buckskin with Jay in Bodega," she told me. (Jay Sliwa is well-known on the California skills circuit, a guy who lives the off-grid, close-to-nature life with his wife and two kids and makes his living selling buckskin creations.) What she said next really surprised me. "My grandma and aunt didn't talk to me for two years when they found out I was tanning buckskin, because that is not women's work, it was what men would do, they said. They were very upset that I wasn't observing their tradition."

I paused, puzzled. "They didn't talk to you for two years?! But you were reviving a Native skill," I said.

She explained that she couldn't find any Native teachers, and she would have preferred to have learned from someone in her family line. But given the prohibition on women working with skins in her tradition, that might not have worked at all, even if she had found someone. Plus, she wasn't sure that she believed her grandma and aunt. "Who is to know who did what?" she asked. "The tradition changed so much over the last few hundred years; we can't really know. And these are just cultural ideas about who should do what. They're not biological."

Curious about this conflict she had, I later researched the statement her relatives had made. The information I found told a different story. Every source I consulted about the Sierra Miwok people confirmed that women, before European contact, were primarily responsible for working animal hides, as they are in most Indigenous cultures that wear skin clothes and make skin shelters.[5] Yet I realized how brave Tiśina was to go against her family and suffer the consequences of their ostracization.

"It's a tiny, tiny group who still have the traditional skills," she explained. "Look, we are very impoverished. We live literally at the bottom of the economic rung; we don't have much choice about how to live. Some of us are working multiple jobs and just trying to survive in the system."

I nodded, understanding that we came from vastly different worlds. "And the skills were outlawed during the days of the missions and native boarding schools," I added.

"Well, these are everybody's traditional ancestral skills," she went on. "We all did this in our communities, no matter what the color of your skin. But people who have access to them now are white people of the upper middle class. Not many Native people go to the gatherings. They don't want to learn from the teachers there.

They would prefer to learn to tan a hide from an elder who had it passed on from their elders," she explained. While there are camps and workshops specifically for Native folks in the old ways, these are just enrichment, she said.

It's people with money who have access to land and access to time, she explained. "Native people have to fight to get gathering rights on public land because there is so much privately owned land where we aren't permitted to go and gather. But that's the land that was stolen from us."

I thought about how frustrating and unjust this situation was. To be told that you can't go and gather basket materials where your family had been going since the beginning of time. Or to be informed that in order to hunt on your ancestors' land, you have to pass examinations, use the right kind of (expensive) weapon, and purchase a license and tags for the animals you wanted to hunt.

"Sure, there are good reasons that we have these restrictions. But Native people should have the right to go and gather and hunt without getting those permissions. They don't want to participate in a government system," she said, as it was the same one that took away everything their ancestors had.

I brought up an instance where the Kashia Pomo tribe—related to her grandmother—had recently been able to purchase some private coastal land in Sonoma County to resume their ceremonial and foraging activities on. It was cause for celebration, Tiśina said. "But we should be getting a lot more land back. Even if it's just an acre in a city somewhere, we need places to go and connect with the land that was ours."

I thought back to Kule Loklo, the fantasy village in Point Reyes that was meant to recreate the coastal Miwok way of life where I had played with my girls. Tiśina didn't even know about it, let alone spent time there in ceremony and connection. Her people were the Sierra Miwok, whose range extended across the foothills and slopes of California's biggest mountain range. Linguistically, the two bands were related, though their political entities are now separate.

With the opportunity to open up to her, I asked what she thought about my learning so many nature-embedded cultural traditions since I have no Native ancestry. I could cherry-pick various traditions and dabble in them for fun. I can fashion my own Tarahumara-inspired sandals and weave Oaxacan rugs and make Ohlone-inspired acorn flour. Wasn't I just appropriating cultures?

"It's okay, because you're not profiting from it," she told me in a pat answer I wasn't expecting. "You're learning it from the teachers who genuinely want to share their culture, and they expect that you won't turn it into a commodity."

I wondered if other Native leaders would agree with her assessment of my activities. At Saskatoon, I had talked with Delmar Williams, a Squamish instructor, during the trade blanket evening session. He had run a friction fire workshop earlier in the day, and we had started talking about his life history and his thoughts about Natives and non-Natives learning skills together. His wife, Tracy, had taught my daughter and me how to make hats from woven cedar bark, which is one of the most recognizable Squamish traditions. Delmar told me that a white woman had taken what she learned from his wife and started making her own versions of the hats and selling them on Etsy for hundreds of dollars. He said he didn't think it was right for her to do that, but he genuinely wanted to know what I thought. He said that he and his wife love teaching their skills at the gatherings, but seeing someone making money off it made his wife angry.

Indeed, I had noted that his wife was a keen observer of colonizing trends. When I asked her where she lived, she said "I don't live in Vancouver; Vancouver lives on me," driving the point home that she doesn't willingly accept the impact of settler conquest. I respected what she felt and what she had taught me about the cedar tree's sacred power for her people. I told Delmar that I had to defer to what his tribe said about the issue of selling the cedar hats. I certainly had no business judging the situation. But his questions pointed to a bigger issue dealing with what groups felt comfortable in the rewilding scene. There's a lot of discussion about who isn't at the gatherings and why.

People of color, particularly Black folks, make up a very small percentage of participants, and they aren't well represented among instructors. I was told by a Black skills instructor that many don't have good associations with some of the conditions at the gatherings or with the practices of rewilding in general. When rewilders advocate a return to the land or working with the materials of nature to provide for basic needs, it can sound like a step backward for people whose ancestors were enslaved or impoverished.

Furthermore, the American property and conservation laws of the last two hundred years have prohibited Black, Native, and poor people from gathering wild food, with extreme consequences.

While the preservation of wildlands in national parks that began with the creation of Yellowstone in 1872 is regarded as "America's Greatest Treasure," many of these lands were simply stolen from Native people who were stewarding the spaces and subsisting off of them.[6]

In this same era following the Civil War, strict property laws were drawn up in the existing states at the time, partially to prevent former slaves from foraging wild food on white-owned land. Some slaves had previously been able to tend their own gardens and provide much of their diet from wild sources near plantations. Prior to 1860, unfenced land was open to "wanderers," but in 1865, racially motivated trespassing laws made it criminal to hunt game, fish, and gather plants in a movement called "closing the range." Much of this legal action was meant to pressure Black folks to return to laboring on plantations, because it was clear that freed people could subsist mostly outside the market economy because they had the skills of self-sufficiency. Entry onto enclosed land was made a misdemeanor, with extortionately high fines as punishment. If a Black convict could not pay the fine, their labor could be sold at auction by the sheriff.[7]

As a result of this legacy of disenfranchisement, going out into natural spaces may still feel uncomfortable for Black people, and equally so for people of color. I thought about how blithely I ignore "No Trespassing" signs when I'm on a trail run and feeling adventurous. I just imagine that if caught, I could easily talk my way out of an encounter with an angry landowner. But so many people would never dare press that line.

I learned more about race and open spaces by following Alexis Nikole Nelson on Instagram. She's a Black forager who lives in a mostly African American neighborhood in Columbus, Ohio, close to where I grew up. In an interview, she talked about how she is very conscious of how she looks when she is gathering plants in public spaces and says she is often questioned, which makes her behave very carefully. "I will go out of my way to look as soft and as harmless as humanly possible. You will catch me climbing a tree in a dress because, well, I feel people are going to be way less intimidated by this like, six-foot-fall Black person very close to them, doing an action they can't identify, if I look very cute, very sweet," she said.[8] Nelson grew up fascinated by plants and attended environmentally oriented schools. She's developed a large social media following and is regarded as an expert forager, even though within that mostly white expert cohort, she said she is questioned more often than her peers, especially about where she chooses to forage. She spreads her knowledge around her neighborhood, where there are no grocery stores. She's motivated to help her community find local, wild food and to make it easier for people to gather in urban spaces, national forests, and national parks.

Because wild skills are everyone's birthright, we all should feel welcome and included in access to abundant natural spaces, especially for subsistence, though this is most often not the case. When I consider these dynamics, I'm filled with questions and uncertainties. I want the dominant culture to change and incorporate the strengths of Indigenous worldviews and the perspectives of people who have experienced racism. I love the work that Tiśina, Samuel, and other BIPOC educators are doing, boldly expressing and teaching the beauty of their heritage, advocating for their people. The fact that they openly share their traditions is a testament to the powerful healing process they are engaging. Yet even as they offer up their cultural heritage, those who have no strong connections to the people and lands where their own ancestors originated from might find it easier to be inspired by what is more accessible to them. It's far easier to adopt a practice being handed out and taught than to go searching for a long-lost connection that might lead nowhere.

Ancestor tracking, however, is a kind of wild skill that can be regained. Its closer to us on the timeline of history than the Paleo-Indian tracking that Jaime and I did in Wyoming. In my journeys, I encountered a lot of rewilders who were seeking to revive aspects of their ancestral cultures as a way of finding historical commonality with the Native people of their bioregions. Many people have lost the knowledge of who and where they came from, which is the legacy of colonial conquest, immigration, and assimilation into the American melting pot. I kept hearing stories from attendees at skills gatherings who had been prompted to look into their own origins after a moving experience with one of the traditional skills on offer. They want to know how people from their lineages approached survival.

I met a woman named Janey Sea at Saskatoon when she was teaching a workshop on leather engraving. Right away, I knew she had a deep story because of how she wove spiritual observations into her instructions. "You have to feel what the material wants to do," she advised as my daughter drew a fanciful design of birds and mushrooms onto a bracelet band. Janey is a Chinese Canadian woman whose Hong Kong–born mother remarried an Irish Canadian man who brought the blended family to live in an all-white neighborhood of Vancouver. There, Janey became acutely aware of her otherness and felt pressure to assimilate. But, she said, "Little did I know that the letting go of my cultural heritage would send me into an identity crisis and tailspin in my adult life."

After years of working as an outdoor educator, Janey got invited to attend Saskatoon Circle. She tried a workshop on tanning salmon skins, one of the more esoteric offerings. Yet leather made from fish is quite durable, similar to alligator or snake skin, and it has been traditionally used to make clothing, footwear, and containers. As she was working with the skin to remove the scales and scrape the skin clean of flesh, she said she felt great comfort, joy, and a strange sense of familiarity. "I felt like I had done this before and that the salmon and I had a connection that was truly special," she said. When her leather was finished, she was so enamored with it that she kept it close to her body for the remainder of the gathering.

Excited to understand her feeling of recognition, she researched her paternal family, who were from a fishing village called Yantai on China's Yellow Sea. Her ancestors had subsisted on fish, though she doesn't know if they made leather. She started looking into the people who have continued to practice fish tanning throughout cold ocean regions, from Japan to Iceland, Scandinavia, Alaska, and throughout the Pacific Northwest Coast of North America. After developing friendships with a number of Coast Salish people in a cross-cultural environmental awareness project, she acutely felt the conflict of living on land that had been colonized. The Squamish, Tsleil-Waututh, and Musqueam people had been decimated by European settlers and deprived of their livelihood—fundamentally linked to the salmon.

When she discovered a way to connect with this most totemic fish by salvaging their skins from a local seafood restaurant, she said she began to deeply connect to the land she calls home. "I am not a visitor, because I don't have plans to leave. I am not a guest, because I wasn't invited," she said. "And so I earn permission to be on this land that I call home through a process of honoring and recognizing the land and local Indigenous communities and by learning some of the Squamish language."

Janey now teaches Indigenous and non-Indigenous adults and youth the skill of fish and hide tanning, and she promotes understanding about how the salmon, as a keystone species, nourish the ocean, rivers, forests, and animals of her bioregion. Her teaching incorporates stories about the importance of salmon from around the world. She tells students about how she carefully gathers up the scrapings and returns them to the river with words, song, and thoughts of appreciation and honoring. Her students are often moved to tears when they witness how deeply she connects with this skill and often feel a similar connection emerging within themselves. "They develop a newfound reverence for salmon leather that started out as a mere curiosity," she said. "Unexpectedly, I found my calling in the remembering, reviving, and teaching of this skill."

Through a similar path, Rye N. Flint, a soil scientist and

mushroom forager whom I traveled with from Northern California up to a gathering in eastern Washington, delved into his family's Celtic heritage as a result of learning about the painful dynamics of cultural appropriation at the Buckeye Ancestral Arts Gathering in Concow, California. He brought his partner and stepdaughter, who is half African, to the gathering and became sensitized to the implicit white bias in these spaces where folks who experience racism are minorities. As he explained it, he became wary of non-Native people of European origin grasping on to Native practices to fulfill their need to feel rooted in place. "People have this deep need for customs that connect you to the land and the place, and they see that some of the Native cultures here in the Americas have these connections and have continued some of these customs. So they reach out, and unfortunately they take, because that's what they know how to do," he said.

Comparing what he knew about Native American traditions with what he learned about Celtic culture, he found overlap and similarities in how people interacted with the nonhuman world and their experiences with genocide and cultural persecution. Take the thrill of the hunt, he said. "In the Pomo [Northern California Native tribe] tradition, their primary symbol is the elk. But in Ireland, it was the boar. There's the same use of symbols to describe that charged experience of chasing game." After attending a pine-needle basket weaving session at a gathering, Rye heard the legend that the abundance of Scotch pine in Celtic areas and the well-known practice of weaving the straight fibers into plaid-like patterns might have been the origin of tartan clan fabric. "Different tribes pick different patterns, which is similar to Southwestern tribes like the Navajo and Hopi, whose distinct identifying designs would show up in their blankets and baskets," he said.

I had done my own ancestral investigation decades before I started attending gatherings, and having a solid tradition to ground me allowed me to also offer informal sessions on Jewish practice at some events. My quest was originally launched when I was nineteen, living in northeast Brazil on a college semester program with mostly students of color. We were engaging the African, Spanish, Portuguese, and native mixture of peoples around us, and many of the students could relate to these traditions from their personal histories. I felt bereft, uninteresting, and sanitized by comparison. Everyone had strong cultural traditions in their lineage, but mine had evaporated in the American melting pot.

I returned to the United States that summer with a passion to learn all things Jewish from my dad's side of the family, to whom I had always felt a strong link. I took Jewish history classes and started going to Friday night Shabbat dinners with the college Jewish group. I received a year-long fellowship to study Hebrew and Jewish life in Israel, and the following summer. I taught art at a Jewish camp while undergoing an official religious conversion, which was necessary in the Conservative Jewish community I joined, because my mother wasn't Jewish. I kept going deeper. A couple of years later, I celebrated my bat mitzvah at age twenty-five instead of the customary age of twelve or thirteen, where I read the Torah in front of a congregation in North London.

The fellowship in Israel created a ready-made network of

well-connected people in cities across the country who had all done
the same program. Many of us would gather annually at a Jewish
retreat center in Connecticut to reconnect and launch new projects together. This group helped me get my first apartment in New
York City when I moved there in 2004. They set me up with jobs,
friends, and social events and gave me places to stay wherever I
traveled. It was a tribe—mutually supporting, mutually uplifting.
In 2005, I met my husband at the retreat, and we were married
two years later in the Los Angeles synagogue where he had per-
formed his bar mitzvah. I had fulfilled the promise of the Jewish
people by settling down with a nice Jewish guy, and within two
years, we had a daughter whom we enrolled in Jewish preschools
and sang Yiddish songs to. Our social life revolved around Jewish
celebrations, Shabbat dinners, and the friends we had made at these
events. I had completely embraced the Jewish path, and it gave me
a moral code, a tribe, a controversial homeland, and a link to my
deep past. Jewish wisdom and ritual would inform my experiences
in nature, such as when I found myself in need of a way to sanctify
the slaughter of the goat during my survival training week.

But as I encountered rewilding ideas, Judaism didn't sit as well
with my changing consciousness. I had never approved of the
inequality between the sexes that Jewish life promotes in its original form. The lifestyle that an observant Jew follows also didn't
feel that healthy to me; in fact, it worked against my instincts. On
a beautiful Saturday, we stayed inside all morning at a synagogue
service, praying in a language I didn't completely understand, reading a book frozen in time, scrupulously observing what seemed to

me to be arbitrary rules for the Sabbath, and above all supplicating to a patriarchal superpower. I started to distance myself from these aspects of the tradition that didn't resonate with my rewilding. Jewishness is my cultural inheritance, it is half of my ancestry, and I want to honor the five-thousand-year tradition that wound its molecular path into my DNA. But there is a history that goes even further back, a perspective that does serve my instincts to be outside, moving, communing with other wild beings, and that was what I needed to pursue.

I also found that Judaism didn't give me the skills to survive on the planet apart from agricultural civilization. Jewish celebrations and prayers were based on a way of life embedded in a hierarchical society of planting and raising livestock that did not take the more ancient human egalitarian approach to gender. As Jews, we prayed for rain, we accepted the nonparticipating status of women in many rituals, we celebrated harvest crops, we slaughtered domesticated animals, we acknowledged inequality by giving to the poor, and we never abandoned the quest for more wealth and an ever-increasing population.

When I brought these issues up in my community, there was no end to the competent rebuttals I heard. (Remember, I was arguing with Jews. As the famous joke goes, if you have two Jews, you have three opinions.) Some took my objections to mean that I was becoming even more Jewish, because at the basis of our tradition is the capacity to question everything. As the story goes from the Torah, when Moses was leading the Jewish people into the promised land of Israel, the Hebrews never stopped complaining and critiquing the whole endeavor. "What's with this manna from heaven?" they asked. "It tastes terrible...and the portions are so small."

Of course, there are nature-based aspects of Judaism, as there are of every monotheistic, institutionalized religion, and I took every chance I could to learn more about the strains of influence that remained from previous animist traditions in my religion. For instance, the original story of Adam and Eve eating from the tree of knowledge in the Garden of Eden had frequently been interpreted as a metaphor about how humans chose to transform from an easy, hunter-gatherer subsistence (the abundant garden) to a world of hard-toiling farm work.

Our entire modern lifestyle unfurled, like a giant scroll, from that moment. It's a religion of civilization, as are all the others, with the one exception of animism, which is the spiritual orientation of all the contemporary immediate-return hunter-gatherers that have ever been studied. For them, everything in nature is imbued with spiritual power.

I don't want to throw out my genetic, ethnic, and cultural heritage, and there's so much to appreciate about Jewish life, like the family-like support that had launched my adulthood, the pastrami at Katz's Deli in Manhattan, and Adam Sandler's "The Chanukah Song." But once I understood more about wildness, I could no longer base my morality or my daily habits around a tradition that perpetuates my domestication. If I still need to go to the grocery store and pay an electric bill, it doesn't matter to whom I pray; my real religion is civilization. My relationship to the Jewish quest for liberation, celebrated every year at Passover

through the Jewish escape from Egyptian slavery, had transformed for me. Living in modern society is not true freedom. It
is only the liberty to be ecologically destructive and dominated
by technology.

It was becoming clear to me that rewilding meant not only
learning wild skills but resisting the system that deprived us of these
skills. When the Ohlone were expelled from their oak groves, when
the Squamish lost access to old-growth cedar and salmon, when
freed Black slaves were cut off from their former hunting grounds,
these people were denied their birthright to live close to the earth.
For all people, learning and teaching others to find food, make
fire, shelter, and clothing, and walk the land with kin are the most
important things we can do in life. Our ancestral traditions, wherever they came from, seemed to provide a path to flourishing.

CHAPTER 7

Approaching Collapse

One of the biggest reasons I pursued my interest in rewilding was to address my fears about environmental destruction in the form of climate change, forests on fire, swirling plastic in the ocean, mass extinctions, and the weak and unrealistic responses I saw from the folks I worked with in tech. *If* they cared about these catastrophic outcomes, they usually trumpeted solutions involving sustainability measures like green building, efficient cars, alternative energy, and more responsibility from corporations. I did what I could to participate in and advocate for these ideas. But nearly every metric by which sustainability is measured continued to get worse over a few years. We weren't reducing emissions, we weren't producing less trash, and we weren't halting the decimation of the environment. All indicators seemed to be pointing to one thing: extinction.

Over the last seventy years, our atmospheric carbon dioxide has increased to the highest level ever in the last fifteen million years. Already, we've seen the global average temperature rise by nearly two degrees Fahrenheit. By the year 2300 (about ten generations ahead), scientists project that our atmospheric CO_2 could reach 1400 parts per million, warming the earth forty-six degrees

Fahrenheit or more.[1] This heralds a near certain catastrophic collapse and massive die-off of not just our species.

And we seem incapable of taking meaningful action to lessen this horrific eventuality. For any proposed solution, gridlocked political processes delay or stop its implementation. New technologies such as massive scale mechanical carbon capture and seeding the atmosphere with sulfur dioxide to stall the warming also bring unforeseen challenges, which will most likely hamper their success. There is a substantial quorum who believe that our future lies in colonizing other planets rather than rehabilitating the only place we evolved to exist on. It's a sad commentary on our species that so many would rather launch a mission to Mars than a mission to Earth.

Like a lot of people, I tend to fret about collapse and the numerous ways it might transpire when I'm thinking about my kids' future. Surfing the booming genre of future climate speculation, I've learned that the best option is that we manage to avoid a total breakdown of industry and finance by maintaining small villages that depend on local resources. However, we will still need a massive decrease in the human population and a reduction of all our negative impacts on ecosystems to avoid the worst impacts of climate change and the destruction that has already occurred. This could happen through a decline in food production, which might provide a kinder, gentler crumbling of the capitalist nation state. But there is no way to keep growing and consuming and emitting at current levels and not experience drastic consequences. Resource depletion will eventually become more pressing, to the point where we are unable to mine the materials that would form the speculative technological solutions to climate change.

Call it compassion fatigue or data burnout, but after fifteen years of thinking and talking and teaching in an alarmist fashion about our global environmental crisis, I much prefer using humor to get the message out. I think we need fewer books with titles like *The Uninhabitable Earth, Notes from an Apocalypse,* and *The Water Will Come,* and more *Onion* headlines like "Encouraged Marine Biologists Project Oceans Will Be Nice, Simmering Seafood Bisque By 2040." Now that's an image you can remember!

Unfortunately, dark humor isn't catching on, except for the dark part. One approach to extinction is to acknowledge that there is little an average Western consumer can do about it except to develop an attitude of "deep adaptation." The leaders of this movement encourage people to accept that we will soon face the collapse of water, power, and food systems by getting spiritually comfortable with this reality. Rather than focus on any actions to take for the future, we can work through our despair and learn to appreciate what we have in the moment while the world burns and people starve, migrate, and fight over resources.

This doomist narrative enraged me, however, since so many of the rewilders I knew were working to release themselves from dependency on industrial systems, and they were not despairing. They were preparing for a hunter-gatherer future. It seemed to me that the deep adaptation folks suffered from a serious lack of imagination (and humor!) because they were so mired in the addictive comforts of civilization.

I knew people who understood that they were complicit in all these unfolding atrocities that state institutions were incapable of stopping, and they were willing to give up every modern convenience to find their own solutions. In their company, I could stop listening to the techno-optimists and the doomsday prophets and entertain instead the almost heretical view that the impending collapse of civilization might be what the earth and all life need. Rewilders weren't committed to maintaining the industrial life support system at any cost, unlike most environmental policy experts. Some individuals and small collectives were preparing for a radically different future outside industrial life if the worst predictions about climate change were to come true. From their perspective, there is only one viable direction for humans to take in response to overpopulation, peak resources, and climate change: we need to be wild and build a self-sufficient, nature-embedded egalitarian culture. As philosopher John Zerzan put it in an interview, "Every past civilization has failed and this one, the only one left, is rapidly on the road to self-destruction. If the future isn't somehow primitive, there won't be a future."[2]

Jaime, my anarchist hunter pal, had purchased land in Alaska specifically for this primitive future. According to climate science projections, during his lifetime, the sub-Arctic region will never warm to uninhabitable temperatures, and the local water supply was not threatened due to overconsumption and drought. He could still drink out of the river below his cabin. He had access to abundant hunting and gathering opportunities and was preparing himself to be able to live off the land and teach his daughter how to do so if he managed to get custody of her. If civilization collapsed, he had a good chance of surviving, possibly unaffected.

Surprisingly, the potential resurgence of hunter-gatherer culture doesn't only occupy the margins of political thought. More and more, mainstream experts speculate about the possibility of a future society that carries on our species' genes, earth-based knowledge, primitive tools, and wild skills. In 2019, John Gowdy, professor of economics at Rensselaer Polytechnic University in New York, published a paper in a multidisciplinary journal called *Futures* in which he spelled out exactly this scenario, based on the current understanding of the impacts of climate change. He stated plainly that it is unlikely that human civilization can survive the impacts of the predicted increase in global average temperatures because we will see massive crop failure. And he agreed with the wild approach to withstanding collapse, writing, "We became human as hunters and gatherers, and we can regain our humanity when we return to that way of life."[3]

As a general principle, the damage that nomadic foragers caused to the environment was never on the scale of industrial society; ecosystems could almost always be repaired through natural processes throughout the long period of the Pleistocene. Also, unlike industrial society, hunter-gatherer patterns of social behavior did not require abstract notions of ethics or a legal system of enforcement; they were instilled in the culture. Given that our bodies and brains are still running on Paleolithic genetic code, we might feasibly recreate a social order more consistent with our evolutionary past. As psychologist Mark Seely wrote in *Anarchist by Design*, "Modern systems of power and authority are technologies of control that have emerged extremely recently in terms of our species tenure on the planet, and as such, they are not themselves meaningfully reflected in our natural development programs or evolved behavioral pre- dilections." [4] The wild way of life is still open to us. But unless we prepare for that possibility now, I don't think a twenty-second- or twenty-third-century hunter-gatherer society can exist. Could the key to our species' survival lie in relearning wild skills and protect- ing the world's living immediate-return cultures that maintain the ability to live outside civilization?

Even with various experts proposing this possibility, I couldn't help but ask if the primitive future is just another fantasy to enjoy during this chaotic chapter in history. I once discussed this with Chris Begley, an anthropologist and survival skills instructor from Transylvania University in Kentucky. He told me that our culture likes to imagine life after civilization collapses because it is a way for us to simplify a way of life that has gotten too complex. "Like wiggling a loose tooth, it hurts in a good way to think about starting over with a blank slate after the apocalypse. Life would be easier in that scenario because our needs would be more immediate," he told me. Immediate, eh? That sounded familiar.

Indeed, the simple, deconstructed way of life sounds promis- ing, and I'll never know in my lifetime what will transpire. Still, I wanted to hedge my bets with the extreme rewilders and the grow- ing body of experts proposing a necessary revival of the Paleolithic way of life, of which Gowdy is only the most recent authority. Many anthropologists and social critics throughout the past century have speculated that civilization, running amok with atom bombs, viral pandemics, and constant warfare, would have no possible extended future. That would be left to those who never engaged technology. In 1949, British historian Arnold Toynbee wrote in *Civilization on Trial*, "I personally should look to the Pygmies of Central Africa to salvage some fraction of the present heritage of mankind... They might be able to give mankind a fresh start." [5]

The Pygmy forest people and other groups like them would undoubtedly be well-equipped to survive this eventuality, but would the rest of us? With more developed muscles and stronger bones than Olympic athletes, wild people, present and past, demonstrate enduring physical prowess. While we are in many ways still Pleistocene people, the past generations of domestication have decreased our strength, bone density, and the acuity of our senses. Could we civilized folks, for example, run away barefoot from a tsunami? That is exactly what the Native Andaman and Nicobar Islanders did when they tracked the movement of wind, sea, and birds to flee the shores where they were fishing in time to escape the brunt of the giant waves that devastated the area in the 2004 Indian Ocean tsunami.

Political scientist and anthropologist James Scott studied these types of anarchic clans living on the edge of civilization. He found that some small-scale remote societies deliberately choose to evade control by authority, and it is their reliance on foraging knowledge that allows them to survive apart from civilization. They are not failed farmers or refugees from factory life as we might think, Scott explained. Rather, they are resisters who responded to conquest attempts by escaping and reverting to hunting and gathering.[6] Their refusal of civilized life was a political choice, one we could make again to survive.

Jaime helped me understand that groups like this are found everywhere and all throughout history. Despite the totalizing forces of colonialism, slavery, and the global market economy that have pressed most of the world's hunter-gatherer groups to integrate into civilization, they persist. There are an estimated one hundred "uncontacted tribes" across the globe still living as they have for thousands of years. This last category is well mythologized in our culture. Contrary to what most believe, these secluded bands are well aware of outside society and fiercely reject it to protect their autonomous way of life.

We tend to think that there is an inevitable direction in human cultural evolution from hunter-gatherer to democratic state citizen. The more likely reality is that small groups of humans will always revert to or maintain some basic subsistence practices. This is the only proven way to guarantee survival amid environmental pressures and violent state oppression as long as our species exists. I was always excited to find people who understood this relatively hidden tendency in human history, and attending several skills gatherings made it easier to learn from them.

At the Sharpening Stone skills gathering outside Grants Pass, Oregon, in spring 2019, I was trying my best to become one of these resisters. Scanning the sunlit spring meadow before me, I was attempting to distinguish small, blue, six-petaled clusters of flowers from similar white flowers, both about seven inches off the ground.

Five others were following me, all with the same mission. I knelt down and, with my fire-hardened digging stick, started poking at the earth around the blue flower, careful not to touch any part of the white one. As my stick plunged about four inches into the dirt, I started applying leverage to wedge out the root. Appearing like a small oblong onion, the camas bulb is the staple food of numerous Native groups across the American West: blue camas, *Camassia quamash*. Ethnographic evidence showed that camas bulbs were not only gathered, steamed, and stored but also traded among groups. Across vast areas, they were the only abundant source of starch. Natives were careful about not overharvesting, leaving smaller, immature bulbs to continue growing and only taking the larger ones. Additionally, they would stimulate regrowth by inserting stems back into the hole and burning the fields, which increased future yields.

More nutritious than a potato but just as filling and starchy, this root guarantees survival. Unless you dig up the wrong color. The white one, a different species, *Anticlea elegans*, is deadly poisonous. A bite of it could contort your insides; a meal of them could do you in after full paralysis. Many, many people have learned this the hard way, including countless Natives. Ranchers look out for this flower in early spring, as it can also kill livestock that graze on it.

As I pulled the root from the ground, I made sure to keep the blue flower attached, which was the best way to know for sure that I had gotten the right one. I brought my prize over to Kyle Chamberlain, our group's instructor. "Yep, you can eat it," he assured me, and I tentatively tested it with my teeth. It tasted like a moist, bland garlic clove. If I had collected a whole basket, I could make a meal, kind of like mashed potatoes. Our group moved on from the foraging Russian roulette, and Kyle talked to us about lomatiums, the various species from the carrot family that all have tiny umbrella-like flowers standing guard over crunchy edible roots. These too have poisonous look-alikes. We gathered some of the wild carrots, dug out some dandelion roots, and headed back to our campfire.

Along with the digging stick I had made out of a small cedar branch, I was also carrying a rudimentary hafted knife that Kyle had shown us how to make from a sharpened rock, a slim willow branch, and some bear-grass cordage. The knife was designed by the Coast Salish people to process fish—the handle kept the user's hands from getting too greasy, while the rock blade made clean cuts. We had started that morning by making a friction fire kit from bigleaf maple tree shoots.

"You all look like happy little hominids!" he praised us as we set about roasting the roots around the fire. I was thrilled—in one day, I had made a stone tool, whipped up a fire, constructed a knife, whittled a digging stick, and then used all these tools to make a (tiny) nutrient-rich meal. No longer was I speculating about grilling up seagulls while running on the beach or counting on a car to kill my dinner for me. The exercise had proven that I could wake up with nothing and live like a wild human.

Meeting Kyle was also sort of a feral accomplishment. I had been following him on social media, obsessively studying his blog, and corresponding with him, so I was eager to learn from him at the relatively small, one-hundred-person gathering. I loved this event because it was scrappier than most. It was run by Adam Larue, a reggae-loving, dirt-bike riding, back-to-the-lander dad who had been able to purchase his land with the settlement money he received after almost dying in a motorcycle accident at age eighteen. While his family emphasized science and institutional achievement—with one of his brothers working for Tesla, the other pursuing genetics— Adam set up a rewilding homestead and builds feral community. Adam has the perfect personality to host one hundred people in the middle of the woods who were using sharp tools, setting fires, and getting curious about his dozens of homestead projects. He was unruffle-able. He cooked all the meals, watched his two kids, gave lessons on DIY steam engines and rabbit processing, and still had energy to find lost kids, wrap up people's sore ankles, and dance late into the night. He and Kyle went way back, and he greeted us both as if we were some of his best friends when we arrived.

Kyle was almost Adam's temperamental opposite. A grouchy, antisocial, self-proclaimed "macho botanist," Kyle lived off the land in eastern Washington where he was haphazardly developing what he called a "Human Habitat." On a twenty-acre parcel of ranch land, he was experimenting with hardy, climate-change-adapted fruit and nut trees and setting up an edible ecosystem for easy gathering. The idea was to create a hybrid cultivated and wild experience for meeting human needs. He had spent over a decade mastering hunter-gatherer skills and studying how Natives had survived in his area, even living entirely off the land for a month when he was seventeen and newly emancipated from his strict Mormon family. At age thirty-one, he said he was "post-rewilding."

Since I was so recently pre-rewilding, I wanted to know what he meant, because his knowledge and insight about the Paleolithic lifestyle was at a level I could rarely find, especially blazoned across the internet. Having previously abandoned modern technology, he now embraced it for typical millennial purposes: to create a glamorous self-image and find women on dating sites. But he had also catalogued all his thoughts on such things as hardy *Prunus* variations (the genus of cherries, almonds, peaches, and nectarines), bone density decline in *Homo sapiens* over the last few millennia, and government land management practices. Checking his Facebook profile regularly, one day I saw a picture of him cradling a bleating goat against his bent knee as he hoisted his rifle into the sky, bearing his teeth. Another day, his grubby hand was splayed out for measurement next to a giant pile of bear scat. He knew he was entertaining, lining up his naked rump in front of a rather buttocks-looking mountain range and captioning it "ass mountain." Frequently, he'd pitch ponderous queries about his psychological state, like "How common is it to be almost totally uninterested in contemporary human endeavors?"

I surmised that he was deep into the cerebral experience of depression. He also seemed committed to dissuading anyone of the romance or pleasures of rewilding. When I pinged him for advice on how to process a roadkill squirrel, he only wrote, "I hope you don't get the plague, a couple years back a BOSS student died after getting it from a squirrel with fleas." I didn't eat that squirrel.

I kept coming back to his pages, though, because his observations were so astute—if sometimes mean—and he was so easy on the eyes. He relished objectifying himself, like a woodsman Zoolander. As handsome as he was, he was equally awkward and off-putting in person. But he was the best iconoclastic wild skills public intellectual I could find, and we both agreed that civilization was in a steep decline. Around the fire that afternoon, as the light faded and misty rains started up, I got to satisfy my curiosity and get his story.

He said that eastern Washington was a place of extreme contrast to grow up in. There was vast uninhabited forest, high desert, and in the cities, crowded Mormon churches, where his family was embedded. He rebelled every chance he got, but he was devoted to Mother Nature's strict rules. "I identified more with coyotes and sagebrush than with my classmates," he said. He honed his wild skills through experimentation, teaching himself how to make friction fire, how to forage, and how to tan animal skins. "Often against my mother's wishes, I would go out and live wild and free for days at a time on whatever land I could find." He said he wanted to get away from his fractured family and a society that was destroying the places he loved. In a Facebook post, he once lamented his heartbreak at witnessing "the rampant development of open lands, the sprawling hideousness of new roads, buildings, and moronic abuses of the land."

When he was finished with high school, he wanted to test himself, so he spent a month in the foothills of the Eastern Cascades living from nature only, building a shelter, setting up a bed, hunting small game, collecting edible plants, and practicing his flint knapping. He said he felt more fulfilled than he'd ever been. But the sacrifices he had to make were not ideal. "I lost a lot of weight. Mentally, I was shaken. I'd gone further than anybody I knew in isolating myself from human company," he told me. His obsession over that kid classic *My Side of the Mountain* took him a little too far.

And it wasn't just the loneliness or the food scarcity that disillusioned him. It was the reality of the degraded environment in which the camas bulbs and salmon that had sustained hundreds of generations were declining. The regulations governing subsistence were arduous and expensive to comply with. He explained how taxing it was not to have a mentor, let alone a social group with a place-embedded culture. The Indigenous practices he had studied weren't sufficient to meet his needs because the ecology was so damaged, he said. He had to give up his dream to live as a completely wild man— it wouldn't be survivable. Having sat crying in the movie theater at the conclusion of *Into the Wild*, I was relieved by Kyle's story. If only Christopher McCandless, who died inside that Alaskan bus, had been as prudent as Kyle.

For a few years, Kyle drifted, but then he got hooked on permaculture, which he saw as a way to apply ecological thinking to agriculture. He thought it held promise as the way to resurrect the hunter-gatherer way of life. Permaculture promised ample food production while remediating the environment. He married his girlfriend at age twenty-two, bought the twenty acres, and set about growing a garden and designing an energy-efficient home. But a few years later, she left him. He descended into depression, and all the homestead projects crumbled.

He told me he thought many rewilders were deeply wounded

people running away from trauma. Certainly he was, being totally distanced from his Mormon family. I had seen many folks at the gatherings whose quest to abandon civilization was motivated by abusive situations. In a sense, they were already in survival mode, so pursuing survival skills was fitting. Some aspects of rewilding, like ignoring modern norms of hygiene, skipping sociable small talk, and making every aspect of life a DIY project, attract people who are so focused on their self-sufficiency that they don't put much effort into understanding the feelings of others.

Exhibit A is the Unabomber, Ted Kaczynski, who despite his objectively heinous acts still inspires some rewilders by virtue of the fact that he advocated for the total destruction of civilization and a return to preagricultural ways of life. For this convicted criminal, all technology was bad technology, and Kaczynski would go to any length to make this point. Separating himself from a society of rules and ever-dominant technologies, he lived a self-sufficient life in an off-grid Montana cabin for twenty-five years. About eight years in, he started feeling encroached on by increasing numbers of hunters and hikers, so he planned a nearby retreat to what he called a "sacred plateau." Upon arriving, he saw that a road had been built right through it, ruining his mental and spiritual escape. He vowed to start fighting back, shifting his focus from wilderness skills to revenge. Over the following seventeen years, he sent bombs in packages to unsuspecting professionals in technology industries that ended up killing three people and injuring twenty-three, all innocent of any crimes except those Kaczynski decided they had committed.

While there are plenty of folks out there today who claim to be anti-civilization (anti-civ) or are intrigued by the idea—perhaps a hundred thousand across the world, according to one *New York* magazine journalist's estimate [7]—the Unabomber is one of the only ones who carried through on violent revolutionary action, earning himself terrorist credentials and a lifetime in prison. The anti-civ stance (also known as anarcho-primitivism) critiques the idea that humanity's adoption of agriculture, industrialization, labor specialization, and large-scale technologies is all positive progress. Anti-civ thinkers view domination, social alienation, and social inequality as effects of humanity's shift away from subsistence toward the oppressive hierarchies needed to sustain agriculture, cities, and industry. They identify as anarchists because the term means "without rulers," and it also describes the longest enduring form of social organization. All immediate-return groups were leaderless and prized individual autonomy. But anarchism is a difficult word to associate with, since most people think it means erratic, violent public displays or the brand of political action that arose in the early twentieth century as a working-class response to the exploits of capitalism. However, the anti-civ movement doesn't advocate for violence or any kind of political organization, state institutions, or formalized markets. The only social arrangements that fulfill their criteria are local, place-based, and directly participatory, like a small hunter-gatherer clan. They argue that the only way to achieve this is through rewilding activities.

Frequently, anti-civ proponents write about the psychosis that they claim civilization induces in humans, who are fundamentally wild beings caught in the cage of our own making. They believe that the human instinctual search for a nurturing, egalitarian environment is constantly impinged by the social technologies and institutions we must operate within today. "In our minds and bodies, even when lost in some ridiculous app, we are trying to reconcile the world of the hunter-gatherer with the path that Modernity has set us on," wrote one of the most prominent anti-civ writers, Kevin Tucker, in *Gathered Remains*. "We don't just want others, we need them. This [social media and bureaucracy] is our animality being torn from us, repackaged, and then sold back to us." [8]

A growing body of psychologists argue that everyone is suffering the trauma of being separated from nature and our evolutionary lifestyle. I knew I was, to some degree. Perhaps extreme rewilders and the anti-civ crowd are just the coal-mine canaries of this mass grief, or they have had worse experiences than most. Kaczynski was found to suffer symptoms of schizophrenia, possibly as a result of his experience with what were found to be unethical and damaging psychological experiments while he was a sixteen-year-old undergraduate at Harvard University.

When I first heard rewilders quoting the Unabomber, ironically called "Uncle Ted," I was alarmed because of what I knew about his murders. Some of them said his anti-technology diatribes provided a surprisingly clear critique of civilization. In the twenty years since the Unabomber wrote his manifesto, groups of rewilders had (unlike him) successfully and peacefully experimented with lifestyles outside civilization. They openly discussed the difficulties they encountered along with the glorious moments of community coexisting with nature. Listening to Kyle's story helped me add color to the black-and-white arguments that surrounded the Unabomber's horrific legacy. Kyle's story of alienation was similar, yet he had never resorted to violence.

By his own account, Kyle was not heroic in his rewilding attempts, and he had doubts about the viability of long-lasting feral community. At the time I met him, his days were taken up with sorting apples and pruning fruit trees for local orchards to get out of debt that he owed on his land. When he had free time, he enjoyed trolling public figures he suspected were "Mormons in disguise" on Facebook from the comfort of his tarp-covered sleeping bag laid out near an unfinished shed on his Human Habitat. It was only because I had specifically petitioned him to come to the Sharpening Stone gathering that he was back to teaching. He'd prefer to stay away from community of any kind, he said.

But at one time, postdivorce, he had found a buckskin-clad crowd to organize foraging adventures with, and many of these folks I'd met and admired. From his reports of these forays, they seemed to be living out the rewilding dream for weeks at a time. They'd set out on seasonal rounds to gather wild food—feral apricots, native roots, green shoots, and wild rice—in a merry crew of pack-toting, llama-pulling, scientific name-dropping nature nerds. The women, in particular, had serious animal processing skills. Kyle anointed them the "Meat Mamas" and described them as uncommonly nurturing people who were comfortable dealing with the mess and gore of birth and death, which he ascribed to their deep connection to the creative power of the feminine. So many men would turn away from bloodiness, he said, but these women confronted morbid, visceral realities.

I knew the Meat Mamas from the skills-gathering circuit. Frequently, the three of them and a group of friends would take a few weeks to live out of a wall tent on forest service land, hunting and processing a lot of the meat they needed for the year, sometimes with Native hunters who culled buffalo from Yellowstone National Park.

Kyle didn't exaggerate; these women are phenomenally confident and skilled, and each has found a way to make a living while existing cooperatively on the land with others. Katie teaches wild skills to kids and runs the gathering Saskatoon Circle. Harmony—fierce looking with dreadlocked hair, piercings, and tattoos sprawling across her face, neck, and hands—is a butcher of wild game, servicing rural hunters and fashioning her own jewelry from the remains. Epona is a striking albino mother of one who is legally blind; she tans hides and writes songs inspired by her Celtic forebears while raising her son on a rewilding commune. They have all spent time with the grand doyenne of the Paleolithic skills world, Lynx Vilden. As participants in her long-term program, after they had made a full ancient human survival kit, they went out into the mountains. I heard that it was often hard for Lynx's groups to get the meat they needed just with longbows and slingshots. Their aim was to live off the land for six weeks, but Kyle said they often came back earlier because they couldn't get enough food. He saw their excursions as vanity primitive camping trips on lands ravaged by mining and logging that just applied additional stress to the ecosystem. "They prioritized pursuing some kind of anachronistic Stone Age purity over their own survival and the health of the land," he quipped.

Whenever I found an example of an activity to admire, he was always ready to shoot it down. I couldn't tell what his motives were with me, as he would vacillate between flirtatious and rude. Clearly he found my rapt attention, probing questions, and need for advice satisfying, so he would indulge me with long phone conversations, footnoted emails, and text streams late into the night. It got personal, as he'd tell me about his on-again, off-again much older girlfriend, and I'd lament how my husband had no interest in the wild. Kyle would empathize to an extent and then surprise me with a harsh rebuke. "I've never met a woman who resists the routines of motherhood as much as you do. It's unnatural," he told me once.

After that, I pulled back, realizing that any far-fetched fantasy I had about what our relationship could become was just a projection. Much of what he expressed to me seemed intended to provoke me, deride my level of skill, or point out how I was to blame for my discontent with married life with kids. He didn't really care about me or many people at all. But when we talked about the Meat Mamas, I didn't sense an ounce of criticism or contempt from him. He held them up on a pedestal, which helped me see that maybe he wasn't a complete mansplaining chauvinist.

Ultimately, he admired that the Meat Mamas took a realist approach to living wild. They know that hunting wild game virtually guarantees failure if traditional weapons are used in today's hunting environment. This is because hunting traditionally takes much longer to master and also requires so much more time in the field, and the governmentally regulated hunting seasons for various animals are relatively short. It might take ten years for someone to finally take a fatal shot with a longbow, but guns allow immediate return, so to speak. The Mamas teach other women to handle a rifle, shoot to kill, field dress, and process wild game. They've also mastered the skills of preparing and canning, making broth, drying jerky, and preparing sinew and bone for tools. When I sat down with Katie for a couple of hours during Saskatoon Circle, she told me her backstory

A self-proclaimed "strong Viking woman," Katie uses her big bones and bold personality to great effect. If rewilding had celebrities, she'd score a magazine cover, with the caption "Wilderbabe," a nickname bestowed on her by troubled teens at a wilderness therapy camp where she previously worked. Having grown up in a rural area with a brother who was a hunter, she had always felt comfortable with using animals for meat and processing them to make all sorts of useful crafts. She received a thorough education in wild skills by majoring in anthropology as an undergraduate, training with Lynx Vilden, and constantly experimenting with meat and hides. Now with a young daughter and husband, she says she's more ranch mom than Wilderbabe, but she's still a trailblazer. "I've traded in my buckskin because it's easier to wear jeans when there's a baby puking on you," she told me with a giggle. Her email handle was "fightswithmilk," and everything about her was larger-than-life badass female energy. "I'm big, awkward, Aquarius, and I have an overabundance of confidence." She hooted with laughter.

Katie told me how she used to date Tom Elpel, another notable figure in the rewilding world who runs his own school for primitive living and has published top-selling books on botany and bushcraft. When she and Tom were driving through Yellowstone National Park in the winter of 2013, they noticed heaps and heaps of buffalo carcasses just outside the park perimeter. A little investigating revealed that these were the remains of a hunt conducted by Native hunters in order to keep the population of the park within manageable numbers—according to a mandate by the state of Montana, under five thousand. These are known as the last wild and free bison in the United States.

That was the first year that federal agencies began allowing Native American tribes to shoot bison in Beattie Gulch near the national park border. A treaty in 1855 had granted perpetual hunting rights to the tribes who traditionally hunted the Yellowstone country, but the treaty was annulled when the bison were exploited almost to extinction by non-Native hunters in the early twentieth century. But in the mid-1990s when conservation efforts allowed buffalo numbers to rise to the point of overpopulation, the tribes reasserted their hunting rights. Now, each winter, around fifty hunters follow the herd as the animals search for new sources of food.

On the day she spied the buffalo entrails, Katie jumped out of her truck and started poking around in the gut piles. One of the hunters nearby took notice of her buckskin clothes and asked if she knew how to tan hides. He was Lee Whiteplume, the conservation officer for the Nez Perce tribe, and the two hit it off instantly.

"Seeing all the materials that the hunters weren't processing made me want to help," Katie said. "They were concerned about getting the meat home to their families, and it's a huge job to make use of the rest of the animal, and you need a team to do it." The hunters gut the animals, cut off the heads, and then quarter the meat to make it easier to transport the load home. Everything else they generally leave as carrion.

Whiteplume invited her to return the next year to make use of the hides, skulls, bones, and innards of the bison that were usually left behind. Katie brought the Meat Mamas and other friends who had some experience with large animal processing to camp right outside the hunting grounds in the frigid Montana winter. They were on call to help in any way the hunters wanted. A photogenic group, they might have been mistaken for a wilderness punk band. In the below-zero weather, they wore fur coats and buckskin layers they had made themselves. Their tangled hair flew out from under raw wool caps they had knitted. Among the leg warmers and mukluks and fingerless gloves, not a North Face logo was to be found, but they displayed plenty of piercings and primitivist tattoos. They called themselves the Buffalo Bridge project because they were creating a bridge between themselves and the Native buffalo-based cultures and also between present and past.

In earlier times, when the people of the buffalo hunted, there would have been plenty of hands available to help with harvesting all the parts of the animal, Katie said. Today, there are rarely enough people with the skills to do it, though the hunters and their families benefit greatly from the meat and animal parts. So Buffalo Bridge is there to help by offering their own skills and trying hard to use every part of the animal.

Across the Western prairies, buffalo herds once numbered in the tens of millions. Their roaming, feeding, and excreting on such a large scale increased the fertility and abundance of the grasslands. The bison were ecological engineers, dispersing seeds, prolonging the season for early green vegetation, and creating ponds to wallow in, which in turn makes the habitat more hospitable for innumerable other creatures. Native people harvested them for food, shelter, and materials for clothing, blankets, containers, and more. When the buffalo were nearly destroyed through market hunting, the buffalo way of life died, which was one of the intentions of the attempted extinction.

Today, very few people have the knowledge, stories, and skills needed to reclaim the buffalo traditions. Katie had been tanning hides using the traditional brain tanning technique, which takes weeks and requires massaging the animal's own brain into the hide to soften it. She dove into the opportunity to teach the method to the Native folks who had lost the skill. She called it "making brain milkshakes."

When not in the field with the hunters, the Buffalo Bridge crew gleans meat from bones that is canned or ground up for hamburger, sausage, and pemmican—a high-nutrient paste of fat, dried meat, and berries that stores well. They also clean bones to create hide-processing tools and make buttons, spoons, and bowls from the horns. The buffalo wool gets spun into yarn, and the copious fat gets rendered for cooking later. The collagen-rich hooves are combined with hide scrapings to make a strong glue. All this is easy to itemize here, but regaining the knowledge required is hard work that often fails because the knowledge is so fragmented. No one has written the *Idiot's Guide to Buffalo Processing*, so the Buffalo Bridge team patches techniques together from reading old ethnographies, talking to Native elders, and seeking out the few mountain men in the area who have buffalo hide-tanning experience.

Buffalo Bridge folks also innovate new uses for the remains, like sleds made of buffalo ribs or cooking sacks made of stomachs used like primitive sous vide. I heard talk of scrotum leather purses, which I've learned not to mention around nonfemale people. All this processing happens in and around a large wall tent with a wood-burning stove but with no modern infrastructure in freezing conditions, sometimes in blasting blizzards. I asked Katie why she does it, given the immense challenges. "I love meat!" she yelled. But then she talked about how good it feels to feed people with wild food, "like we are ingesting the land around us, becoming part of it again," she said.

Over the past decade, Buffalo Bridge has built an enduring temporary foraging community that attracts new people each year and furthers our knowledge of how to live with and off the herds as Native people once did. One of my closest rewilding friends, Fern, whom I had met at Saskatoon Circle, had very little experience processing animals before she joined the Buffalo Bridge crew for a month. When she visited me shortly afterward, she showed me dozens of jars of buffalo fat and meat that were the result of her days of assiduously cutting, packing, and boiling buffalo while listening to stories about the animals. I was amazed that cooking up broccoli in buffalo fat made my kids actually want to eat it.

The Meat Mamas aren't just about taking game and processing though. Harmony told me "we're at the point where we can't live off the land without tending to its wounds and our own." She believes that learning to acquire meat was what allowed her to heal from an eating disorder. As for the land, she makes sure to bring along seeds and starts for native fruit trees, grasses, and wildflowers to plant that will provide food for the wildlife they harvest and speed the land's restoration after centuries of extraction. After their training with Lynx, Katie, Epona, and Harmony had gone on to learn these restoration ethics from a well-known rewilding mentor, the transgender white woman Finisia Medrano, affectionately called "Tranny Granny," because she was in her sixties.

Ever since I entered the rewilding scene, I had been hearing about Finisia and running into people who had spent time with her on her nomadic journeys, some embittered and vitriolic when they talked about her, some glowing and grateful. Fin, as she was also called, was strikingly attractive, like Kyle. Similarly, she courted controversy and spoke her mind about the ecocidal, genocidal effects of civilization, calling everyone a colonizer and insisting that the folks who travel with her "bring gifts" and practice a good "reach-around" technique when harvesting wild food. Applying porn lingo to horticulture was one of her trademarks. What she meant was that you had to pleasure the plants too by giving them what they needed and stop just getting off "like a selfish lover." Her friends said she was like Coyote, an ancient Native trickster spirit who disobeys convention and stands at the threshold of sanity to spur the rest of us on to moral action.

Apprenticed under Native Shoshone elders, Finisia traveled a circuit of public lands across the Great Basin every year, harvesting and planting native seeds, starting in 1977. This route was called "the hoop," and she derived its path from stories and ethnographic information about the seasonal migrations of Western Native tribes. Her wild tending was sometimes not legally permitted, but her tradition of living off and giving back to patches of native edible species like yampah, biscuit root, and camas is ancient, perhaps going back millennia in certain spots. She trained scores of young people to manage a horseback and pickup truck itinerary across Idaho, Wyoming, Oregon, and Washington.

Unlike the more purity-focused rewilders, Fin and her group had no qualms about engaging with the trappings of contemporary society—Facebook, Walmart, cigarettes, casinos—if it served their goal of promoting the abundance of wild foods and reconnecting people back into the web of life. The native plants they were concerned with are able to grow in place and reproduce without extra input or intensive management, and they can improve the health of the soil and surrounding ecosystems. It's hard to find anything ecologically wrong with what they do, but unfortunately Finisia had been in jail several times for trespassing and violating park regulations. She was a conservation policy analyst's nightmare, unpredictably strewing edible seeds in areas that may have been designated for other purposes by land management officials. Yet she was participating in a human activity that predated American governmental authority and was possibly more appropriate for what the ecosystem required to flourish. Her ethics came from Native understanding of mutually supporting relationships between humans and the nonhuman world.

By contrast, regulations governing foraging and planting along with the hiker's creed of "Leave No Trace" presume that humans inevitably exert a negative influence on nature, but many Indigenous communities voice the view that without some care and attention (which means leaving beneficial traces—everywhere!), native species become less abundant and, today, crowded out by invasives. Fin and her "hoopsters" talked about how our interactions with living things must become partnerships once again, with reciprocity and balance. That's the feel-good part of her credo that almost everyone can get behind. But she also had some words from the dark side.

Before I met her in person, I read all I could about her from her self-published book *Growing Up in Occupied America* (2010) and her Facebook posts, and I spoke with several people who knew her well. Fin was known for calling civilization "Babylon," in reference to the name of the ancient city of sin and luxury that has become a stand-in for any kind of oppression. She might have adopted the term popularized by roots reggae of the 1970s. According to her, if you're not planting back to pay for what you take, you're living in Babylon. And if you're in Babylon, you're in denial of your participation in ecocide. Fin would tell people that they were just lying to themselves if they thought any action they could take within cities and towns could help the earth heal. To her, any green product, alternative energy scheme, carbon tax, organic farm, or nature reconnection program was just another way to preserve the illusion that global capitalism is the only way to live. Fin said we have to see that we have other choices. She cautioned that sooner or later, we would learn the hard way, because civilization is beginning to break down, and it will continue crumbling over decades while the planet rages at us with rising oceans, massive wildfires, devastating storms, and desiccating droughts. *We can't win this war*, she preached. *There is another way.*

Hunter-gatherers from the Great Basin and many other spots across the world lived like grazing animals, crossing back and forth through a massive territory. When snow lay on the mountains, people were in the lowlands getting fresh plants by the rivers and digging up roots. When the snow started melting, they'd gain altitude to collect the fresh new plant growth and follow a ruminant herd. They would pass through the same areas during the same parts of the year, hitting up pine nuts in the fall, hunkering down to repair and craft tools and clothing in the winter, and then setting out in the spring for the newly replenished herbs and roots. Every place had a time and a task, and the tasks benefited not only the people but the plants and the animals.

The hoop was like a vast low-maintenance garden. When roots are dug, the earth is opened up and made more receptive to the seeds scattered by the digging process or deliberately shaken back into the uprooted holes. When people eat seeds and defecate them, plants are also spread to new territory. The act of harvesting stimulates new growth in many types of plants. Migrating people carry water and fertilizer around the land in the form of their own waste. Every activity promotes continual rebirth, and the cycle continues. This is the way to extract from an environment without depleting it but rather regenerating it. Civilization also regenerates certain plants, like corn, soybeans, cotton, and wheat, yet it requires huge fossil-fuel inputs and toxic by-products to keep going. Fin once asked, "What if we replaced these mass crops with camas, tule, and lomatium instead in their original habitat?"

Many Indigenous people believe plants and animals thrive when we engage them in meaningful relationships in a process known as "wild tending." They say that no one is gathering anymore, which is why the land is so degraded. To my Western mind, this seems kind of fanciful, but science is verifying this long-held principle. When Indigenous cultures are displaced from their land, the ecological composition shifts, usually toward less abundance and diversity. Humans have prehistorically been powerful positive actors in the ecological web, even though many of us are accustomed to thinking of humans as great destroyers.

In a study published in *Human Ecology* in 2019, a group of anthropologists analyzed how an Aboriginal Australian community shaped their land through traditional hunting. This community of Martu people had been pushed out of their traditional territory by nuclear testing facilities and other development. A wave of extinctions followed their departure in the 1960s, which seemed counterintuitive. You'd think that if you remove the hunters, the wildlife will flourish, but no. The Martu practiced a form of hunting with fire in which they would burn parts of the land, uncovering the burrows of their prey and creating productive patches that became appealing to lizards, dingoes, and insects. Without periodic burning of the landscape, these open-patch dwelling species had to find more suitable places to inhabit. When the Martu reclaimed their land in the 1980s and began to hunt again, the species diversity gradually returned due to the presence of the beneficially burned habitat and its positive effect on the greater food web.[9]

Kyle Chamberlain and I explored these ideas as I tried to figure out the practices and methods for living wild that would be the most beneficial for people and the planet. He believes in the principle of wild tending, but his approach is much more deferential to science rather than Native practice. He stayed on top of ecological journals with current research coming out of nearby universities to understand the factors affecting the land base he wanted to steward. He thought that industrial development had changed the land and wildlife habitats too much to be able to revert to precolonial ways of tending the land. He said that we needed the tools of data collection and peer-reviewed studies to make sure human interventions weren't causing more damage. State regulations on wild spaces were necessary, he said, because we are now dealing with the aftereffects of possibly two hundred years of bad livestock grazing practices and wildfire suppression. He believed that Fin was beholden to a delusion about restoration that stemmed from her appropriation of Native culture and didn't address today's realities. "Her plantings are doomed to get eaten by cattle or shaded out by encroaching junipers," he said. Furthermore, he didn't agree with what her philosophy meant on an ideological level. He saw her reinstating a one-truth narrative—that only Native ways were correct—that was just as toxic as the Mormon church was for his wild youth.

"On the level of ideas, I embrace irony, uncertainty,

contradiction," he said, "while she believes in herself as a savior." He would seize any chance he had to tangle with Fin and her crew online and in person, and I heard about these encounters from a number of people. Ever the prankster, he once dressed up like a cowboy, grabbed a paintball gun, and drove several hours west across the Cascades where he knew she was camped with a bunch of her hoopsters. He knew where they were because he had been invited to join them in a sort of rewilding detente. But Kyle wouldn't abandon his opposition to the hoop. If they were going to "play Indian," then he would play cowboy to put their activities in stark contrast.

"I waited a long time in the cold, squatting by their wood-burning stove in my black cowboy hat. At the right moment, when they were all discussing something about the hoop, I burst out and spattered the wall with paint. They all looked so perplexed. Couldn't understand what I was trying to show them," Kyle gloated. He said that Finisia kicked him out and said she never wanted to hear of him again. Peter Michael Bauer, who was there at the time, said that he didn't know what Kyle was trying to prove except that he might have been envious of the fact that Fin and Peter had attracted lots of people to their projects, and Kyle's Human Habitat project wasn't successful.

Trying to understand Kyle's post-rewilding mindset a bit better, I wondered if all his trolling and pranking was about pushing beyond anyone's prescription for living wild. He was a contemporary Coyote. You're not doing it right, but you also can't ever do it right, he says. Yet I saw both Fin and Kyle sharing the same credo, that adhering to the norms of mainstream liberal environmentalism is never an option. But what could I, a mom with financial responsibilities and a need to nurture a positive vision of the future, learn from their experiments in wild living? Could their lessons enrich someone who was equally dissatisfied with contemporary life in civilization but not about to cut ties with family and most social norms? Or did extreme rewilding only belong to...extremists?

I finally met Fin at Saskatoon Circle in 2019, the last year she attended. She clocked me immediately with a raunchy nod. I gaped at her as if she were royalty. She wore a silk Japanese robe over a sleeveless summer dress, and even though her canvas cowboy hat shaded her deeply crevassed face, her eyes pierced into me: the married-with-children professional who could afford to live in the heart of Babylon and visit a primitive skills gathering for fun. I knew that I'd have my own reckoning with her before the week was up. But before I did, I got to observe her in action.

She entertained the crowd nightly, even presiding over the legendary trade blanket session. My daughters were upset by her behavior, making me wonder if she should even be around kids. "Get the hell off my blanket or I will sell you into the slave market!" she yelled at a group of under-twelves who were encroaching on the ritual space. My friend Raven had told me that Fin had blown pot smoke directly into her son's face at a previous gathering when he asked her a question. When we were all gathered around to bless the evening meal, she ran and danced around our circle, urging us to toss anything we could donate onto her blanket. "Grass, cash, and ass is what we need, folks! We're gonna be spreading native seeds in Hells Canyon, Northern Oregon. Don't suspect I'm trying to hustle you," she yelled. "I *am* hustling you! I wanna show you easier ways to care for each other besides throwing a raffle. Just give back." I submitted to the hustle, dropping forty dollars onto her blanket. She gave me a nod of approval.

I met with her the next day in a group that went on a hike to harvest wild roots with several of her followers to learn about how they plant back native perennial foods on public lands where they are most likely to flourish. After we walked way out to their camp (they didn't pay to attend the gathering but just occupied the out-skirts, which Katie Russell allowed, unlike a lot of other gather-ing leaders), they showed us the beat-up bags of seeds collected throughout the West. Fin stayed to smoke in her tent with a friend while our group hiked uphill for about a mile and found the famous fritillary. This member of the lily family stores its nutrients in the most extraordinary, sweet, flattened bulb with little rice-like nod-ules that you could easily dig out with your fingertips. Some people found biscuit root, another energy-dense and portable food that can be boiled or ground into flour and baked until it tastes like an unsweetened shortbread cookie.

The experience helped me further understand the impor-tance of the age-old tradition of digging roots. Under the ground lie nutritious treasures that take much more effort to yield than gathering leaves or berries. I recalled watching a documentary by the immediate-return anthropologist James Woodburn, which fol-lowed a tribe of Hadza people for a day as they hunted and gath-ered in gendered groups. The women of the clan searched half the morning to find the ekwa plant (*Vigna frutescens*), a member of the pea family that produces giant tubers that grow nearly three feet into the ground. Once the adult women identified the plant, they expended tremendous effort to retrieve their roots, resting in between ferocious bursts of hand-digging for over an hour. While watching, I wasn't sure it was actually possible to dig them out, the tubers were so tightly rooted and deep. After they had collected a sizable amount, the women roasted the roots over the fire, feeding a group of twenty adults and children, who ate with their hands from a communal pot. I felt a sense of satisfaction on their behalf. Their lifestyle was hard and demanding, but in the end, every belly was full.

Similarly, Fin and her crew harvested roots day after day, performing similar exertions and preparing their harvest into porridge and dried cakes. I could see how the activity brought them health on multiple levels. It required physical fitness, perceptive acuity, social coordination, and guidance from an elder who knew how to locate the roots. They had successfully revived one very key part of the hunter-gatherer life, and it was tasty. One of Fin's acolytes had told me during our harvesting walk, "It's difficult to grasp how we might be able to eat without relying on the industrial agriculture system until you've visited a landscape where you are literally surrounded by free wild food everywhere you step." Amazing densities of wild food still exist as remnants of ancient Native gardens along with old plantings that have been naturalized and now grow without inputs. "These can be home to us once again," he urged.

The next morning, I had my chance to sit down with Fin,

steeling myself for what she might say to me. She seemed outwardly friendly and gregarious and laughed heartily, but she could quickly turn angry. She gazed at me with icy blue, penetrating eyes while in the process of rolling a joint. I'd heard that she'd made men cry, sparked existential crises in lost souls, and above all, pissed off, insulted, and degraded her interlocutors. I sat expressionless, cross-legged at her feet, and she began telling me how she wasn't there to absolve me of my lies and guilt, even though I had given her money.

I would never be okay, she said, as long as I lived in ecocidal, genocidal Babylon. "I use Jesus technology to fight Geronimo's war," she said in a complicated point that meant that she aligned herself with Native resisters but also saw herself as their savior. She admitted that she was trying to fuck with my brain in these fifteen minutes, which made me wince a bit. "You think these gatherings are wild?" she questioned me. "This isn't helping anything."

I was holding her gaze while nodding intently. I didn't try to rebut anything, ask any questions, or defend myself. I knew everything that she said carried some truth—our civilization perpetuates a destructive way to live, so why fight her over it? A young woman then came and sat down next to me, interrupting Fin's diatribe. She presented Fin with a bag of Pacific nori seaweed that she had collected and looked at her expectantly. I was thinking that I would love to have that seaweed. But Fin glared at the woman with venom dripping from her lips.

"Why are you apologizing for the corporations, thinking you can harvest this radioactive shit from the trash pile of the ocean?" she spewed. The woman looked visibly shaken. She asked Fin what was wrong. "Leave the ocean alone. It is gone; they destroyed it. This is a bag of Fukushima. Everywhere on the Pacific coast is a red level of radioactivity. Don't you know you have to get over the Sierras and the Cascades before you get into safer levels? Look it up on the federal website."

The woman started crying. Fin said, "If I loved you, I'd tell you to get away from the Pacific. But I don't." With that, she grabbed the bag of seaweed and walked away. "Someone I know will eat this, thanks."

I stayed to comfort this gentle soul whose generosity had backfired. "You can't ever take anything she says personally," I said. This kind of behavior was what people had warned me about. Fin was relentless in her quest to throw people's innocent intentions back in their faces, opening them up to a different way of thinking. She did this through her transgressive costumes, her gender fluidity, her speech, and her actions on the land. There was no category available to her—she defied them all, and by defying categories, she was able to permanently stick it to the man.

I later searched for evidence of what Fin claimed about the radioactivity of the seaweed resulting from the 2011 explosion of the Fukushima nuclear reactor and found that there was negligible impact on all seafood beyond a certain radius of the reactor. But because Fin had spent time with the Western Shoshone of Nevada, who had lived near nuclear power test sites in Nevada, she was sensitized to the issue and deeply felt the injustice of corporations poisoning the air, land, and water in pursuit of energy to fuel Babylon. Her statements about the seaweed were not true, but the larger argument did carry moral weight. It also related to the way many Indigenous folks view the contemporary debates around climate change.

Understanding how rising temperatures, erratic weather events, and melting ice caps might initiate a total ecological and economic collapse disturbs people who have never endured a catastrophic breakdown of their way of life. Yet for every Native community that was eradicated from their land and deprived of their livelihood, the apocalypse has already occurred, and they are still here, living in a dystopian present, still gambling with the chaos of the world and adapting to it. Many Native folks see environmental anxiety as a symptom of privilege that erases how Indigenous people have already resisted and survived through five hundred years of collapse.

This perspective provides a counternarrative of what climate change means to human culture. At issue is which groups are actually responsible for causing this potential future collapse. It's been estimated that up to one-sixth of the human population has had no part in creating our surging greenhouse gas emissions.[10] This large, impoverished segment does not consume or produce enough goods to have any significant climate impact, nor will they likely do so in the future. Furthermore, looking at global historical Indigenous resistance to industrialization also suggests that these groups have never consciously chosen to partake in environmental destruction. This calls into question how most experts speak about "humanity" in relation to environmental issues. They're really only referring to the five-sixths of the global population who live in a destructive manner.

Take the newly coined geological era of "the Anthropocene," a designation that supposedly accounts for how drastically human activity has impacted the biosphere since agriculture and industrialization. According to anthropologist Joshua Sterlin, assigning all people, or "anthropos," responsibility for the present era of mass extinction and climate change is patently incorrect.[11] Finisia made it very clear in all her teaching that what Babylon does and what she and the wild tenders do are not simply separate but equal ways of life. Babylon is the destroyer, and she and the wild tenders continue the legacy of the nature-embedded cultures who came before.

After I left Saskatoon Circle, I reached out to a few of the people who had traveled on the hoop with Fin. Zach Elfers, who propagates native seeds near the lower Susquehanna River in Pennsylvania, filled out some of her story for me. He told me that when Fin was twenty-seven, before her gender transition, she was about to commit suicide because she had suffered so much abuse in straight, Christian society and was utterly done with the dominant culture of destruction. As she was walking down a rural road, a pickup truck gave her a ride. It was full of Native Americans who said she could camp with them. They were digging yampah roots all over the West. This changed everything.

Fin went on to learn from a lot of Nez Perce, Paiute, and Shoshone Indians about their traditional ecological knowledge. These elders, Zach told me, often wept in Fin's presence because their own kids had no interest in the old ways and were only "interested in booze and TV." Fin was the only one who came with a passion to learn the old ways. Zach explained to me how he had visited a Native Paiute reservation with Fin. "She is so polarizing. They hate her because she is a white man who is now a woman, and she is practicing their culture better than they are. A lot of hard feelings there. But she is also a hoot, a riot, and somebody keeping their tradition alive, so they enjoy her too."

He said that Fin initiated him into this traditional ecological knowledge which might be as much as fifty thousand years old. When they'd visit gardens out on the hoop, it was clear to him that they had been tended for a very long time, possibly thousands of years. The plants were deliberately protected by piles of rocks, growing near gullies to deliver rainwater efficiently. He said this made him feel like whoever planted them there, the ancestors, were still providing for us today. "We can also provide for generations to come if we keep planting back," he said.

I agreed that Fin's practice on the hoop was wildly inspiring. But she certainly wasn't a nurturing mentor and had very unstable relationships. Fin's crowd was volatile, people came and went from her orbit regularly, and she was always falling out with folks. After I had spoken (I thought confidentially) to one of her closest hoopster guys, she sent me messages attacking me for calling her an abuser. He had told her all about what I said. Still, I wanted to spend more time with her but not with my kids along, so I kept track of her wanderings on Facebook to see when she might be close to my area. But when I checked social media in early April 2020, I saw that she had died. At age sixty-three, she had a heart attack while traveling in Nevada with a couple of hoopsters and refused to go to the hospital because it was overflowing with COVID-19 patients. I waited for the eulogies to flow in for this elder with knowledge and skills that very few had; she was an irreplaceable resource.

By this time, I had stopped talking to Kyle because he had made it clear that he was better off without all my questions. I was relieved to be free of his bouts of intense criticism, but I also wondered if I'd ever find anyone else with his singular combination of scrutinizing intellect and wild skills mastery. Our correspondence had blurred the lines between researcher and informer, between married woman and unattached bachelor, and his rejection of my interest in him stung me more than I should have let it.

Cutting off from him left me depressed for a few months. Then, during a social media memorial service for Fin, he popped up in my feed, insulting Fin's legacy of seed dispersal across the hoop that dozens of people were effusively praising. "I hope hoop culture will die next. It's an embarrassment to ethnobotany," he wrote and then hounded the hoopsters. "Stoners flinging seeds willy-nilly everywhere risks diluting the native biodiversity that people in conventional conservation roles spend lifetimes protecting... Playing Stone Age in the contemporary context is a frivolity of white privilege."

Fin's followers posted many pointed retorts to his comments over the next days (which, in the way of schadenfreude, finally made me feel better about not being in his life). It surprised me how many people piped up to ostracize him online, given the basic conditions and social circles many of them live in where internet access is hard to come by and technology is scorned. Yet the wild tenders, in particular, embrace the contradictions of the capitalist economy, knowing that one of the most profound human needs is for community and social support. As the prominent anti-civ writer Kevin Tucker had said, corporations sell our social needs back to us. So social media use is a compromise they are willing to make. Yes, there are rewilders who don't own handheld phones or computers, but I've never met one under forty who doesn't engage social technologies at some point. What else could they possibly do to stay in touch, spread out across the West as they are, attempting to carry out their planting missions? What's inspiring about Finisia, her followers, and also Kyle is that they grapple hard with every question, delving into and dancing with contradictions, yet they remain committed to an ideal of reciprocity with nature.

With Fin no longer around to organize the hoop migration, the wild tenders have taken individual paths. Today there are over a dozen people, none of whom evidence the kind of antisocial behavior that Fin was known for, who carry on her planting work in humble, creative ways. One man in his twenties, Michael, lives alone on the hoop with his horse, making the rounds as the seasons change, collecting and distributing seeds for the survival of future generations should Babylon finally crash. Another couple, Gabe and Kelly, travel on foot to spread seeds and visit what they planted on earlier trips, documenting the progress of the precise spots and keeping data on what flourishes and what fails.

One woman, Nikki, spent twelve years on the hoop and has advanced Fin's thinking about how humans propagated plants across the West. She believes biscuit root gained its widespread territory across the United States only because it was carried by humans and planted everywhere they went. Human-assisted migration is the untold story of modern botany, she said. I met up with her in 2020 at Winter Count, a skills gathering in Arizona where she taught me and my kids how to scatter chia seeds by the handful across grassy areas. Nikki was in the midst of a West Coast journey, living out of her van by herself and making stops at important spots on the hoop. I envied her complete self-sufficiency and her devotion to her calling.

She demonstrated how to plant deliciously sweet nutsedge seeds by pressing them one inch into the soil near seep willow stands, where they will be protected and watered by the willow's moisture-storing roots. Nikki emphasized that there is a season for every wild-tending practice to ensure reciprocity. Harvesting roots, for example, is best done when the plant has gone to seed so that you can immediately replant what you've taken. She also believes that if you eat wild foods, especially seeds, you really should defecate into soil to continue the cycle. She said that she even collects seed-containing scat from bears in order to deposit it in the most receptive spots she can find, sometimes taking it very far away, in an attempt to regrow what bears like to eat in territories they've migrated away from.

I asked her why that was better than simply planting seeds. "If it's been run through the mammalian digestive tract, it's prefermented, so the seeds germinate easier," she explained. "I call it 'poo-pagation,'" she laughed. Our waste that we usually flush away into a labyrinth of chemical treatment plants can be transformed so simply into wild-tending earth nutrition, with a catchy pun to make it all fun. The way the wild tenders spoke, I could tell they had been influenced by Fin's brash insight-germinating language, or "priest craft," as she called it.

Despite his show of opposition to hoop culture, I think that Kyle's vision of a human habitat for happy hominids merely adds more dimensions to that of the hoopsters. Food was and should be freely available all around us if we are humble enough to tend to it and reciprocate its gifts. He had told me that he believes—like some of the climate scientists—that our only future on the planet is one in which we live in tight-knit tribal groups, not as solo emissaries for ecological causes in consumer capitalism. He once wrote on his blog that he wants to see "a future rich in healthy relationships between people and the natural world…in a place where food falls from the trees, where you are immersed in a rich company of living things, where you can be part of a self-sufficient family and be completely and [un]apologetically human." [12]

This vision was worth pursuing, especially under the threat of societal collapse, and it defiantly contrasted the refusal and negativity of Babylon hating and Unabombing. It preaches that we can accept the realities of the worst possible climate change outcomes yet seek a harmonious way to ensure future human survival.

Kyle's desire to be part of a self-sufficient family gnawed at me in particular. He knew that he lacked that family growing up and that he hadn't yet been able to create his own clan the way he wanted. But was I any different? While I was gaining skills of self-sufficiency and venturing out in search of a hopeful rewilding future that my children could mature into, I had to face the fact that my marriage was fracturing. On a microscale, this challenge presented me with a rehearsal for the possible global apocalypse. I would soon confront a breakdown of my entire way of life as my dependency on my husband extended to all my basic needs. Without his support, how would I feed, clothe, house, and transport myself and my children? Would I lose the community that he and I had built together? Would I see the total destruction of my finances and security, or could I persist through the collapse of my family with a similar vision of a sustainable future community?

CHAPTER 8

Self-Sufficiency

Over the past three years, my husband had not joined me and the kids on our adventures as we traveled to the skills gatherings, took weekend camping trips, and hauled ourselves around the state for family wilderness treks. Our growing divide was no one's fault. Well, it was probably mine. I was going deeper than I ever imagined I would go with my rewilding journey, and he needed to live the life that was best for him. We still had a strong bond and a united view of what was beautiful and good, which was embodied in our children. Yet through all the adventuring in which I was functionally a solo mom, I felt lonely and lacking support. When I was home, I was frustrated and overwhelmed by what I had to do to keep my kids thriving while keeping up with my work. Meeting people who wanted to build their lives centered on nature was such a relief; it was validation for my passion to recover my human roots and leave my dissatisfying arrangements.

Twelve years married—most of them delightful—and we decided to split up. I grew apart from my husband and lost my longest and most secure adult relationship. I exacerbated the painful end by acting immaturely, doing things I regret, hurting him and me. Isn't that how it has to go? You have to feel the pain in order to grow and mature. You have to metabolize your angst, guilt, and shame into more constructive forces.

I felt the wise spirit of my mother guiding me during this transition from nuclear family life to something new. She had worked for over two decades as a divorce mediator, helping children succeed after family breakup, and I had grown up with stories of horrific battles between parents and the behavior problems that ensued for the kids who lost their peaceful homes. I knew how to avoid that outcome because of her words to me as a child. At times, I could hear her voice in my head, urging me to release my anger, drop my resentments, and focus on coming to agreement.

Because my parents had similar professions to each other, they enjoyed a more equal relationship than what I experienced as a parent, given my husband's line of work. My expectations of how a partnership should be shared were not met. I had spent years feeling inadequate and less important than him because I wasn't achieving professionally at the level afforded to him. When our first daughter was born, I was so drawn to be with her and so flexible with my career that I chose to take care of her full-time and then part-time as she started going to nursery and preschool—part of a widespread trend among mothers like me who experience significant career interruptions so they can care for their families. Since the precedent had been set, I continued to be available and highly involved in our second daughter's early childhood, but the feeling of lagging behind in the professional world was ever-present.

That was when I leapt into opportunities to write for tech

companies and completed a 180-degree shift in my orientation toward family and work, #supermom style. This period of my life built my confidence that I could take on tough challenges, but I was starting to see that becoming a part-time single mom would be less stressful for me and therefore better for my girls. Even though they would never receive the human ideal of a loving intergenerational clan, my children would receive full, equal participation from their mother and father, and I might get enough time alone to feel satisfied in my other pursuits.

I also wouldn't have to be bound by our community's expectations of what I should do or be. The obligations of our social circle that I didn't enjoy, like attending birthday parties, PTA meetings, and office parties, would decrease or disappear. I could parent the way I saw fit, with much less interference on a daily basis. I could do what I needed to do to radically transform. I was prepared, like the rewilders I met, to lose the comforts and conveniences that I had gotten used to as half of a high-earning urban couple. But I would gain my freedom and choice about how I wanted to live. Having raised my children through early childhood with my husband's support, I could rely more on my children's growing mastery with meals, going to bed, and getting ready for school, those times when he previously stepped in to help.

We agreed to avoid the litigious path and sought a mediator to help us work out our marriage settlement and custody arrangement. I had always been the lower earner in our partnership, so a lot of our negotiations involved how much support he owed me. In conventional family law, the lower-earning spouse is supposed to be given a runway to establish "self-sufficiency," at which point they will no longer require financial support from the former spouse. Most people view this as progressive, generous, and good for the kids, and it is. But I objected to the use of that term, sitting at a conference table with two men in business attire under artificial lighting in a climate-controlled office discussing when I might foresee becoming "self-sufficient." I had just foraged salad greens for my dinner and was wearing earrings I had fashioned out of roadkill squirrel pelts. In my bag was a knife, a sharpening stone, some dried berries, and a tin of cottonwood salve I'd made for my dry skin.

"I'm the most self-sufficient person in this room!" I nearly shouted. "Can either of you feed and shelter yourselves in the woods or survive without an industrial life-support system? Why do you get to decide what *my* self-sufficiency is?" It took a lot of composure not to storm out of the room in my buckskin moccasins.

The mediator, who was a cool guy beneath his stiff attire and had survived years in the Israeli army during which he successfully refused going on any violent missions in Palestine, allowed me this concession. "Okay," he said, "let's not use that word. When do you think you'll be able to earn what you need to live in the Bay Area?"

"How about never?" I muttered to myself.

Over the ensuing months of the divorce process, my ex and I worked everything out amicably, and I accepted the fact that I'd lose the house, my health care, the car, and all my expectations of a successful financial future. But I'd receive some financial support and eventually get back my investment in our house. In the winter of 2019, I moved out and took up residence in a 112-square-foot tiny home loaded onto a Ford F-350 truck that was once a U-Haul. I minimized my belongings down to what could fit inside the truck. I was done with the American script of consumerism and finished with the pressure to provide all the things that are considered normal nowadays for my kids' happy childhood. Instead, I relied on an ethnographic benchmark. Hunter-gatherers don't accumulate any personal goods that they can't carry around themselves. They do barely any housekeeping and have tiny structures, if any, in which to sleep and take shelter. In the case of the !Kung San people of Southern Africa—likely the oldest culture on earth—their tools, apparel, and adornment are handcrafted and able to be packed away in one leather cape that can easily be hauled to the next camp.

My truck was this cape. As Jessica Bruder chronicled in *Nomadland*, an account of the rise of van dwellers, also called vanlifers, across America, many others had come to the same conclusion I had. One of the book's interview subjects, who lived in a Ford truck with her family, even speculated, "Is this the evolution of the former middle class? Are we seeing the emergence of a modern hunter-gatherer class?"

My truck had already been broken in by inveterate vanlifers who understood the freedom and reinvention that a mobile lifestyle offers. A surfer couple had lovingly refurbished and decked out the truck with a double foldout bed, a compost toilet, a wood-burning stove, solar panels to operate a set of lights, a phone charger, and a running sink. That it had given them two years of nomadic living made me feel more confident that I could make the lifestyle work. Long-term, I didn't know what I was going to do, if I'd adjust to living in the truck or if I'd need to get an apartment near my kids. I knew that I couldn't afford nor did I want to encumber myself with a property in the Bay Area and to resume paying bills to an industrial system of power, gas, internet, and garbage.

At the gatherings, I had met several badass women who lived out of their trucks who told me the tricks of the trade. *Wear baggy clothing when you're traveling alone,* Kelly shared. *Try to look androgynous. Carry Mace in the cab,* Nicole advised. *Don't ever park under a pine tree at night—the pitch and resin that fall down can damage the solar panels,* Temra said.

I slowly mastered driving a massive vehicle amid narrow avenues after some initial scrapes and dents. I learned the best spots to "work from home" while still taking care of my kids half the week. I asked for permission from people I knew to park on their land adjacent to nature preserves so I could practice my naturalist activities, forage, and scatter seeds. Still, the hostility I encountered from well-to-do property owners who didn't like me parking in their neighborhood led me to keep searching for little patches of land near my old house that I might be able to purchase and bring the truck onto as my living quarters. But I found out that this proposal was highly irregular and most likely illegal.

Living in urban civilization requires that residents play by all the system's rules, which may not be in the urban dweller's best interest but rather to the advantage of the municipal tax base and utility companies. Having a self-sufficient method for creating power or dealing with waste must be secured with a costly permit. Disconnecting from the water and sewer main or the electric grid is highly discouraged and can constitute unfit living conditions according to Child Protective Services. If I wanted to continue to raise my children, I'd have to stay plugged into the machine.

The tragic irony is that officials endorse the substandard, unhealthy conditions of living next to polluting trash incinerators, toxic fracking mines, and clear-cut mountains. Poor communities are disproportionately affected by these environmental hazards, in some cases potentially more negatively than if their plumbing and electric systems didn't work. Urban living requires residents to be dependent on mass infrastructure, whether it's for basic daily needs, high-tech communications, or emergency health care. This dependence is also what keeps us obedient to authority, which in our culture is established by our parents, drilled into us at school, perpetuated by our bosses and law enforcement, and reinforced by "experts" whom we come to trust more than we trust ourselves. Each of these institutions produces the effect of lessening our self-sufficiency and increasing dependency on industrial solutions.

Or perhaps the design of bureaucracies was intentional—constructed, as some social critics contend, as a way for elites to extract wealth from the masses. It is not just obedience that is produced by bureaucratic institutions. They instill in us the perceived need to work, to perform tasks that we would not otherwise be inclined to do. Since the dawn of the Industrial Revolution, the virtues of a highly disciplined work ethic have been touted by social and religious authorities despite the fact that most work doesn't contribute to the health of people or the planet. Work is what we must do in order to earn future rewards and avoid punishment and poverty.

At the time, I was reading *The More Beautiful World Our Hearts Know Is Possible,* in which author Charles Eisenstein described how "most of us have grown up in a society that trains us, from kindergarten or even earlier, to do things we don't really want to do, and to refrain from things we do want to." We naturalize this self-control and shame ourselves for being lazy and unmotivated. Yet as Eisenstein pointed out, "most of the tasks of industry were not anything a sane human being would willingly do."[1] Here was more justification for me to drop out.

Some people who recognize their subjugation in this system of industrial control have tried challenging their dependency with age-old principles of natural law, a set of ideas purportedly based on values inherent to all humans, that predate any kind of state-enacted law. One Montana mountain man, Ernie Tertelgte, was caught fishing with his son without a license in 2013. He refused to show his ID and insisted that he was within his rights to fish in a public waterway. The game warden had him arrested, and Tertelgte represented himself in court against misdemeanor charges. He used a natural law argument to justify feeding himself from the wild.

Tertelgte is as eccentric as one would have to be to try this maneuver—his old-timey glasses, bushy beard, tricornered hat, and felted coat formed the perfect costume for a Tea Party radical. His court appearance went viral on YouTube because of his over-the-top theatrics. He refused to show customary respect, wouldn't remove his hat, and yelled back at the judge. "I was searching for something to put in my stomach as I am recognized to be allowed to do," he said. "I am the living man, and I have the right to forage for food when I am hungry." He was fined $150 and in further proceedings was sent to jail for thirty days.

I noted that he was entirely peaceful during his arrest and his court appearances. He just wasn't obedient, so he became a public enemy (according to the Southern Poverty Law Center civil rights advocacy group) because he tried to get food through a means that spilled beyond the strictures of state legislation. In some ways, his politics were irrelevant, because his argument challenged the contradictions of civilization. He also provided humorous entertainment to mock the legal system. He refused to officially enter a plea. "I never plead," he scoffed. "Animals plead, [with] sounds like baaaa, oink," he said.[2]

I wanted to believe that there was still a way to live off the land with natural law in a community without modern technology and agriculture, one that did not disrupt ecosystems or abuse people further. Yet everyone I researched or spent time with who tried to live this way encountered challenges that made them compromise their dreams of self-sufficiency. Peter Michael Bauer had decided to live an urban life in Portland so he could build a rewilding organization and educate people. Kyle Chamberlain lived with questionable mental stability and low social support and had given up on pursuing any kind of communal goals. Katie Russell of Buffalo Bridge married a marijuana entrepreneur and moved into a ranch house to raise her child more easily. Finisia Medrano spewed venom at everyone who tried to get close to her and likely expired from her two-pack-a-day smoking habit. Lynx Vilden ultimately sold her eastern Washington property and permanently moved to Europe during COVID-19.

I had interviewed and hung out with dozens of others who wanted to live with wild skills. Some had formed communities and seasonal camps modeled on happy hunter-gatherer settlements, but not a single one lasted. People had conflict, resources were scarce, or families and jobs pulled them away. Who was I to judge any of these passionate, knowledgeable people who had decades more experience in thinking about how to dismantle human domestication? My basic needs not only included food and water but also excellent Wi-Fi and an endless supply of pasta for my kids.

It's easy to point out the giant delta between the ideals and realities of rewilding because of any one individual's required dependency on gasoline, trips to Target, and iPhone apps to function in this society. Advocating publicly for living wild and rejecting interactions with corporations and bureaucracies as rewilders and anti-civ theorists do makes them obvious targets for critics. *Wired* editor Kevin Kelly took an easy jab when he wrote, "As far as I can tell from my research, all self-identifying anarcho-primitivists live in modernity." He railed against how they compose rants against the machine on high-tech computers while sipping coffee. "They have not relinquished the conveniences of civilization for the better shores of nomadic hunter-gathering."[3] This is all true and is discussed at length in the journals and publications that these thinkers put out. What Kelly missed, though, is that these folks feel significant discomfort about their continual reliance on industrial technologies, which further reinforces rather than negates their critique of civilization.

In my year and a half of keeping up with Jaime Van Lanen, I

was encouraged that he refused to get distracted by these critiques and questions about hypocrisy. As he put it, he didn't waste time worrying about how much fuel he used or if he should get a smartphone. He didn't entertain arguments about cultural appropriation, the most effective seed dispersal methods, or whether he should spend a day ritually fasting before he went out hunting. He just got wild food, however he could. His understanding of how immediate-return and small band hunter-gatherer culture functioned was deep, and he knew what kind of life humans would have to prepare for should civilization collapse, since he had lived like that for seasons at a time. He'd had years of accumulating solo, low-tech hunting experience through which he had built up the endurance and strength to attempt dangerous tracking feats that yielded him hundreds of pounds of moose, caribou, elk, and bighorn sheep. He couldn't be steered off his course, though there were very powerful forces arrayed against him.

Once, he called me from his office cubicle at his government wildlife job to tell me about how he had nearly died from hypothermia the weekend before when he fell into a river while hunting sheep in the wilderness. He had barely managed to haul the eighty pounds of meat four miles on foot back to his vehicle. His job as a government anthropologist that he worked at for half the year allowed him to set up a self-sufficient lifestyle during the time he didn't have to be in the office. But he was growing increasingly dismayed by the sacrifices he had to make in order to benefit from participating in a bureaucratic system. He wanted to leave the job, but he couldn't. Not because he needed the money, the benefits, or the security of employment during a recession. He needed to prove to an Alaska family court that he was capable of maintaining custody of his baby girl.

A few years earlier, he had met Millie, a like-minded woman who worked in his department, who was enthralled with the wild life and seemed to have insatiable energy for processing animals, trekking out to remote locations, and staying out in the night air as the sub-Arctic winds raged. She was the one he had been waiting for to help him tan the moose hide that he had carted around for years. They eventually made him a winter coat from it. Even still, the two never fell in love but developed a project-based relationship that occasionally became romantic. They went out hunting together, explored the land, and spent hours discussing how to escape civilization.

Because they were so aligned—and like-minded people were difficult to find—they decided to have a child together. The plan was to co-parent in Alaska and teach the kid all the skills they were developing to live more like hunter-gatherers. Millie behaved strangely during her pregnancy, which she chose to spend mostly away from Jaime, putting him increasingly on edge. He didn't fully understand his baby mama's character. When their daughter was born, Jaime was floored that Millie didn't even call him and did her best to block him from contacting her.

It appeared that she had never intended to share the child with Jaime, whose pursuit of co-parenting seemed threatening to her once she had become a mother. She then used the law, with its contemporary bias against men and fathers in custody cases, to take the most meaningful part of Jaime's life away from him. What is known as "the tender years doctrine" ruled that maternal custody for young children, even when all things were equal between the parents, was thought to express "the best interest of the children." [4] By the 1980s, nine out of ten custody awards went to mothers, and men were generally required to pay child support. Joint custody gained currency in the 1990s, but this was mostly for legal decision-making because physical custody by the mother is still the default award across most states. "I feel discriminated against because I'm the father," Jaime told me.

What ensued was an epic character assassination of Jaime and a vicious, expensive custody battle. Millie claimed that Jaime was abusive to her, and she moved with the baby girl back to her family in Washington. Jaime became embroiled in a court battle to win any amount of time he could get with his child while being permitted a few hours of supervised custody in a Washington state facility each month to see his daughter. "I had a lot of trust. I thought she was a primitivist," he said of Millie. "But those ideals fell apart, and now everything I built for my daughter was for nothing."

The legal battle was draining his bank account and his peace of mind. A close friend advised him to give up and let the baby go to allow total autonomy for the mother. This friend advised him that his daughter was going to need a dad at some point when she came of age, and then Jaime would be ready for her. But Jaime wouldn't let go. "If I am a human responsible for bringing a child into this precarious twenty-first-century world, I want to give that child every possibility to be raised in wildness," he said, but he lamented that he was not being allowed to give her this birthright.

He figured out his own wild path around age twenty-eight, but he wanted his daughter to know it from early years. Even more importantly, Jaime believed that by giving her the opportunity to survive and thrive in the wild, she would have a better life during the unraveling of civilization. Yet the more he sunk in and protested the custody arrangement, the worse he was viewed by the court, and he couldn't back down. "I'm a very proactive person; I have to make strong moves that make a difference. Hunting is a great metaphor for that. You have to take a radical action in the right moment, and there is a major result," he said.

As parents, Jaime and I both felt thwarted by the structures of civilization in our desire to help our children build a connection to the wild and live in a supportive community. We looked for insight from ethnographies of egalitarian cultures, trying to understand how we could make social changes in our lives to align more with our evolutionary heritage, besides practicing wild skills. The designation of "egalitarian" applies to people who never developed rigid hierarchies in their relationships beyond the natural progression of age and seniority. For small bands of twenty-five or so individuals, widely dispersed over large territory in search of food sources, the most reliable survival strategy for the entire group was to share resources equally rather than compete. Cooperation was an adaptation that allowed them to persist in their lifestyle for tens of thousands of years.

Jaime was very specific about which groups embodied egalitarianism and insisted that we look at ones with the longest uninterrupted track records of using the same subsistence methods, like the !Kung San, the Hadza, and the Paleo-Indians we had tracked in Wyoming. "We need solid evidence that these cultures don't manipulate people or turn food surpluses into power that they could hold over people and other outside groups," he said. Adding nuance to the original distinction between immediate- and delayed-return societies posed by James Woodburn, Jaime pointed out that simply storing food seasonally is not the trigger for social inequality among humans. Like many animals do, it is possible to store food for the winter and maintain an immediate-return lifestyle.

Despite the fervor for Native American tribal lifeways that I had encountered in the rewilding community, most tribes from the past millennia were not fully egalitarian, he said, even if their engagement with the environment was sustainable. Because the majority of tribes either held slaves, waged war with other tribes, or built tiered political structures led by chiefs, they are more appropriately termed "complex hunter-gatherer societies." The extent to which many Native American tribes sought guns and industrial goods shortly after colonial contact revealed that they were already operating with an orientation toward accumulation of resources beyond what they needed day to day, he said. What's more, despite the inspirational aspects of wild tending for a feral future, Jaime believed that practice originated within complex hunter-gatherer society and wasn't a key component of the most ancient and enduring way of human life.

"Immediate return" means relying on available resources without manipulating them directly. The need to share these resources equally gets enforced through cultural norms that downplay competition and hoarding. For instance, the Hadza never openly celebrate the man who made a big kill. As he returns to camp with big game, he might even be criticized, lest he feel too proud. But he is given the honor of dividing up the animal for the group. Sometimes generosity doesn't flow freely, and individuals have to be assertive to receive their portion of the group's food or materials in a practice (that every parent of a toddler knows) called "demand sharing." On the flip side, if someone is greedy and takes more than their fair share, they are openly mocked and humiliated until they give some back.

The group as a whole disapproves of bossiness or manipulative moves. Those who consistently behave in antisocial ways can be banished or even executed. Yet scrounging and laziness are not openly disdained as they are in our culture. For example, some members of the Hadza society rarely participate in productive activities. Some men spend their days playing gambling games with spearpoints, and they say they fear damaging their gambling "chips," so they never go out on the hunt. But they don't starve because they continue to demand and receive their shares of game animals that are killed by other hunters.

Egalitarianism also extends to male and female roles that are distinct yet often overlapping, based on individual preference. Neither sex is more valued than the other for what they contributed, and both were necessary to sustain the group. While stereotypes still abound about hunter-gatherer societies in which women raise children and men provide resources and maintain higher status, this is more a reflection of our culture's patriarchal bias than of reputable ethnographic data. In these societies, the work of raising children, like the work of procuring food, is shared among many adults and older children. Women do the majority of gathering plant foods, while men are mainly responsible for hunting, but men could also affectionately care for children, and women could pursue prey. Every individual is free from the authority of others, and women made decisions about their own lives and often for the whole group in the same way that men do. Regardless of sex, individuals are expected to be self-sufficient for short periods of time, and they enjoy direct access to resources to meet their basic needs from the environment.

I was getting closer to individual self-sufficiency, and I thought that I was approaching a more egalitarian relationship with my ex-husband because our divorce agreement gave us each 50 percent custody of the girls. But this arrangement was based on equality, a political construction and legal priority of modern times. Egalitarianism is a very different social reality in which the tasks that women usually perform (nurturing, tending, foraging, crafting) and that they generally still prefer to perform in contemporary life aren't downgraded. They're viewed as vital to the band's survival. Our culture prioritizes the work that men are inclined or trained to do, evidenced by the significant pay gap between the sexes.

The more I learned about how humans have been socially organized for the vast majority of our evolutionary history, the more comfortable I became with a division of labor based on fluid definitions of male and female traits, as long as these were equally valued. The real contention in our current society is the lack of prestige and power of the female role relative to the male role. Like many women, I had internalized my lower status as a mother, and I did not value my nurturing activities as much as my income-generating activities. But studying how women behave in immediate-return societies boosted my self-conception. I recalled the Hadza women digging up roots for hours. They were badass.

Choosing to leave my spouse was made more difficult by the legal structure of marriage that we were embedded in and that took so much time, money, and paperwork to undo. Hunter-gatherer partnerships, while generally enduring, can be dissolved simply by walking away. The membership of these nomadic groups was constantly fluctuating based on the seasonal availability of food, which also helped with human conflict. If difficult situations arose, it was relatively easy for individuals or families to split apart (fission) and join another group (fusion) in a practice known as "fission-fusion."

This is not to say that egalitarian humans don't have fits of jealousy, reputation battles, or the drive for retribution that spirals into lethal violence. Homicides happen, yet they are for the most part between people familiar with each other rather than warfare between groups. Compared with rates of violence today across the globe, existing immediate-return hunter-gatherers exhibit the lowest incidence of violence of the possible human social arrangements across the world. So much for the myth of the brutish, club-toting caveman!

The emergence of the kinds of hierarchy, violence, and domination that we experience today didn't occur until *Homo sapiens* developed more social complexity, which some see as the most significant change in human history, around thirty-five thousand to forty thousand years ago. Storing surplus food for the purpose of wielding power over the rest of group was the first step our nomadic foraging forebears took toward building a civilization that would see the rapid rise of inequality, the subjugation of women and captives, higher rates of violence, and mass warfare.

Yet the egalitarianism of immediate-return life is still embedded in our consciousness, according to Leonard L. Martin, an evolutionary psychologist who spent his academic career at the University of Georgia. His work tested the psychological premise of rewilding and was directly inspired by Woodburn's concept of immediate return. Martin contended that our mental processes are the same as the earliest *Homo sapiens*, but we're living in an extraordinarily delayed-return world that forces us to wait for decades to reap the benefits of long-term crops, education, loans, wage accumulation, and retirement investments. He posited that when people experience this mismatch between their immediate-return consciousness and the delayed culture they live in, they take steps to reconcile the two.

Individuals in delayed-return societies cope with the uncertainties and long timelines presented to them by their culture by developing structures that give them confidence that their efforts will pay off in the end. Marriage, legal contracts, debt arrangements, and formal job arrangements do this, as do ideologies like the Protestant work ethic. According to Martin, when someone consistently works hard for future payoffs and social prestige, that not only permits rampant selfishness and inequality but it also turns self-aggrandizement into a desirable trait. Formal structures based on delayed return reduce an individual's autonomy, give one person power over another, and keep people from practicing fission-fusion because they are tied to one place with significant resources, such as a farm, factory, or university. "Our current delayed-return societies may be requiring us to behave in ways that are discordant with our natural tendencies, that overemphasize our individualistic dynamic," he wrote.[5]

But he said that we can do a few things to make our social worlds more like an immediate-return society. I was already learning how to view my role as a woman and mother in a more powerful way, and it's also possible to socially engineer our way out of evolutionary mismatch. When we maintain friendships with more than twenty-five people (the size of a typical early *Homo sapiens* clan), we have less satisfying and more superficial interactions. But keeping our close contacts under that number allows our connections to grow deeper and provide true support and resilience. I put this idea into action by radically reducing my number of social media contacts and saying goodbye to friends who I didn't genuinely want to spend time with anymore. Facebook suddenly became a much more intimate, supportive venue.

Martin also advises pursuing work with a high degree of autonomy to simulate self-directed subsistence activities. I had experienced so much relief when I stopped working for a boss and started seeking my own writing contracts. Martin says that environments such as co-ops and cohousing that require the same resources from everyone can also alleviate some of our unease about inequality. Though he sounds like a Bernie Sanders campaign rep, his research into human evolution reveals that our original programming was not for the unequal society we live in now. Our modern systems of power and authority have developed so recently in the long time frame of human evolution that they don't reflect our innate nature, and some humans are less adapted to these modern systems than others. Martin provided grounding for why Jaime and I as well as so many other rewilders I knew who were modern people nonetheless felt wired for egalitarianism, self-sufficiency, autonomy, and small-group interactions. Hunter-gatherer consciousness was still encoded in our DNA.

I have not yet succeeded in creating a caring community around my children (and other children) that doesn't involve exchanging money. Yet we are managing to build a supportive network with the individuals and families crossing paths several times a year at the skills gatherings. Myron Cretney became a mentor for me, and I would travel to spend time with him where he'd teach me forestry techniques with hand tools, perfect my hand-drill skills, and crack way too many lewd jokes around the fire at night. He always has a project ready for my kids, like making willow bark toy animals or sharpening pencils with penknives. When my kids and I met buffalo-braising Fern at Saskatoon Circle, we instantly bonded with her like family, and now she regularly visits us as she travels around the West Coast doing anthropological fieldwork. Most of the folks I interviewed and spent time with for this book have met each other—our common interests unite us as a temporary clan, with epic rivalries and passionate love stories. I know that if I show up at a gathering, I'll find old and new friends. We have the same gripes about politics, parenting, and living expenses that I might have discussed at Berkeley dinner parties in the past, but then we'll tan a hide together, roast a wild boar, or dry our foraged herbs by the fire until the owls and bats guide back to our tents.

Jaime is also finding ways to live in a more egalitarian manner, and I'm a part of his transformation. He had to endure a grueling series of court dates that pressed him beyond his edge. He could have lost custody of his daughter and might have been forced to pay tens of thousands of dollars of Millie's legal fees. He believed he was suffering emotional damage from the trauma of this extended uncertainty and often told me he didn't know how much longer he could fight the situation. His boss at the agency, his lawyer, his daughter's mother, and even some of his friends ripped into him, telling him to stop pursuing the wild life because it was ruining his chance of being a father to his child. He was encouraged to get a job, an iPhone, and a Zoom account in order to be seen as a fit parent in the eyes of the judge. That didn't go over well. He regretted getting entangled in the legal system, but by staying committed to his visitations with his daughter, and yes, even connecting with her on video chat, he prevailed. While he had to see her in a state facility under the watch of a court-mandated supervisor, he would bring her caribou roasts and salmon jerky he'd made. She started saying "Daddy, Daddy, meat, meat!" whenever he walked in the room.

Nevertheless, he struggled to reconcile his understanding of his role as a father in today's society with how his family might have fared under Paleolithic conditions. He believed that Millie could never have restricted his access to their child had they been living in a small, nomadic group. There would be no indifferent, institutional power that could intervene to keep a family from negotiating their own arrangements. This was what tore at him—that his daughter's mother, an avowed back-to-the-land nature lover, had tried to use the modern legal system to deprive him of his paternity.

After his case settled, Jaime gained the ability to take care of his daughter for unsupervised visitations several days each month. When she turns four, he will be able to bring her up to his Alaska base and teach her everything he knows. She'll help hunt caribou, wear fox pelts, and watch the salmon swimming upstream in the spring, Jaime hopes.

At one point while he was preparing for his custody trial in 2020, Jaime called me with an urgency in his voice I had never heard. "I'm about to crack, Jessica," he told me. He was in the middle of two weeks of visitations with his daughter. He would be seeing her for four hours, two afternoons a week. "I don't know how I'm supposed to finish prepping all the materials for the trial, stay on top of the work my boss needs from me, and be with my daughter this week. It's too much."

Here was a man who had been in confrontations with four aggressive grizzly bears, who had smashed open his forehead while shooting caribou to bring to his kid, who had survived avalanches and roiling river rapids, and dispatched an eight-hundred-pound moose with a primitive bow. But the pressure of work plus child care was bringing him to his knees.

"Where are you right now, Jaime?" I asked him.

"I'm on a beach in Puget Sound getting ready to grill some meat. I was planning to stay out here another night before I head back to the city," he said.

"Go back now," I told him. "Get to work."

I'd been in his situation too many times to count. There was no way out of it. He had to just push on through. No one was going to rescue him from these responsibilities. I thought to myself, *Jaime, stop whining and just be a mom.*

CHAPTER 9

Wild Community

About half a year later, in May 2021, Jaime and I met up in Chelewah, Washington, for Between the Rivers, his first skills gathering. There, I introduced him to the friends I'd made over the years who had helped me on my rewilding path. He brought ten pounds of freshly harvested moose roadkill that he grilled up at the campfire on the first night, sharing it with Raven, Fern, Myron, and two of the Meat Mamas, Katie and Harmony. Jaime fit right in, appearing to relish showing off his flint-knapping and animal-processing skills and diving into deep conversations about subsistence strategies and emergency preparation. He was so popular in that crowd that several folks pledged to come visit him to go hunting later in the summer when the Alaskan season opened. He fantasized about one special woman staying up there with him, telling me that this feral female might just be the one for him.

In the ninety-degree heat of an unseasonably warm Western spring, I worked all week fleshing and scraping the hide from my roadkill deer under the tutelage of Finisia Medrano's former acolyte Alex, softening it into buckskin to make moccasins for my girls. I was glad to be back with my wild people after a year and a half of missing gatherings due to COVID-19 closures. On the second-to-last day, I met a woman who looked a little out of place, wearing bright athletic attire and toting around a notebook to all the workshops. Asking her how she liked the gathering, I found out she was there to research how learning ancestral skills might positively affect mental health. She had planned a summer itinerary of traveling around to gatherings to immerse herself in rewilding culture. I invited her back to my truck, where we spent an evening with Jaime. We showered her with our ideas about immediate return and anti-civ philosophy while serving up a dinner of nettles and roadkill that she politely declined. She listened to us, absorbing our untamed enthusiasm, pausing to scribble notes for her upcoming book. I wondered if she would take it all in, perhaps transforming just as I had.

For a year after I left my marriage, I struggled to find housing because of the enormous expense of West Coast real estate and the fact that I couldn't give up my dream of living in a community based on wildness, which I had only been able to find at skills gatherings. During time with my kids, I had to shuttle them around to various situations, while the rest of the time, they enjoyed stability with their dad. For six months, we lived both in my truck and in a five-hundred-square-foot cottage on the property of a family I had hoped to share daily life with, but the restrictions surrounding COVID-19 left us unable to interact with anyone at all. During the lockdowns, I did my best not to spread the culture of fear to my children despite the closure of all state parks across California—an unnecessary overreach meant to keep people safe from the virus.

We played "outlaw" and snuck past the gates and enjoyed our time outside as others stayed home.

Still looking for community, we tried living with a family friend who had an extra bedroom, but I felt that the noise and mess of two lively girls was disturbing her more than she let on. Another rewilder who lived on fifty-six acres previously decimated in the fire that razed the town of Paradise invited us to come up with the truck whenever we wanted. I was completely enamored with his lifestyle. Sixty-year-old Carl slept outside on a buffalo skin, bathed in a pond, cooked on an open fire, harvested local animals, raised bees, and collected seeds from native plants. He was healthy and tan and didn't look a day over forty-five. Munching on piñon pine nuts he had collected and touring his shady groves of juicy figs, I thought I had hit the jackpot of rewilding opportunity. I pledged to spend half my time helping him repair the land so I could learn his skills. He needed help pulling up invasive Scotch broom, clearing fields of star thistle, watering baby oak trees, and harvesting other wild foods and materials.

One week that I brought the girls, we spent our days naked, sweating, and fighting mosquitoes in the one-hundred-degree heat. At night, ants crawled over us as we slept in our sweat. My effort to stay positive and keep them cheerful was a total failure. They were miserable. Then, back in the foggy hills of Berkeley, I heard from Carl that he had spotted a rattlesnake, quickly beheaded it with a shovel, then got bit on the ankle by another that was hiding down by his kitchen pond. As he zoomed to the hospital, he felt his throat closing up. Narrowly making it, he required eighteen vials of antivenom and three weeks in care to start healing. Three rattlers at the pond where we ran around naked! I couldn't handle the idea of my kids battling snakes, and while I cursed myself for acting out of fear, I also decided that we weren't going back to Carl's.

I started booking hotels and guesthouses for our family of three. After the girls fell asleep, with the three of us packed into one bed, I would scour the web for any available place I could afford to buy that would let me live as close to nature as possible. After months of this, I finally found the right spot on the edge of the Eldorado National Forest in the Sierra foothills. A small house sat in a clearing amid twenty acres of cedar, fir, and oak forest that surrounded a year-round creek studded with giant stones, just a two-hour drive from their dad's place. I planned to spend half my week alone there, setting up a wild skills workshop that I could eventually invite folks to join me at.

It took me three months to secure a home loan, since self-employed folks like me aren't enticing mortgage holders to banks that were skittish after the 2008 financial collapse. I was grateful that my father was able to help me with the down payment and cosign the mortgage, but even these measures didn't win us instant bank approval. I remember more than one night I spent sobbing into a shot glass of whisky, wondering if I'd ever be able to provide a home for my kids like their dad could give them. Finally, after frantic calls during the winter holidays to my dad's employer, requesting that they verify his teaching position of over thirty years, I received the loan.

I rushed to pack the truck with my things and drove myself 120 miles east to set up my new country home. No one was available to help because it was in the middle of a COVID-19 surge, so I muscled through the ordeal like a seasoned long-haul driver. I was glad I didn't have any items that I couldn't heave, push, wedge, or roll by myself. That first winter, my girls enjoyed romping in the snow and following deer tracks across our yard while I was rapidly learning to adjust to rural living with no mail delivery, no garbage service, water from a well, and heat from a wood-burning stove.

Just a month into my new situation, I met a neighbor, Will, while I was running, and he was grading the gravel road that about a dozen of us share. He told me that the county didn't maintain the road, so we all had to help each other figure out how to keep it passable. It was a good thing too, he explained, because it meant that the authorities never came down to us. We were less under government control. "Out here, we all look after one another," he said with a slight twang, winking at me from under the brim of his grungy cowboy hat.

I felt an odd nervousness wash up my chest. This guy was really cute. Too good-looking and charming to just be sitting on top of a tractor in the middle of the nowhere I had escaped to. He should be in a Western movie. Why was he so friendly? Then he dropped that key piece of info I couldn't believe I already wanted to know. His girlfriend had recently taken off, leaving him on a massive piece of land they used to share. He proceeded to tell me about all the far-flung neighbors I hadn't yet met, including his son, daughter, and stepson, all of whom I'd come to know very well in the coming seasons.

My closest neighbors, Monica and Dan, own horses and maintain a series of mountain trails behind our properties. My girls
learned to ride on their gentle mare and docile gelding, traipsing up
hills that they would have never climbed otherwise. Nearly retired
Opie works for the railroad and brought me a cord of firewood for
the coldest months when my supply was running low, so I tried to
repay him with baked goods. Jerod and Cidney host raging parties
and were always ready to pop up their inflatable waterslide for all
our kids during the heat of July.

Running on the wooded trails, I met many others, including
our furry and feathered residents: bears, mountain lions, turkeys,
jackrabbits, hawks, and skunks. The neighborhood gossip extended
to all of them, and Will made a point to keep me informed about
everything going on, bringing me eggs from his chickens and warning me to stay alert for the mountain lions when I ran. Actually, he
said, I needed a gun. Every time he'd drop by, I'd get that queasy
crush feeling that I'd try to brush off, thinking that it would be the
height of stupidity to get involved with someone who lived so close.

As my girls and I got to know this place and these people better,
they were amazed at the contrast with their city life, where they only
casually knew a few people from school and ignored everyone in
nearby addresses. But now, on any evening, we can stop by someone's house, bring them foraged blackberries, hang out with their animals, go swimming in their section of the creek, and promise to water
their gardens when they travel. My neighbors are less tethered to the
safety nets of insurance, health care, electric grids, and sewer systems
because they have practical know-how and faith that other people will

show up for them. They hunt, fish, and take their vacations locally in the beautiful mountains that surround us. Their self-sufficiency is bolstered by community. Unfortunately, it took one harrowing event for me to fully understand the resilience that comes from rural bonds.

It was early in the morning in August 2021 when Jerod texted me that a fire was spreading quickly just a few miles south of our road. Three nights earlier, I had been up until 5:00 a.m. at his place, listening to bands with dozens of people and gazing up at the stars with Will next to me in the grass. Now, we were all going to be evacuated as the Caldor Fire erupted across tens of thousands of acres, consuming the drought-ridden forest and threatening hundreds of homes.

I rushed to pack my truck with supplies and precious items in case the house burned, thankful that my kids were safe with their dad. Into a homemade basket, I placed the fox skull, my mother's ashes, and my first knife. I threw our clothes and books into the back and took off for Will's house, where he, his stepson, and a friend were packing all his tools and hunting guns into a trailer. Will rents his house, and if it all got destroyed, he'd also lose his ability to make a living as a home builder because he would no longer have his valuable tools and machinery. As we drove out of our canyon, giant pyrocumulus clouds billowed behind us, hovering like gaseous cauliflowers.

Fifty thousand people were evacuated in the Caldor Fire, and we weren't allowed to return home for three weeks as the inferno raged across thirty miles of national forest. I was lucky that friends took me in, and I was able to keep up some semblance of regular life for my girls. But the severe wildfire was further proof that giant climate changes are afoot and we all must adapt. I believe that rewilding in all of forms is growing because of the robust answer it presents to the pressing question: What now? Get ready to be nomadic, rely on your small group, and stay in the present moment.

As I learned through trial and error, a fully rewilded lifestyle seems preposterous and dangerous to most of my peers and family members. Debating its merits has thus become a regular occurrence in my life, and some themes have emerged. At one skills gathering, I met a photographer who pressed me to admit that a lot of rewilding practices don't scale. "Earth's 7.2 billion people can't hunt and gather anymore," he said. "There isn't enough quality habitat, and there are too many of us to live in ecological balance."

I responded that it is true that we civilized folks vastly out-number our nomadic forebears. But the idea of "scaling" is a con-cept based on agricultural civilization and popularized by tech. It assumes a mechanical replicability, which is only something indus-try can do. The immediate-return lifestyle doesn't scale; it grows according to the carrying capacity of the environment, and it adapts based on the particular species available in that ecosystem. The more important point, I said, was that not everyone needs to rewild right now. We just need some portion of the population to retain wild skills and the ability to forage in whatever radically different environment emerges from future global upheaval.

Others lament that we can't possibly feed everyone on the planet with wild food. But this statement is based on an illusion that we're feeding everyone on the planet right now with industrial agriculture, which we most certainly are not. We have enormous rates of malnourishment and hunger. Kyle Chamberlain once took on this argument, saying that it assumes that the only thing we can do is commit to the trajectory of the industrial food system and that figuring things out for yourself somehow denies other people the food they need. "But we're already starving millions of people," he said. "Why can't individuals or small groups figure out how to get wild food? They will either figure it out, or they won't. The real issue is guilt, which these people feel because they're hoarding a disproportionate share of the world's resources."

While it's doubtful that a large mass of people can successfully rewild, it is certain that not everyone on the planet can consume like we do in wealthy countries. But as I found, rewilding in an immersive, total sense is not yet a reality even for committed individuals, let alone for everyone. Most Western consumers—including my closest family and friends—won't be able to disengage from modern comforts, conveniences, and addictions without some tragic precipitating cause.

Another point that comes up frequently questions the legality of rewilding practices. Someone like Philip Stark, the Berkeley forager, can talk about himself as a "scofflaw" when it comes to picking up greens from the side of the road, but the same wouldn't be true for someone who didn't look like the professorial type. Penalties are always harsher on the poor and people of color. Hunting and fishing without proper licenses is illegal—even for Montana man Ernie Tertelgte. Harvesting food from public or private land is trespassing, and simply collecting rainwater is not officially permitted in most areas. Native American communities have suffered the consequences of laws made against subsistence throughout colonization and into today, and they have paid dearly for this in the loss of their vital traditions.

Others ask about the consequences of masses of rewilders going out onto the landscape. We've already seen populations of highly desired wild foods like ramps, mushrooms, and seaweeds declining in areas where people are going out to forage them for the commercial market. There could be so much more damage from this approach, which is about extraction rather than regeneration.

If human rewilding is to happen, we have to respect the lands by planting back, ensuring the reproduction of native species, and providing a positive benefit to ecosystems as humans once did across the earth. The consequences would be devastating if a generation of wannabe wilderness wanderers decimated our already taxed landscapes by pulling up all the edible roots, killing all the tastiest fauna, and mishandling their own waste. The land has to have the capacity to regenerate from our impact, which means our footprints must spread widely, with low population density. If there is no reciprocity and regeneration that comes from humans living off the land, then there is no rewilding, only more destruction and domestication.

As anti-civ writer Paul Shepard recommended, we must take our cues for how to live from primal cultures, who have the longest time-tested wisdom traditions. We have to rewild our minds and ask ourselves in any situation, *What would a hunter-gatherer do?* Then we must do our best to approximate that. Whittle your social group down to twenty-five key players. Pursue good relationships, not money. Eat wild food. Make your kids play outside, and spend as much time as you can outside yourself. Don't buy stuff that you can make yourself, even if it takes more time than tapping and swiping on your Amazon app. Try to master a few skills of our ancestors, even if you only use them on those long, minimalist camping trips. The notion that hunter-gatherers live a heathier and more balanced life than we do in civilization becomes an opportunity to imagine what a better life might look like and allows us to critique the short-comings of our consumer habits and industrial dependency. If more of us understood how humans lived for most of our tenure on earth, we could make better decisions about how to live now.

What I know for sure is that the more I unleash myself from the tethers of domestication, the happier I feel. Though I still live in a single-family home far from my relatives, get many of my basic goods from strangers, and use the best hours of my day to work for money, I know better how to return to a state of connectedness in nature, and I live in a mutually supportive community. Knowing that civilized life is just the most recent, flawed iteration of how humans have chosen to live helps me lessen the power that institu-tional ideas have over my choices. I'm grateful that I now live in a place where no one thinks it's strange that I pick berries from the roadside, carry a tarp in my trunk in case I find a deer on the high-way, and feed my chickens acorns from the tree above their coop instead of buying feed at the store. I hang out with my neighbors every day, whether we're riding horses, building gardens, or playing card games late into the night.

I'm also grateful that I met a wild man, Will, who calls himself a redneck but seems more like a cowboy who ran away with the Indians, *Dances with Wolves*–*style*. Driven to desperation when the mother of his two kids left him several years back, he went to the woods to find himself. He told me how he set out to Desolation Wilderness near Lake Tahoe with his dogs, a gun, a hammock, a knife, and a fishing pole. "I was thinking all day about all the stuff people don't usually think about," he said. For forty-two nights alone, he just survived, "eating off the fat of the land," and giving up his pain to nature, setting deadfall traps for squirrels, fishing, and sheltering from the rain. Listening to this tale on one of our first dates, I saw how his kind brown eyes lit up when he talked about the freedom of leaving the daily grind. "We are meant to live that way," he told me, and I couldn't have agreed more.

Up until that point, despite my intense attraction to him, I didn't see how we would ever merge our vastly different worlds. But hearing about his wild wanderings while enjoying an extended courtship made me realize that the motivation for my rewilding journey wasn't entirely about living wild or changing my life with my kids. I also wanted romance, companionship, and a mate who could adventure with me. I had been attracted to many of the rugged men I had met— Gabe, Kyle, Jaime, and others—but I couldn't see them reciprocating my intense fascination with them. I had resolved myself to enjoying whatever amorous distractions might pop up for me on my path, but I was beyond seeking out partnership. It just seemed too hard, and I had ended my most meaningful one.

But Will and I just kept hanging out. For one of our first hikes out on my land, he showed up wearing a holster (in case of bears), toting two beers (in case of boredom?), and smoking an American Spirit. We hiked down to the creek and then bushwhacked up to a meadow ringed by buck brush and dotted with strange concentric circles of stones. I had probably brought a dozen visitors up there, and no one could explain this open field in the middle of the forest. After grumbling about all the poison oak he'd had to boot stomp, Will walked out to the meadow and confidently proclaimed, "This is lava cap!" Millions of years ago, the Sierra Nevada mountains harbored volcanic activity that spilled lava out all over the foothills. Even though much of it eroded away, there were still open rocky areas on ridgetops where nothing but wildflowers would grow.

Will's local knowledge gave me the dose of realism I sorely needed to understand my land. But before I could thank him for solving that mystery, he was challenging me to fire the gun—I had to be ready to defend myself against mountain lions and bears, and he was going to help me learn that wild skill. He set his two empty beer cans on one of the big volcanic stones, and I was to bring them down, from fifty feet away. I missed, but I think it was just because he was plugging my ears with his big fingers.

Over many months, we realized that our differences brought us closer together—we were mutually intrigued by our polarity. He works with his hands; I work with my mind. He never went to college; I spent too much time sucking up to professors. He knows how to hitch up a trailer, weld steel, mine gold, grade a road, and build a house. I beat him at any game involving words, and I once trounced him in a swimming race. At his worst, he's belligerent and rough. At my worst, I'm pretentious and demanding. But we both know how to skin a deer, start a fire with flint, and build a rain-proof shelter. My overall practical skills are juvenile in comparison to his, and he doesn't shy away from letting me know how much I have to learn, and I can't help but make fun of his spelling. We share a deep understanding that we are rooted on this land, we are children of the mountains, and we are never going back to the lives we had before. Love happened.

It's not my rewilding paradise, but it's close. Living in Gold Country still feels like the Wild West sometimes. People out here retain an extractive mentality toward the land, as if it's their right to use what's here, however they want. I've been schooled in a regenerative way of thinking that says we've got to give more than we take from nature, but I'm careful about how I present this to my neighbors, lest someone call me a "hippie flatlander." Will is somewhat on board with my dream to wild tend my wilderness of oak and Douglas fir forest by planting hardy perennial edible species like biscuit root, wild carrot, and nutsedge, which grows sweet, crunchy root tubers. I want these plants to flourish on their own so that anyone in the future will be able to forage what they need; it's my gift to my descendants. To do this, I have to plant some seed starts and protect them until they are more robust.

"You want more rabbit food, eh?" he cackled when I brought this up and then stared at me fiercely. It was nearing midnight, and I didn't want to fight. I just wanted to go to bed. But he was juiced up. "Then you're gonna need guano, and we gotta get it right now while the bats are out," he said. I protested.

"Let's get fertilizer tomorrow. I'm tired."

"No, no, nope. We're going. Get your boots on."

There's an old Bureau of Land Management mining claim across the dirt road from Will's house that he toys around with, handpicking out tiny nuggets of gold with his buddy and dreaming of the abundant gleaming veins that might lie deeper in the tunnel. We loaded up buckets and shovels and headed out to the mine, donning hard hats as we entered the four-foot-tall cave that extends deep into bedrock and stretches down into a one-hundred-meter-long tunnel that miners carved with pickaxes over a century ago. We submerged into water in the deepest parts, up to our thighs. Our headlights illuminated the sparkling gold dust embedded in the cobble ceiling. The guano lay at the very back of the enclosure, and we scooped it into the buckets, swearing when it got close to our mouths. "This is the best shit for your seeds to grow strong," he told me. "Nothing better."

As we were leaving the mine, I stumbled and grabbed for a ledge on the wall. It cracked off and threw a thirty-pound rock shard toward my foot while more rocks rained down. He pushed me out of the way, keeping me from getting crushed as I screamed. Horizontal, we looked at each other and burst out laughing. We could just glimpse the Milky Way blazing an arc in the sky through the arch of the cave entrance.

What launched me on my rewilding journey was a desire to leave the nine-to-five grind, soothe my ecological anxiety, and reconnect to nature and my health, but what I found was that my life became more fun (and badass!) as I started replacing industrial goods and activities with wild ones.

When my mom died, her best friend called me the next day and shared her grief. The one word her friend used to describe my mom was "authentic." Mom had to do what she felt she needed to do, regardless of what anyone thought. She wasn't a people pleaser, and she didn't dwell on the trivial. She had done many transgressive things in her life, and I'd like to think she would enjoy how I've gone from reciting prayers to a paternal god and writing for CEOs of AI technology companies to dunking my kids in sacred rivers and scavenging my meat with a good ol' country boy at my side. If I call out to her spirit, I hear her praising me for living authentically. When I access the freedom and pleasure of a wild life, nature provides an immediate return to who I've always been.

Acknowledgments

Thank you to Mother Nature for all beginnings and endings.

I give gratitude to my ancestors who came from far shores to secure my life in the West; my mother, Virginia Petersen, who showed me how to be a strong, fun-loving matriarch; and my father, Robert Kraft, who gave me the gift of language, wonder, and walking in the woods.

While writing this book, I was endlessly energized by Opal and Odiya, who will always be my adventure girls, making me a better human and mother. JE, you are in my heart forever; I am so pleased to have your enduring support of our family. Sam, Erin, and Ciel, my closest and most cherished trio, your love and care keep me grounded. Amy Kolen, thank you for inspiring my career in art and writing with your beautiful work. Raychel, Daniel, and Paul, you took me on some of my first nature adventures and made me a hungry mushroom forager. I give top-shelf praise to Scott Kirschenbaum, who constantly urged me to rise to my ladybeast best.

There are many folks who provided boosts of creativity, editing, and sources during my research and writing: Phil Stevens, Christopher Daradics, Dmitri Novomeiski, and huge praise for Fern

Thompsett, who put every part of my journey into glorious, loving perspective. Dear friends have held space for my changes over these transformational years: Janice Gallagher, Deborah Orosz, Fiona Aboud, Blair Perilman, Heather Harrington, and Shoshanna Kirk, thank you for your love.

I am lucky that I have a community of writers, creators, and editors who encouraged me through ups and downs: Vanessa Hua, Rachel Lehmann-Haupt, Jaime Schwalb, Sarah Durham Wilson, Larry Smith, Mark Welte, Robert Scott G., Jane Metcalfe, Jason Bardi, and Laura Mazer. My agent, Ted Weinstein, believed in this project from the very beginning and never gave up. To Anna Michels and Diane DiBiase at Sourcebooks, you are both extraordinary editors who found missing pieces and spaces for a more personal story.

Jolie Elan taught me about the magic of the oaks; may her memory always be a blessing for the acorns. To the naturalists who showed me how to see through the wall of green, you changed my perception: Brad Balukjian, Marley Peifer, Suzie Woolhouse, Meghan Walla-Murphy, Kyle Schulteis, Jack Harrison, Rye N. Flint, and Hazel Ward. Rick Berry, Robin Bliss Wagner, and Matthew Forkin gave me many hours of rich description of their experiences with living wild. Thanks to Etai Wolins and Maya Katz-Ali who kept my girls entertained and joined our family adventures.

Tom, Ayla, and Tenaya were our first gathering friends who helped guide my journey with tales and knowledge. Tamara Wilder's enduring contribution to the world of wild skills helps me in my everyday life. Myron Cretney's knowledge, humor, and mentorship helped me gain a nicenheimer vision of community. I am indebted to Velton V. Fry, who showed me how to take my first shot.

I cherish the ancient skills of these craftspeople: Delmar and Tracy Williams, Janey Sea, Julia Parker, Tiśina Parker, and Samuel Lazer. Nicole Apelian and Philip Stark provided grounding for my foraging practice. Finding Jeremy Koster's anthropological work and friendship twenty-five years after we met has bolstered my belief in lifelong connections.

This book would not have been possible without the prior work of Kevin and Natasha Tucker as well as Gumby Montgomery and Teresa Forlotti, whose podcasts are first on my list. I couldn't have written so many words without these rewilders: Jaime Van Lanen, Glenn Helkenn, Peter Michael Bauer, Raven Gray, and Adam LaRue.

Steven Milani, existing in your reality helped me see another side of anarchy. Rachael Soroka, you're the mama pal who I aspire to emulate. Dori and Roni, your sisterhood and insatiable curiosity have shown me a new reality. Jerod, Kayla, Jeremiah, and Jon—I'm so happy to have my home among you. Will, I'm deeply grateful that the land called me to you and this beautiful life in the woods.

Reading Group Guide

1. Had you heard of rewilding prior to reading Why We Need to Be Wild? What did you know about it? What was the most surprising thing you learned while reading?

2. How do emerging technologies aim to "transcend" biology? What might the proponents of these technologies learn from the perspectives of rewilders?

3. Can we succeed at creating a sustainable society in social groups as small as the nuclear family? How does collaboration improve success in both wild and modern environments?

4. Jessica notices that the primary selling points for items at the trade blanket are their functionality and durability. How do those compare to mainstream consumer values? Why are these mindsets so different?

5. Eating meat and cutting trees down are activities that are often criticized for their negative environmental impacts but are

necessary for wild living. What variables determine the immediate impact of these activities? How can they be sustainably experienced?

6. Some rewilding proponents often reject advancements like renewable energy, urban permaculture, and electric cars because they see these as "half-measures." How do such uncompromising views benefit or inhibit the growth of the rewilding movement?

7. What does a strict "Leave No Trace" policy suggest about the contemporary human-nature relationship? Is that assumption correct?

8. What role do laws play throughout the book? What causes the most disconnect between our legal system and the principles of rewilding?

9. What drew Jessica toward rewilding? What would persuade you to try it yourself?

A Conversation with the Author

Although many people find rewilding empowering, they might find themselves in conflict with their acquaintances and even close friends. How have your relationships changed since you began your journey?

It's been encouraging to see a lot of my friends and family get curious about my new passions. A good friend of mine started foraging and now regularly cooks with wild food that she collects. I've brought a bunch of pals to primitive skills gatherings and watched them get hooked on something they never imagined they'd learn, like hide tanning or herbal medicine. Since moving out of the urban center, I do find that I have more in common with rural people who have a close connection to the land, but I'm frequently visited by old city friends who want to get away, enjoy a campfire, take a long forest hike, and hang out with my rowdy neighbors. I don't take it personally if someone thinks rewilding is nuts! I know it's not for everyone, and I don't try to create conflict about it.

Rewilders expect to do better than their domesticated counterparts in an apocalyptic scenario. Do you think some kind of societal collapse is necessary for people to recognize the value of these skills and renounce the unsustainability of convenience?

I think that if a massive breakdown of society happened soon, there could very well be a surge of people interested in wild skills. The rewilding growth curve is already shooting up, as the number of people seeking training at wilderness schools and attending gatherings is increasing every year. The small scale collapses we experienced during the Great Recession and COVID-19 incited large numbers of people to seek alternative ways of living outside of the grid and global consumerism. But just as World War II inspired people to plant 20 million victory gardens, which produced 40 percent of all the produce consumed in this country in 1944, a similar global catastrophe that curtails the industrial supply chain could quickly motivate people to create local subsistence communities.

You mention the whiplash of returning to modern society after your wild sojourns. How do you move between those two worlds these days?

I've realized that the forces of modern society are so pervasive that it is hard for even the most committed rewilders to fully opt out of driving gas-powered vehicles, picking up food at grocery stores, and using digital technology sometimes. Since our need for community is primal, we will do what we must in order to stay connected to the people we love, even if it goes against our ideas about how we'd ideally like to live. I do make sure to venture into natural areas for extended time every day and forage wild food, and I constantly challenge myself to forgo one or many modern conveniences. Rewilding is the life raft off the sinking ship of civilization, though, so I hope that within a decade I'll be sailing that raft full-time.

You mention living your life by a "hunter-gatherer benchmark." What does this mean, practically?

When I understood that our ancient human ancestors weren't motivated by fear unless there was an immediate threat to their lives, which could come in the form of a predator, extreme social exclusion, or a rare situation of physical danger, I realized that living in a generally fearful state wasn't helpful or healthy for me. Our natural psychological baseline is to be happy, low-stress, and socially supported. Gaining more wild self-sufficiency allows us to be less dependent upon experts, institutions, technologies, and financial systems that retain power over us by stoking our fear. While I used to worry about getting lost, losing electricity, running out of money, being deprived of possessions, letting my kids take risks, going without a shower, or taking on big physical tasks, I now see these possibilities as interesting challenges that require courage and resilience, qualities that wild humans develop in abundance.

What one primitive skill do you think everyone should learn and practice?

Some plants that are often called "weeds" or "invasives" are easy to recognize and offer a lot more nutrition than the veggies you can buy at the grocery store. You can save money, improve your diet, get exercise, and promote biodiversity by searching for dandelions, Himalayan blackberries, kudzu vine, and any other common wild edible in your area. You also tap into your hard-wired instinct to find food from your environment, which offers the same type of dopamine reward that we moderns are used to getting from phone alerts, fast food, and sweets. Warning: foraging is addictive!

Notes

CHAPTER 1: MISMATCH

1   Jane Desmond, "Requiem for Roadkill: Death and Denial on America's Roads," in *Environmental Anthropology*, ed. Helen Kopnina and Eleanor Shoreman-Ouimet (New York: Routledge, 2013), 60–72, https://doi.org/10.4324/9780203403341-12.

2   J. Lalo, "The problem of road-kill," *American Forests* 93, no. 9/10 (1987): 50–52.

3   Benjamin Franklin, Mr. Franklin: A Selection from His Personal Letters, ed. Leonard Woods et al., (New Haven: Yale University Press, 1961), 481–482.

4   Christopher Ryan, *Civilized to Death: The Price of Progress* (New York: Avid Reader Press, 2019), 274.

5   Richard Lyons, "A Doctor in the Amazon Probes for Genetic Links to Disease," *New York Times*, November 8, 1983, https://www.nytimes.com/1983/11/08/science/a-doctor-in-the-amazon -probes-for-genetic-links-to-disease.html.

6   Paul W. Turke, "Childhood Food Allergies: An Evolutionary Mismatch Hypothesis," *Evolution, Medicine, and Public Health 2017*, no. 1 (January 2017): 15460, https://doi.org/10.1093/emph /eox014; H. Pontzer, B. M. Wood, and D. A. Raichlen, "Hunter-Gatherers as Models in Public Health," Obesity Reviews 19, no. S1 (December 2018): 24–35, https://doi.org/10.1111/obr.12785.

7   C. M. Turnbull, *The Forest People* (New York: Simon & Schuster, 1962), 25–26.

8   Daniel Lieberman, *The Story of the Human Body: Evolution, Health, and Disease* (New York: Vintage Books, 2014), 47.

9   Michaeleen Doucleff, "Secrets of a Maya Supermom: What Parenting Books Don't Tell You," NPR, May 11, 2018, https://www.npr.org/sections/goatsandsoda/2018/05/11/603315432 /the-best-mothers-day-gift-get-mom-out- of-the-box.

10   Ronald Jurek, "Nonnative Red Foxes in California," State of California, Department of Fish and Game, Wildlife Management Division, April 1992, https://nrm.dfg.ca.gov/FileHandler .ashx?DocumentID=2949.

11   Cathryn H. Greenberg, Kendrick Weeks, and Gordon S. Warburton, "The Historic Role of Humans and Other Keystone Species in Shaping Central Hardwood Forests for Disturbance-Dependent Wildlife," in *Natural Disturbances and Historic Range of Variation*, ed. Cathryn H. Greenberg and Beverly S. Collins (New York: Springer Cham, 2016), 319–53, https:// doi.org/10.1007/978-3-319-21527-3_12.

12   Robinson Jeffers, "Shine, Perishing Republic," in Roan Stallion, Tamar and Other Poems (New York, NY: Random House, 1935), 95.

CHAPTER 2: WEAVING

1   L. D. Bissonette, "The Basket Makers of the Central Californian Interior," in *Women and Plants: Gender Relations in Biodiversity Management and Conservation*, ed. Patricia L. Howard (London: Zed Books, 2003), 197–210.

2   Urban Scout, Rewild or Die : Revolution and Renaissance at the End of Civilization (Portland, Oregon: Urban Scout, 2016), 7.

3   Urban Scout, Rewild or Die, 19.

4   Yuval Noah Harari, *Sapiens: A Brief History of Humankind* (New York: Harper Perennial, 2018), 32.

5   Dor Shilton et al., "Human Social Evolution: Self-Domestication or Self-Control?," *Frontiers in Psychology*, February 14, 2020, https://doi.org/10.3389/fpsyg.2020.00134.

6   Harari, Sapiens, 32.

CHAPTER 3: GATHERING

1   The word "primitive" was used not as a disparaging term but as a way of denoting that these skills were "primary" to the human experience. Yet as the political tolerance for this word has waned recently because some groups perceive the word as derogatory, many of the organizations that promote these skills have rebranded as natural living skills, earth skills, place-based skills, or similar terms. I use them all interchangeably depending on the context.

2   John Coles, *Experimental Archaeology* (Caldwell, NJ: Blackburn Press, 1979), 11–12.

3   George C. Frison, "Experimental Use of Clovis Weaponry and Tools on African Elephants," *American Antiquity* 54, no. 4 (October 1989): 76684, https://doi.org/10.2307/280681.

4   David Wescott, "Gathering: The Modern Primitive Skills Movement," *Bulletin of Primitive Technology*, no. 49 (Spring 2015), 31–94.

5   Wescott, "Gathering."

6   Sarah Pike, "Rewilding Hearts and Habits in the Ancestral Skills Movement," *Religions* 9, no. 10 (2018): 300, https://doi.org/10.3390/rel9100300.

7   Alex Langlands, Cræft : An Inquiry into the Origins and True Meaning of Traditional Crafts (New York: W.W. Norton & Company, 2019), 293.

8   Michael Balter, "World's Oldest Stone Tools Discovered in Kenya," *Science*, April 14, 2015, https://www.science.org/content/article/world-s-oldest-stone-tools-discovered-kenya.

9   Hannah Smith Schiller, "'You Just Make a Buckskin Laptop Case': Identity and Authenticity in the Primitive Skills Community" (bachelor's thesis, Warren Wilson College, 2013), https://nanopdf.com/download/you-just-make-a-buckskin-laptop-case_pdf.

10   Hannah Smith Schiller, "'You Just Make A Buckskin Laptop Case': Identity and Authenticity in the Primitive Skills" (community undergraduate research, spring 2013), Warren Wilson College, https://nanopdf.com/download/you-just-make-a-buckskin-laptop-case_pdf.

11   "Queer Stealthcraft," Queer Nature, accessed January 28, 2023, https://www.queernature.org/queer-stealthcraft.

12   Christian Lander, "#128 Camping," Stuff White People Like (blog), August 14, 2009, https://stuffwhitepeoplelike.com/2009/08/.

13   Chris Clarke, "Untold History: The Survival of California's Indians," *Tending the Wild*, KCET, September 26, 2016, https://www.kcet.org/shows/tending-the-wild/untold-history-the-survival-of-californias-indians.

13   Sabitaj Mahal, "Fishbowl at Wild Roots, Feral Futures: Thoughts on Race, Identity, and Solidarity," *Earth First! Journal* (June 2013): 18–19, https://feralfutures.proboards.com /thread/202/wrff-2012-fish-bowl-report.

CHAPTER 4: SURVIVALING

1   Jon Young, *Exploring Natural Mystery: Kamana One* (San Gregorio, CA: Owlink Media, 2001), 220–221.

2   Derrick Jensen, "Saving the Indigenous Soul,: An Interview with Martín Prechtel" *The Sun*, April 2001, https://www.thesunmagazine.org/issues/304/saving-the-indigenous-soul.

3   Quoctrung Bui and Claire Cain Miller, "The Typical American Lives Only 18 Miles from Mom," *New York Times*, December 23, 2015, https://www.nytimes.com/interactive/2015/12/24= /upshot/24up-family.html.

4   "Study: Elevated Levels of Toxic Chemicals Found in Menstrual Pads and Disposable Diapers," Environmental Working Group, March 2019, https://www.ewg.org/news-and -analysis/2019/03/study-elevated-levels-toxic-chemicals-found-menstrual-pads-and -disposable.

5   Jim Pojar and Andy MacKinnon, *Plants of the Pacific Northwest Coast: Washington, Oregon, British Columbia & Alaska* (Auburn, WA: Lone Pine, 2016).

6   Heather Ohly et al., "Attention Restoration Theory: A Systematic Review of the Attention Restoration Potential of Exposure to Natural Environments," *Journal of Toxicology and Environmental Health, Part B* 19, no.7 (September 2016): 30543, https://doi.org/10.1080/10937 404.2016.1196155.

7   Meredith Root-Bernstein and Richard Ladle, "Ecology of a Widespread Large Omnivore, Homo sapiens, and Its Impacts on Ecosystem Processes," *Ecology and Evolution* 9, no. 19 (2019): 10874–94, https://doi.org/10.1002/ece3.5049.

8   Bibi van der Zee, "What Is the True Cost of Eating Meat?," *Guardian*, May 7, 2018, https:// www.theguardian.com/news/2018/may/07/true-cost-of-eating-meat-environment-health -animal-welfare.

9   Beth Blaxland, "Hominid and Hominin—What's the Difference?," Australian Museum, October 2, 2020, https://australian.museum/learn/science/human-evolution/hominid -and-hominin-whats-the-difference/.

10   Richard Kemeny, "Fat, Not Meat, May Have Led to Bigger Hominin Brains," *Scientific American*, March 31, 2019, https://www.scientificamerican.com/article /fat-not-meat-may-have-led-to-bigger-hominin-brains/.

11   Alexandra Rosati, "Food for Thought: Was Cooking a Pivotal Step in Human Evolution?," *Scientific American*, February 26, 2018, https://www.scientificamerican .com/article/food-for-thought-was-cooking-a-pivotal-step-in-human-evolution/.

12   Vaclav Smil, "Should Humans Eat Meat?," *Scientific American*, July 19, 2013, https:// www.scientificamerican.com/article/should-humans-eat-meat-excerpt/.

13   Ronald L. Grimes, Deeply into the Bone: Re-Inventing Rites of Passage (Berkeley: University of California Press, 2002).

14   Kate Tuttle, "The 'Walden' Effect: Tracing the Myth of the Man Alone in the Wilderness," *Atlantic*, August 4, 2011, https://www.theatlantic.com/entertainment/archive/2011/08 /the-walden-effect-tracing-the-myth-of-the-man-alone-in-the-wilderness/243017/.

15   Amy Morin, "Loneliness Is as Lethal As Smoking 15 Cigarettes Per Day. Here's What You
      Can Do About It," Inc., June 18, 2018, https://www.inc.com/amy-morin/americas-loneliness
      -epidemic-is-more-lethal-than-smoking-heres-what-you-can-do-to-combat-isolation.html.

16   Camilla Power, "Camilla Power: Why Menstruation Matters.15 October 2019," Radical
      Anthropology Group, Vimeo (video), October 14, 2022, https://vimeo.com/372575239.

17   Camilla Power, "Why Menstruation Matters," (lecture, Radical Anthropology, London,
      October 16, 2018), https://vimeo.com/296418390.

18   K. A. Spielmann, "A Review: Dietary Restrictions on Hunter-Gatherer Women and the
      Implications for Fertility and Infant Mortality," Human Ecology 17, no. 3 (1989): 32145, https://
      doi.org/10.1007/bf00889022.

19   Errol Barnett and Tim Hume, "The Himba: Namibia's Iconic Red Women," CNN, May 18,
      2012, https://www.cnn.com/2012/05/11/world/africa/himba-namibia-inside-africa.

20   Camilla Power "Beauty Magic: The Origins of Art," in The Evolution of Culture, ed. Robin
      Dunbar, Chris Knight, and Camilla Power (Edinburgh: Edinburgh University Press, 1999),
      92–112.

21   Christ Knight, Camilla Power, and Ian Watts, "The Human Symbolic Revolution: A Darwinian
      Account," Cambridge Archaeological Journal 5, no. 1 (April 1995): 75–114, https://doi.org/10.1017
      /S0959774300001190.

CHAPTER 5: SUBSISTENCE

1   Philip B. Stark et al., "Open-Source Food: Nutrition, Toxicology, and Availability of Wild Edible
      Greens in the East Bay," PLOS ONE 14, no. 1 (2019): e0202450, https://doi.org/10.1371/journal
      .pone.0202450.

2   James Owen, "Humans Were Born to Run, Fossil Study Suggests," National Geographic, May 4,
      2021,   https://www.nationalgeographic.com/science/article/humans-were-born-to-run-fossil
      -study-suggests.

3   Michael J. Wheeler et al., "Distinct Effects of Acute Exercise and Breaks in Sitting on Working
      Memory and Executive Function in Older Adults," British Journal of Sports Medicine 54, no. 13
      (2019): 776–81, https://doi.org/10.1136/bjsports-2018-100168.

4   Marley Peifer, Intertropical Impressions, vol. 3, Tanzania (self-pub., 2017).

5   Laurens Van der Post, The Lost World of the Kalahari (Harmondsworth: Penguin, 1962), 21.

6   Richard B. Lee, The !Kung San: Men, Women, and Work in a Foraging Society (Cambridge:
      Cambridge University Press, 1979), 154.

7   "Screen Time and Children," American Academy of Child and Adolescent Psychiatry, February
      2020,   https://www.aacap.org/AACAP/Families_and_Youth/Facts_for_Families/FFF-Guide
      /Children-And-Watching-TV-054.aspx.

8   Stephanie Pappas, "What Do We Really Know about Kids and Screens?," American Psychological
      Association, April 1, 2020, https://www.apa.org/monitor/2020/04/cover-kids-screens.

9   Richard Louv, Last Child in the Woods: Saving Our Children from Nature-Deficit Disorder
      (London: Atlantic, 2010), 81.

10   Gail Johnson, "Experts Warn Screens Affect Childrens' Development," Georgia Straight, October 15,
      2014, https://www.straight.com/life/749411/experts-warn-screens-affect-childrens\-development.

11   Lærke Mygind et al., "Mental, Physical, and Social Health Benefits of Immersive Nature-
      Experience for Children and Adolescents: A Systematic Review and Quality Assessment

of the Evidence," *Health & Place* 58, (July 2019): 102136, https://doi.org/10.1016/j.health place.2019.05.014; Mathew P. White et al., "Spending at Least 120 Minutes a Week in Nature Is Associated with Good Health and Wellbeing," Scientific Reports 9, (June 2019): 7730, https:// doi.org/10.1038/s41598-019-44097-3.

12 Dmitry Orlov, *Shrinking the Technosphere: Getting a Grip on the Technologies That Limit Our Autonomy, Self-Sufficiency, and Freedom* (Gabriola Island, BC: New Society Publishers, 2017), 480.

13 Four Legged Human, "The Wind Roars Ferociously: Feral Foundations and the Necessity of Wild Resistance," *Black and Green Review*, no. 3 (2016), http://www.blackandgreenreview .org/2016/04/bagr3-wind-roars-ferociously-four.html.

14 Andrew C. Janos, *Politics and Paradigms: Changing Theories of Change in Social Science* (Stanford: Stanford University Presss, 1986), 44–64.

15 Four Legged Human, "Wind Roars Ferociously."

CHAPTER 6: BIRTHRIGHT

1 "Canceled: Tindra Skills Gathering," Living Wild, accessed January 28, 2023, https://www .lynxvilden.com/classes/tindra-skills-gathering.

2 Peter Michael Bauer, "On the Path toward Living Wild," Peter Michael Bauer, November 5, 2015, https://www.petermichaelbauer.com/on-the-path-toward-living-wild/.

3 Jacob W. Gruber, "Ethnographic Salvage and the Shaping of Anthropology," *American Anthropologist, New Series* 72, no. 6 (1970): 128999, http://www.jstor.org/stable/672848.

4 M. Kat Anderson, "Indigenous Uses, Management, and Restoration of Oaks of the Far Western United States," U.S. Department of Agriculture, 2007, https://directives.sc.egov.usda.gov /OpenNonWebContent.aspx?content=25907.wba.

5 Lisa Frink, *Gender and Hide Production* (Lanham, MD: Altamira Press, 2006), 200–204.

6 Kollibri terre Sonneblume, "A Century of Theft from Indians by the National Park Service," *Ecologist*, March 29, 2016 https://theecologist.org/2016/mar/29/century -theft-indians-national-park-service.

7 Brian Sawers, "Property Law as Labor Control in the Postbellum South," *Law and History Review* 33, no. 2 (2015): 351–76, http://www.jstor.org/stable/43670779.

8 Faith Durand, "The Green, Magical Wild World of Alexis Nikole Nelson, Forager and TikTok Star," Kitchn, Apartment Therapy, updated August 7, 2020, https://www.thekitchn.com /alexis-nikole-nelson-forager-tiktok-the-way-we-eat-23060470.

CHAPTER 7: APPROACHING COLLAPSE

1 John Gowdy, "Our Hunter-Gatherer Future: Climate Change, Agriculture and Uncivilization," *Futures* 115, (January 2020): 102488, https://doi.org/10.1016/j.futures.2019.102488.

2 Brian Whitney, "If the Future Isn't Somehow Primitive, There Won't Be a Future," interview by John Zerzan, *Disinfo*, January 22, 2016, https://www.johnzerzan.net/articles/disinfo.html.

3 Gowdy, "Our Hunter-Gatherer Future."
Mark Seely, Anarchist by Design: Technology and Human Nature (OldDog Books, 2013), 58.

4 Alfred Toynbee, "Civilization on Trial," *Atlantic Monthly*, June 1947, 38.

5 James C. Scott, *The Art of Not Being Governed: An Anarchist History of Upland Southeast Asia* (New Haven, CT: Yale University Press, 2009), 6.

6   John H. Richardson, "The Unlikely New Generation of Unabomber Acolytes," Intelligencer, December 11, 2018, https://nymag.com/intelligencer/2018/12/the-unabomber-ted-kaczynski -new-generation-of-acolytes.html.

7   Kevin Tucker, Gathered Remains (Denver, PA: Black and Green Press, 2018), 46.

8   Stefani A. Crabtree, Douglas W. Bird, and Rebecca Bliege Bird, "Subsistence Transitions and the Simplification of Ecological Networks in the Western Desert of Australia," Human Ecology 47, (2019):1 6577, https://doi.org/10.1007/s10745-019-0053-z.

9   D. Satterthwaite, "The Implications of Population Growth and Urbanization for Climate Change," Environment & Urbanization 21, no. 2 (2009): 54567, https://doi.org /10.1177/0956247809344361.

10   Joshua Sterlin, "The Civilicene and Its Alternatives," in Liberty and the Ecological Crisis, ed. Katie Kish, Christopher Orr, and Bruce Jennings (London: Routledge, 2019), 175–87, https:// doi.org/10.4324/9780429327100–12.

11   Kyle Chamberlain, "About The Author - The Human Habitat Project," Human Habitat Project, accessed March 29, 2021, https://sites.google.com/site/humanhabitatproject/about-the-author.

CHAPTER 8: SELF-SUFFICIENCY

1   David Neiwert, "Montana's 'Natural Man' Defies Courts, Sets Up Another Rural 'Patriot' Showdown," Southern Poverty Law Center, May 1, 2014, https://www.splcenter.org/hatewatch/2014/05/01 /montanas-natural-man-defies-courts-sets-another-rural-patriot-showdown.

2   Charles Eisenstein, More Beautiful World Our Hearts Know Is Possible (Berkeley, CA: North Atlantic Books, 2017), 287.

3   Kevin Kelly, "The Unabomber Was Right," The Technium (blog), February 18, 2009, https:// kk.org/thetechnium/the-unabomber-w/.

4   Jed H. Abraham, "Why Men Fight for Their Kids: How Bias in the System Puts Dads at a Disadvantage," Family Advocate 17, no. 1 (1994): 48–56, http://www.jstor.org/stable/25805660.

5   Leonard Martin, "I-D Compensation Theory: Some Implications of Trying to Satisfy Immediate-Return Needs in a Delayed-Return Culture," Psychological Inquiry 10, no. 3 (1999): 195–208, https://doi.org/10.1207/s15327965pli1003_1.

Index